SOCIAL MOVEMENTS IN THE WORLD-SYSTEM

SOCIAL MOVEMENTS IN THE WORLD-SYSTEM

THE POLITICS OF CRISIS AND TRANSFORMATION

Jackie Smith and Dawn Wiest

A Volume in the American Sociological Association's
Rose Series in Sociology

Russell Sage Foundation • New York

Library of Congress Cataloging-in-Publication Data

Smith, Jackie, 1968–
  Social movements in the world-system : the politics of crisis and
transformation / Jackie Smith and Dawn Wiest.
    p. cm. — (American Sociological Association's Rose series in sociology)
  Includes bibliographical references and index.
  ISBN 978-0-87154-812-2 (alk. paper)
  1. Social movements   2. Globalization.   I. Wiest, Dawn.   II. American
Sociological Association.   III. Title.
  HN17.5.S5863 2012
  303.48′4—dc23   2011039568

Text design by Suzanne Nichols.

RUSSELL SAGE FOUNDATION
112 East 64th Street, New York, New York 10065
10 9 8 7 6 5 4 3 2 1

= The Russell Sage = Foundation

The Russell Sage Foundation, one of the oldest of America's general purpose foundations, was established in 1907 by Mrs. Margaret Olivia Sage for "the improvement of social and living conditions in the United States." The Foundation seeks to fulfill this mandate by fostering the development and dissemination of knowledge about the country's political, social, and economic problems. While the Foundation endeavors to assure the accuracy and objectivity of each book it publishes, the conclusions and interpretations in Russell Sage Foundation publications are those of the authors and not of the Foundation, its Trustees, or its staff. Publication by Russell Sage, therefore, does not imply Foundation endorsement.

Previous Volumes in the Series

⸺ Forthcoming Titles ⸺

Embedded Dependency: Minority Set-Asides, Black Entrepreneurs, and the White Construction Monopoly
Deirdre Royster

Family Consequences of Children's Disabilities
Dennis Hogan

Family Relationships Across the Generations
Judith A. Seltzer and Suzanne M. Bianchi

Global Order and the Historical Structures of Daral-Islam
Mohammed A. Bamyeh

The Logic of Terrorism: A Comparative Study
Jeff Goodwin

The Long Shadow: Family Background, Disadvantaged Urban Youth, and the Transition to Adulthood
Karl Alexander, Doris Entwisle, and Linda Olson

Nurturing Dads: Social Initiatives for Contemporary Fatherhood
William Marsiglio and Kevin Roy

Repressive Injustice: Political and Social Processes in the Massive Incarceration of African Americans
Pamela E. Oliver and James E. Yocum

The Rose Series in Sociology

The American Sociological Association's Rose Series in Sociology publishes books that integrate knowledge and address controversies from a sociological perspective. Books in the Rose Series are at the forefront of sociological knowledge. They are lively and often involve timely and fundamental issues on significant social concerns. The series is intended for broad dissemination throughout sociology, across social science and other professional communities, and to policy audiences. The series was established in 1967 by a bequest to ASA from Arnold and Caroline Rose to support innovations in scholarly publishing.

DIANE BARTHEL-BOUCHIER
CYNTHIA J. BOGARD
MICHAEL KIMMEL
DANIEL LEVY
TIMOTHY P. MORAN
NAOMI ROSENTHAL
MICHAEL SCHWARTZ
GILDA ZWERMAN
EDITORS

Contents

═ About the Authors ═

Jackie Smith is professor of sociology at the University of Pittsburgh.

Dawn Wiest is senior research analyst at the American College of Physicians.

═══ Acknowledgments ═══

This book has been many years in the making and we are grateful to the numerous colleagues who have provided feedback on drafts of the book and its chapters. We are also grateful to countless others who have provided support and ideas that have shaped our work building and analyzing the dataset on transnational social movement organizations. At the risk of overlooking some folks who have helped us along the way, we highlight some of the people who have been key to bringing this book to light.

John McCarthy has been a constant source of support and encouragement throughout Smith's career, and his research on social movement organizations inspired Smith's initial interest in compiling systematic data on transnational movement organizations. He read several versions of the book manuscript and provided critical feedback along the way. This book would never have been possible without his input. Carol Mueller, Sid Tarrow, and John Markoff also played key roles over the years, encouraging our work on this project and providing insightful feedback on early drafts of the book.

Kiyotero Tsutsui was involved in many early conversations about this project and worked with us on some of the initial analyses of human rights organizations. Valentine Moghadam and Peter Waterman helped shape our thinking and writing about the particular contributions of transnational women's and labor movements, respectively. And we are grateful to Rachel Kutz-Flamenbaum and participants in the Higgins Labor Studies Program and the Studies in Politics and Movements seminar at the University of Notre Dame for their feedback on various draft chapters.

A special thanks to the Rose Series editors, our former colleagues at Stony Brook University, including especially Michael Schwartz and Naomi Rosenthal, who initially encouraged us to submit the proposal for this project and provided crucial ideas and feedback as we developed the book. Daniel Levy provided editorial leadership on the project, and we are also extremely grateful to the participants in our seminar at Russell Sage, especially Greg Maney, Timothy Moran, Michael Schwartz, John Shandra, Ann Swidler, and Gilda Zwerman. The input we received from the seminar sent us back to the drawing board and pushed our thinking forward in extremely important ways. Thanks to Suzanne Nichols, our editor at Russell Sage, for her guidance, encouragement, and patience, and to Diana Baldermann for her excellent support as managing editor.

Funds to support the data collection and management were provided by the National Science Foundation (Grant #SES 03-24735), Funds for Advancing the Discipline program of the American Sociological Association, The Kroc Institute for International Peace Studies at the University of Notre Dame, University of Notre Dame Office of Research and Institute for Scholarship in the Liberal Arts, and a faculty research grant from the University of Memphis.

We also want to honor the organizations and activists who have inspired and informed our work throughout the years. We hope to have given something back with this attempt to gain insights into what they have accomplished and how to strengthen their efforts to change the world.

═ Introduction ═

SIGNS ABOUND that the world is witnessing a time of major transitions. Although great uncertainty persists about the direction in which change will go, conflict has mounted in recent years over the future trajectory of the world political and economic system. Transnational corporations, wealthy states, and other influential elites generally support the existing global capitalist order. These actors seek to defend the status quo, or to make only minor adjustments to sustain the privileges that have accrued to these groups in particular. They resist government regulation of capital and advocate for market-based responses to problems like climate change. And, as we show in this book, those in power have access to important resources that help them mobilize support for their vision of how the world should be organized, even among those who are not benefitting from global capitalism.[1]

But whereas some actors have promoted a vision of the world organized around capitalist markets, others have advanced different principles and priorities. Social movement actors have worked to shape the United Nations' (UN) agendas and advance understandings of global problems in ways that challenge market logics and contribute to alternative visions for organizing the world. Increasingly, these movements have converged around demands for a more democratic and equitable global order. Many of these movements are explicitly anticapitalist, or at least offer fundamental critiques of the dominant forms and practices of globalized capitalism. Many others are vague about their preferred economic model, but nevertheless quite clear in their demands that people have a greater voice in the decisions that affect their lives. We argue that the competition among these diverse visions for how the world might be organized has helped shape both global institutions and social movements.

History has shown that major social change only comes when those excluded from power and privilege rise to challenge the existing social order. Moreover, it is in times of crisis that elites are most vulnerable to pressures from social movements and more radical change becomes possible. Thus, to understand contemporary conflict over how the

1

world should be organized, it is important not only to look at the actions of elite groups or challengers, but also to consider this struggle within its particular historical context. In other words, it requires a world-level perspective attentive to the larger processes of conflict, accommodation, and reform taking place between challengers and authorities as well as to the particular issues or movements around which social forces organize. In addition, we must consider how the convergences of movement actors around demands for greater participation and equity affect the character of these movements.

Recent decades have brought a proliferation of transnational associations of all sorts, including rapid growth in the numbers of transnational organizations advocating for social change. We also have seen, over the 1980s and 1990s especially, an expansion in the levels of participation by people from the global South in transnational organizations.[2] Over the 1990s, the networks among transnationally organized social movements have become denser and more vibrant, in part as a result of new technologies that facilitated transnational communication and interaction, but also in response to mobilizing opportunities created by UN global conferences and other developments in interstate institutions.

In 2001, movement activists came together to launch the World Social Forum process. This dynamic process operates autonomously from the interstate system and has become the leading focal point for transnational mobilization and interchange among movements. It has fostered more deliberate work to build transnational and cross-sectoral movement alliances and encourages ongoing efforts to link local struggles with a critique of the global neoliberal economic order (Fisher and Ponniah 2003; Sen et al. 2003; Smith et al. 2011; Smith, Karides et al. 2007; Juris 2008b). This move to emphasize more autonomous movement spaces is not unique, because movements have always sought to escape the limitations of the interstate system as they modeled and advanced alternatives to the dominant social order. However, the World Social Forum is unprecedented in its size and its global scale.[3] Significantly, the process is highly reflexive, building on lessons of past movements as it works deliberately to foster transnational and cross-sectoral alliances in response to contemporary political opportunities and challenges.

We argue in this book that we need to understand these changes in light of both the shifting institutional and organizational setting in which social movements operate and in terms of the much larger world-systemic context. The timing of the changes in these movements is not a mere coincidence. Social movements were becoming more transnational and building capacities for collaboration across differ-ence at the same time as the larger interstate system and world eco-nomic order were experiencing a "long crisis" brought about by the beginning of the end of the United State's hegemony in the world-system. The U.S. decline is seen to begin with the end of the U.S.-backed gold standard in the international monetary system and with the U.S. military failure in Vietnam (Wallerstein 2004b). Elites responded to the financial and energy crises of the 1970s with a set of economic policies that have come to be known as neoliberalism. Neoliberalism was de-signed to restore profitability to the capitalist system by expanding op-portunities for investment and trade (Harvey 2005). But, as was true in earlier periods of hegemonic decline, responses to crises have tended to exacerbate underlying tensions in the system, and thus provide only short-term fixes (Silver 2003; Arrighi and Silver 1999).

The escalation of global crises in more recent years can be expected to bring new openings for groups hoping to challenge the dominant order and advance alternatives to the existing world economic system (Wallerstein 2004a, 37). Of course, although crisis expands opportuni-ties for democratic movements, it also invites challenges from exclu-sive, xenophobic movements (Barber 1995; Moghadam 2008). The pros-pects for any type of mobilization are shaped by movement interactions with other actors and institutions of the world political and economic order. In this book, therefore, we draw from theories of social move-ments, world culture or polity, and world-systems to uncover the ways institutions mediate between political actors and world-systemic dy-namics to define the opportunities and constraints social movements face. We show how in this process social movements introduce ideas and models of action that help transform both the actors in this system as well as the system itself.

Our research leads us to make three basic claims, which we develop and support in the pages that follow. First, the decline of U.S. hege-mony and related global crises has strengthened opportunities for movements to come together to challenge the basic logics and struc-tures of the world economic and political system. The crises the world now faces require basic restructuring of the economic and political or-der to avert ecological disaster and political and social instability. The United States lacks the economic and military dominance it once en-joyed, and it increasingly must compete with counter-hegemonic chal-lengers, including multistate alliances, such as the European Union and the BRICS (Brazil, Russia, India, China, and South Africa), and with nonstate actors (for example, al Qaeda).

Second, the capacities of transnational movements—including pro-

gressive challengers as well as exclusionary and fundamentalist ones—
to mobilize antisystemic challenges has increased over recent decades.
This is in part due to greater global communication and other technological innovations, but also to the accumulation of lessons, ideas, and
organizing infrastructures from earlier civil society engagement with
interstate processes such as the UN global conferences (see chapter 4).
Earlier mobilizations around interstate conferences and political processes have helped fuel the growth of transnational organizations, alliances, and networks. Such networks have become increasingly autonomous from the interstate polity as transnational organizations have
become stronger and more cohesive in their analyses and frames (Pianta and Silva 2003; Alger 2002). The ideological orientations of these
transnational alliances range from explicit antisystemic claims to reformist and service-oriented concerns. These diverse groups are increasingly able to come together—in alliances of various degrees of commitment and intensity—around shared analyses and goals. As they have
engaged in struggle, activists have deepened their analyses of global
problems and learned new ways of acting together. This has contributed
to the antisystemic potential of contemporary social movements.

Third, over time, the bases of power, authority, influence, and legitimacy have shifted from territorial sovereignty claims, based on coercive
abilities and assertions, to normative ones, based on actors' conformity
to international law. This shift expands the "discursive opportunities"
for transnational challengers (Braun and Koopmans 2008; Ferree 2003;
Giugni et al. 2005). It stems partly from states' recognition of limits to
violence as a means of advancing security (that is, from nuclear attacks
or terrorist threats). The gradual strengthening of norms and institutions
of international law, especially in the aftermath of World War II, has contributed to shifting the cost-benefit calculus behind the use of coercion in
international affairs. The organizations we examine in this book and the
larger movements of which they are part have been essential to advancing international norms in global politics (see, for example, Risse, Ropp,
and Sikkink 1999; Kaldor 2003). This normative trend is reinforced by
the fact that military competition among states has become prohibitively
expensive, forcing states to divert essential resources away from basic
social welfare and productive infrastructure of their societies (Kennedy
1989; Reifer 2005). This shift, moreover, should be understood as a long-
term historical trend rather than a dualistic category. Although particular incidents or conflicts may suggest that coercive power generally pre-
vails, the larger pattern of interstate interactions suggests that states'
ability to effectively use coercive power to achieve domestic and international goals has been reduced over time.[4]

Systemic Crisis and
Movement Opportunities

Few would argue that we are now witnessing a time of great crisis. The collapse of global financial markets and increased uncertainty in the financial sector, the growing evidence of large-scale climate disruption and species extinctions, unstable and rising energy and food costs, and large-scale inequality are coupled with growing scarcity of water and arable land and rising threats from international terrorism (see, for example, Davis 2001, 2006; Klare 2001). These multiple and interrelated crises all can be seen to signal the physical and social limits of the existing world capitalist order. Some analysts would argue that we are observing a world-system in the late stages of systemic crisis—a crisis that has been developing since the 1970s and that results from basic contradictions within the world economic system.

For Immanuel Wallerstein, a crisis is "a situation in which the restitutive mechanisms of the system are no longer functioning well and therefore the system will either be transformed fundamentally or disintegrate" (1984, 23). The logic driving the contemporary world economy is one of endless accumulation. In other words, to survive, it requires constant economic growth. Capitalism is thus an ever-expanding mode of economic organization and therefore necessarily global in reach. But the system's need for constantly expanding markets and economic growth contends with the hard reality that we live on a single planet that is not growing, and that, although the productivity of workers can often be increased, there are physical limits to how much surplus value (profit) can be extracted from the planet and its people.

Whether we interpret the enormous problems of our day as evidence of a systemic crisis or not, there is little doubt that they will require dramatic changes in the way our societies are organized. As the signs of ecological and financial crisis become ever more apparent, additional threats to the existing order are also present in the form of large-scale mass protests in many countries and multiple costly and sustained U.S. military interventions, widening cracks in the foundation of the system's organizing logic (Arrighi and Silver 1999).

First, we see challenges to the legitimacy of existing institutions, reflected in increased protests against national governments around the world and in increased military spending and intervention. The leading cause of this crisis is the inability of the system to continue providing benefits to key groups—such as workers and the middle class in the core states. In the past, this bargain between elites and workers in the north has served to mask fundamental contradictions between actual practices and the liberal ideology that justifies and rationalizes the world-system (Silver 2003). The legitimacy crisis is reflected in declining rates of confidence in major political institutions in countries around the world (see, for example, Weber 2011; WorldPublicOpinion. org 2008; Gallup 2008).

The large and growing U.S. military budget and prison population should be seen as indicators that this regime has come to rely more and more upon coercion over consent as a basis for its authority. As U.S. industrial strategies have met with greater international competition, they have become less profitable and less able to generate those benefits for workers that were key to securing both labor's cooperation and the domestic peace needed to ensure global hegemonic leadership. U.S. economic success was also essential to securing international co-operation with the interstate order it favored, and so as the U.S. economy declines relative to others, new international challenges to U.S. hegemony have emerged (see, for example, Reifer 2005; Harvey 2009). This rise in coercion has taken place over several decades. For instance, Pamela Oliver shows how the U.S. government–enacted policies that led to the mass incarceration of blacks stem the demands for equity by civil rights and Black Power activism (2008). Donatella della Porta and her colleagues have also documented a shift in core countries' policing strategies away from more permissive practices that protected citizens' rights to speech and toward more restrictive and coercive forms of policing. This emphasis on security became even more pervasive after the attacks on the U.S. Pentagon and World Trade Center in 2001 (della Porta and Reiter 2006; della Porta, Peterson, and Reiter 2006; Ericson and Doyle 1999; Howell et al. 2008; O'Neill 2004, 243; Gillham and Marx 2000). Peter Evans warns that this shift in state emphasis from providing welfare to coercive enforcement of property rights threatens the long-term viability of the state and the larger neoliberal order it supports (1997).

The threat to the system's legitimacy is, moreover, likely to increase as many—if not most—states of the core confront escalating costs of security and new spending constraints that make "austerity the order of the day not only in Haiti and in Argentina, but in France" (Arrighi, Hopkins, and Wallerstein 1989, 92). At the time of writing, massive strikes and protests have become more frequent and effective at paralyzing European countries such as Greece, Spain, and France as well as countries across the Middle East. Although these protests focus largely on national government targets, the ultimate cause of their grievances lies in the policies of global and regional financial institutions, and thus in the long term the protests are likely to strengthen movements for changes in the larger world-system. In some parts of the global South, for instance, long-simmering popular resistance to the policies of the global financial institutions has been translated into electoral influence, and—aided by global crises—leaders from those countries are becoming more forceful and unified in their demands for new rules for the global economy. Thus, in 2006, Argentina and Brazil repaid their debt to the International Monetary Fund ahead of schedule, putting the institution in a financial dilemma (Bretton Woods Project 2006).[5] Also, the Group of Eight (G8) leading industrial countries has been forced to expand its ranks to become the G20. And recent World Bank–International Monetary Fund meetings have expanded the influence of poor countries in the governance of those institutions. The "development project" (McMichael 2006) launched in the wake of World War II did not produce all the benefits it promised, and a wider range of people and countries are now demanding alternatives.

Second, just as the system is being challenged because of its inability to meet expectations of relatively privileged groups, new groups of people who have been largely excluded from the benefits of global economic growth are also mobilizing transnationally to advance claims challenging the hegemony of globalized capitalism (Sassen 1998; Hall and Fenelon 2009). The rise of global human rights discourse and increasingly broad, formally structured movements of people to support human rights claims thus generates yet another threat to the system's persistence (Sassen 1998, 2007). This threat has become more potent because rising food insecurity and water shortages highlight the incompatibilities between values of human rights and globalized markets. Also, human rights movements have more consistently and clearly come to repudiate the Cold War's separation of civil and political from economic rights (Skogly 1993). Financial and ecological limits illuminate the gaps between the human rights ideals that have justified the existing regime and the actual experiences of growing numbers of people around the world, fueling both nonviolent challenges as well as international terrorism (see, for example, Bergesen and Lizardo 2005; Friedman and Chase-Dunn 2005; Uvin 2003; Moghadam 2008).

Finally, the rise of anti-Westernism outside the core through nationalist and terrorist groups as well as the much larger segment of progressive, pro-democracy groups helps frame the current period as one of civilizational conflict—that is, a conflict over the basic organization and logic of our social and economic systems. As the Western development project (see McMichael 2006)—which has provided the key organizing logic behind the U.S.-led accumulation regime—proves unable to meet the needs of larger numbers of people not only in the global South but also in the core countries of the world economy, more and more people are questioning U.S. leadership and the world-system as a whole. More significantly, as it becomes clear that the basic premises of that system are undermining the livelihoods of poor communities and threatening future generations, more people will find the alternatives offered by antisystemic challengers increasingly appealing (Arrighi, Hopkins, and Wallerstein 1989; Wallerstein 2004a, 37; Amin 2006).[6]

Giovanni Arrighi and his collaborators have shown that this sort of hegemonic decline we are seeing today is part of the cyclical dynamics that have occurred throughout the more-than-500 year history of the modern world-system. These scholars have demonstrated recurrent patterns that marked earlier *accumulation cycles,* one dominated by the United Provinces (sixteenth through the eighteenth centuries) and another by the United Kingdom (eighteenth through the twentieth centuries). U.S. hegemony began to emerge in the late nineteenth century and reached its peak in the early post–World War II decades (Arrighi 2010; Arrighi and Silver 1999, 2001). In the two earlier cycles, hegemonic powers dominated the system through their competitive advantage in accumulating capital and were able to consolidate their influence over the world-system for a time. But, once established, hegemonic powers invited challenges from other actors, and this competitive dynamic fueled both the expansion of the system and innovation and emulation by other actors that gradually undermined the hegemon's competitive edge. These processes contributed to hegemonic crisis, defined by interstate rivalries and competition among business entities, growing social conflicts, and the emergence of new configurations of power—a breakdown that paved the way for the emergence of a new accumulation regime.

This world-historic perspective sheds important light on the current context and can aid our attempts to understand the potential trajectories and prospects for change. If we view the current environmental and financial situation not as a mere setback in the overall forward march of economic globalization—able to be addressed with technological breakthroughs or market corrections—but rather as part of this long crisis of the twentieth and twenty-first century, we might better understand the long-term changes in the organization of social movements that have resisted—in one way or another—the globalized capitalism that is the modern world-system. In many ways, the crises of today are a more potent threat to humanity's future than any others in human history. Yet it is unclear what sort of transformation of the existing system is possible, and whether such a transformation can indeed occur before challenges to the system of governance lead to its unraveling. Will we see the rise of a new global hegemon, or a world-empire based on coercion, increasing chaos and violence, or the rise of a noncapitalist world economy based not on coercion but on more cooperative and mutually respectful relations (see, for example, Arrighi 2010, 377–80)?

It is not our purpose here to speculate on the various potential outcomes of this conflict. Instead, we argue that this context shapes the opportunities that contemporary movements face in organizing across national borders and around visions of fundamentally different world orders. We believe that movements working to transform the world economic and political order into a more democratic and equitable one have greater potential for affecting global change at the current historical moment than they have had at earlier points in history. Thus, we examine changes in the population of transnational social movement organizations within this world-historic context, integrating different bodies of research on social movements and political institutions as we try to explain patterns of transnational social movement organizing during the time of this long crisis of the twentieth and twenty-first centuries.

Trends in Movement Capacities and Arenas

Scholarship in the world-systems tradition has led to an expectation that the contemporary era will see an increase in the number of larger and more transnationally organized social movements advocating for large-scale global change. Evidence that their predictions are indeed unfolding is strong, and it is worth considering how these theories of world-systemic change might add to our theorizing about social movements, much of which has remained within state-centric frameworks. Our analysis supports the argument that the capacities and strength of social movements have expanded over time, and in fact we see a shift in the arenas of contention so that movement energies are now more focused on spaces defined by movements and largely autonomous from interstate politics and agendas. This contrasts with earlier periods, in which transnational activism focused largely on defining interstate norms and institutions and mobilized within arenas defined by states. This is significant to the extent that it liberates activist discourses and imaginations from the constraints of the existing interstate order. Activists' and organizations' relationships with other movement actors thus become more salient than claims of political feasibility and expediency in shaping movement strategies.

In their analysis of successive hegemonic cycles of rise and decline, Arrighi and Beverly Silver show that

> [pressure from below] has widened and deepened from [one hegemonic transition to another], leading to enlarged social blocs with each new hegemony. Thus, we can expect social contradictions to play a far more de-

cisive role than ever before in shaping both the unfolding transition and whatever new world order eventually emerges out of the impending systemic chaos. But whether the movements will largely follow and be shaped by the escalation of violence (as in past transitions) or precede and effectively work toward containing the systemic chaos is a question that is open. Its answer is ultimately in the hands of the movements. (1999, 289)

In other words, as globalized capitalism has extended its geographic and social reach—that is, as it has increased demands upon more of the world's workers through, for example, outsourcing and the casualization of labor, and as it commodifies goods once freely accessible, such as water and public services—we would expect a growing tendency for social movements to develop and to focus attention on cross-sector organizing and transnational alliance-building. This is exactly what has developed considerably over the last few decades, and the deepening networks of transnational association have led to the emergence of the World Social Forum process in 2001, reflecting some of the changes Arrighi and Silver predicted. But these movements are resource-poor and constantly threatened by internal division as well as external repression. Counterposed to this more hopeful scenario is the possibility of a continued escalation of violence developing out of the current U.S. wars, rising instances of terrorism, and expanding nationalist, xenophobic, and racist right-wing mobilizations.

World-systems analysts have understood social movements as acting in response to the underlying structures of the world economy. This frame of reference sheds light on some of the large-scale and long-term developments among and across social movements, including their relations to the larger world-system. "Antisystemic movements" include a diverse "family of movements" working to advance greater democracy and equality (Arrighi, Hopkins, and Wallerstein 1989). According to Wallerstein, "to be antisystemic is to argue that neither liberty nor equality is possible under the existing system and that both are possible only in a transformed world" (1990, 36).

World-systems analysts recognize that many actors and organizations within social movements do not frame their struggles as antisystemic, nor necessarily see their diverse issues and struggles as connected (see, for example, Hall and Fenelon 2009, 120–23). Nevertheless, they argue that these various and sometimes loosely linked struggles have served to shape and transform both the opportunities for antisystemic movement and the world-system itself (Amin et al. 1990, 10–11; Boswell and Chase-Dunn 2000). At times they do so by helping challenge the dominance of particular hegemonic powers by advancing nationalist claims, as the anticolonialist movements did in the middle part of the twentieth century. At times their challenges may be more direct in naming the system of globalized capitalism as the target, such as with international socialist movements of the nineteenth century and beyond. At times their challenges may serve to chip away at the dominant order by calling into question the gaps between the legitimating ideologies of the system—that is, equality, human rights, or even free markets—and its actual practice. This has been a strategy of many movements throughout history, from the early antislavery struggles to today's campaigns for worker rights, climate justice, and food sovereignty. Elites often respond to movement challenges by reforming political institutions in ways that create openings or formal means of access for movements to further their struggles within existing institutions.

Terry Boswell and Christopher Chase-Dunn have described this process as part of a "spiral of capitalism and socialism" whereby structures shape movements and their possibilities for challenging the social order, and the interactions of movements with states and interstate actors then transform the larger set of structures that form the stage on which social conflicts are expressed (2000, 18). They observe that "from the elimination of slavery to the end of colonialism, a rough and tumbling spiral between socialist progress and capitalist reaction has resulted in higher living standards and greater freedom for working people" (2000, 11). Their spiral model of global change suggests that revolutionary movements don't simply emerge in a discontinuous way, but instead build on past successes to parry the next move of those defending the existing world-system.

In short, a world-historic framework can help shed light on long-term trends and patterns in the capacities and forms of transnational social movement organizing over the past few decades. At the same time, we have learned much from other literatures that focus on international institutions and more localized structures and processes, such as those operating within national and interstate institutions and social movement organizations. The chapters that follow offer an analysis of the changing population of transnational social movement organizations that embeds our thinking about the operations of movements and their organizations within theories of global institutions and culture, which is in turn embedded within the context of the constantly evolving world-system.

A key part of our argument is that conflicts over how the world should be organized are articulated within and shaped by interstate institutions. We must therefore consider how institutions have changed alongside the longer-term cycles of economic expansion and contraction as well as the rise and decline of hegemonic powers. We thus consider the geographic makeup of transnational organizations, their articulation of issues, their connections with interstate institutions and other nongovernmental actors, and their organizing structures and how these have changed since the founding of the United Nations. Our analysis demonstrates that antisystemic movements have been inextricably linked to global institutional processes, not marginal to them. Moreover, movements both shape and are shaped by their interactions with states and other global actors. In the course of their interactions, they may adopt reformist, counter-hegemonic, or antisystemic strategies, and their choice of strategies is shaped by the larger global context. Our observations of organizing patterns over recent decades suggests that the interactions between movement actors and global institutions have enhanced the capacities for transnational organizing and strengthened the antisystemic potential of movements. They have done so by creating global focal points and incentives for geographic expansion and by facilitating ongoing communication and exchange among diverse movements and groups.

Shifting Bases of Power

When we embrace this relational and dynamic approach, the usual conceptual boundaries that academic disciplines establish—for instance, between states and civil society, between social movements and other civil society groups, between core and peripheral regions of the world, between reformist and revolutionary paths toward change, and so on—become blurred. Thus we devote some attention to thinking about boundaries and how structures and actors reproduce particular divisions and ways of thinking as well as how they give way to new ideas and modes of organization. If we consider contemporary struggles as questioning the fundamentals of the world-system, the very nature of existing states and institutions is therefore subject to contestation and reformulation. In other words, systemic transformation would require basic reorganization of institutions now largely taken for granted.

One inherent dilemma and source of crisis in the modern world-system is the contradiction between the norms and values used to rationalize or justify the system and the practices essential to the endless accumulation of profits this system requires. We argue that as systemic crises have made dominant actors more vulnerable to challenges and as capacities of counter-hegemonic and antisystemic forces have grown, the bases of power and authority are shifting. In particular, conventional justifications of state authority were based on the ability of a state to control activities within particular geographic boundaries and to defend those boundaries with force, if necessary. But recent years have seen important challenges to these assumptions, as nuclear weapons and terrorist networks can threaten the security of even the most well-armed states. Moreover, the interstate system has developed an increasingly expansive set of norms allowing intervention into a state's formerly sovereign territory to advance human rights claims. At the same time, states' abilities to use coercion against their own citizens as well as others have been constrained by the expanding global human rights regime. Christopher Hill, a former U.S. secretary of state for East Asia and ambassador to Iraq, observed that "the notion that a dictator can claim the sovereign right to abuse his people has become unacceptable" (quoted in Fisk 2011).[7]

The expansion and greater institutionalization of international human rights norms, as well as the articulation of enhanced understandings of the global environment as a commons whose survival depends on global cooperation, have undermined traditional bases of state authority. This strengthens opportunities for nonstate actors whose power stems from normative rather than coercive advantages (see, for example, Friedman et al. 2005; Finnemore 1996; Risse, Ropp, and Sikkink 1999). This shift further strengthens the possibilities for antisystemic mobilization, especially as stronger transnational networks have helped shape new discourses and consolidate energies around a few important and potentially transformative frames.

One area where this shift is apparent is in the critical discourses emerging from transnational movements and their broader civil society alliances in response to contemporary global problems. For instance, although governments have responded to the increased volatility in food prices with calls for greater "food security," activists in transnational movements are increasingly united in calls for "food sovereignty." The former reinforces states' roles in regulating food markets, the latter decentralizes authority and control over food production and distribution to farmers and consumers. Similarly, although states speak in terms of addressing climate change, activists have responded with the slogan "system change, not climate change." They advance claims for "climate justice," and more recently many groups have converged around calls for the "universal rights of Mother Earth." Such discourses challenge state-led efforts to use market mechanisms to address climate change and other environmental problems, and these discourses gain momentum as states fail to reduce greenhouse gas emissions. Another significant form of movement discourse confronts the lingering effects of colonialism through calls for repayment of the global North's "ecological debt" to the global South and for reparations for slavery.

Although subtle, the shifting discourses in both interstate institutions and the growing chorus of movement voices for fundamentally new approaches to international cooperation reflect important changes in the operation of power in the contemporary world-system. States of course remain dominant forces in world politics, but their supremacy is complicated by the emergence of new actors with fundamentally different claims to authority. As globalization challenges states' capacities to both control activities within their borders and to provide for the well-being of citizens, this power shift is likely to become increasingly relevant to explaining global social change.

Chapter Outline

The major theme of the book is that global institutions—including states and international organizations—are best seen as the products of contestation among a diverse array of global actors (including social movements) competing in an arena that is defined by these same institutions and the norms and cultural practices they generate. Global social change results from competition among global actors operating within this institutional context; contestation helps transform identities of global actors and their forms of struggle. Over time, the opportunities and capacities for transnational antisystemic mobilization have, we argue, increased significantly. In addition, the primary bases of power and authority have shifted from coercion and territorial sovereignty to normative claims based on universal rights.

Our study draws heavily from both quantitative and qualitative data in our analysis of the changing patterns of transnational social movement organizing. The primary quantitative data source is the *Yearbook of International Organizations*, and we describe our data collection methods in greater detail in chapter 2. The advantage of this data source is that it provides measures of the general characteristics of the subset of international nongovernmental organizations (INGOs) organized to advocate for some form of social change. Our dataset includes organizational founding dates, issue focus, and geographic scope of membership over several decades. Our database begins in the 1950s and extends into the early 2000s. But we find that this macro-level organizational data, though helpful for discerning general patterns, leaves much room for interpretation. To aid us with this interpretation, we draw heavily on additional primary and secondary research on transnational activism and activist organizations (see chapter 2 for more details).

Chapter 1 reviews the major literatures on which our study draws, including world-systems, world polity, and social movement theories.

We discuss the various contributions each approach makes to our understanding of social movements and explain how our integration of these three theoretical traditions can enhance understandings of transnational social movement activism and global change.

Chapter 2 situates our study of the population of transnational social movement organizations within the context of the historical period following World War II, when decolonization and the rise of national independence movements and the creation of the United Nations and other international organizations altered the institutional and normative context in which states and other global actors competed. We then provide an overview of the general patterns of transnational social movement organizing, summarizing overall trends in the organizational population over the last half century.

Since the 1990s, forms of regional interstate cooperation and integration have taken on a new character in response to declining U.S. hegemony and the end of the Cold War. The superpower rivalry had a significant impact on the ways in which regional bodies such as the European Union and the Organization of African Unity developed into the late twentieth century. But the end of the Cold War and the destabilization of U.S. hegemony opened the door for new forms of cooperation and regional unity that help states assert and protect their interests as they seek more favorable terms of participation in the global economy. Regionalism is thus a counter-hegemonic force in the world-system.

In chapter 3, we analyze the impact of changes in regionalism on transnational social movement organizations. As regional institutions have enlarged their mandates to encompass a wider variety of policy domains, such as human rights, environmental protection, and women's rights, and have adopted mechanisms allowing the formal participation of civil society actors in regional policy processes, they have altered the field of contestation and created new possibilities for movements to engage in transnational forms of struggle. Social movements have thus increasingly mobilized within regions to influence the direction and scope of regional governance. We examine the development of both interstate regional polities and regional transnational social movement sectors over the course of the Cold War and into the post–Cold War period.

Chapter 4 examines relationships between social movement organizing and the United Nations. As the global institution designed to help consolidate and maintain U.S. hegemony in the postwar order, the UN and its various bodies reflect and help reproduce the accumulation logic of the larger world-system. At the same time, it helps advance norms of human rights and environmental protection that are essential to the legitimacy and stability of the system. We focus on the United Nations' global conference processes as particularly important sites of contention over competing values and interests, sites where social movement actors have been particularly active, especially since the end of the Cold War.[8] By creating spaces where activists can come together around a shared agenda and set of targets or goals, we argue that the UN global conferences provided focal points that encouraged transnational organizing on a diverse array of issues. Moreover, because global conferences reinforce particular sets of organizing principles and practices among groups that are developing around the times these conferences are held, the effects of conference-derived norms and practices are likely to affect even those groups not directly engaged in the global conferences. UN conferences thus generate norms and models of action that diffuse through the widespread dissemination of accounts of the conferences by those who participate. Diffusion also occurs through networking among organizations, which is facilitated and encouraged both before and following global conferences, and through movement discourses and practices that relate to global conference processes (Riles 2001).

Although global conferences encouraged movements to engage with global-level political processes, and provided in many cases opportunities for movements to challenge the practices of governments that violated international norms such as human rights and environmental sustainability, they also demonstrated the limits of interstate politics for addressing some of the world's most pressing problems. Institutions are designed to provide stability and predictability in interstate affairs, and therefore constrain prospects for movements seeking structural change. They also contain contradictory norms and logics that both enable powerful actors to elude sanctions for violating global norms and provide leverage for challengers mobilizing against such hypocrisies (Ball 2000; Hafner-Burton and Tsutsui 2005). Global institutions thus create both possibilities for movements to gain political leverage (through what is known as a boomerang strategy) and "iron cages" that constrain movements. Chapter 5 explores these paradoxes of the global institutional context.

The contradictions embedded in world polity norms and practices as well as the fundamental contradictions of the world-economy have generated important contemporary challenges to the world polity. Chapter 6, the final one of this volume, presents a model for thinking about the interactions between social movements and global institutions over time, and the implications of these interactions for large-scale structural change. Building from the analyses in earlier chapters, we show how movements are affected by their relationships with global institutions and other actors and how the interactions among various actors shape ongoing processes of institutional and world-systemic transformation, including the development of antisystemic movements.

Many have emphasized the extent to which civil society engagement with institutions can lead to co-optation, but we argue that a more complex dynamic is at work, and that global institutions are also shaping the antisystemic potential of transnational movement networks. Drawing from experiences in global conferences, activists in contemporary movements have expressed increasing skepticism about the prospects for achieving social change through institutions. This has fueled a process of critical, transnational movement-building that may be heralding large-scale, and perhaps systemic, social change. As the world faces profound financial and ecological crises, and as U.S. dominance in the world political economy is increasingly challenged, it is especially urgent that scholars, policy analysts, and citizens gain a better understanding of the ways social institutions shape social behavior and the distribution of power in the world-system. We hope this book will help illuminate the contentious and complex processes that constitute the global political order and contribute in some small way to helping identify paths toward a more equitable, sustainable, and democratic world.

═ Chapter 1 ═

Theorizing Social Movements and Global Change

A MID THE 1990s celebrations of globalization was a growing rumble of discontent over the effects of global economic integration on the poorer countries of the world and on working people in the rich countries that were championing economic globalization. In the late 1970s and 1980s, few in the global North knew of the increased frequency and militancy of protests taking place in the global South against the punishing conditions imposed on Third World governments by the World Bank and International Monetary Fund, or IMF (Walton and Seddon 1994). Proponents of the loans claimed that conditionalities such as reductions in social spending, budgetary discipline, and lowered barriers to trade would foster economic growth in borrowing countries. Instead, most faced long-term and crippling international debt without the predicted benefits of development, the promise of which justified multilateral lending policies (Goldman 2005; Easterly 2002; Ferguson 2006). Yet, as the 1990s wore on and sustained economic growth still eluded many countries of the so-called developing world, global leaders, including UN Secretary-General Kofi Annan, continued to call for greater openness to world markets as the solution to persistent poverty (Weisbrot et al. 2002).[1] The world saw overall economic growth, but inequities grew and persisted both within and between countries (Korzeniewicz and Moran 2009). Thus, by late 2010 we were witnessing the equivalent of "IMF riots" in countries of the global North.

Outside elite circles, a growing chorus of political activists and academic analysts from around the world were coming together around a shared critique of the policies of economic globalization. By the late 1990s, a growing and more diverse array of social movements was gathering at sites where international leaders met to plan global economic policy. Their presence became increasingly large and disruptive throughout the decade, and with the 1999 Ministerial Meeting of the World Trade Organization, they burst into global public consciousness following the "battle in Seattle," waged by tens of thousands of protesters who shut down the meeting's opening session (see Starr 2000; Smith 2001; Broad and Hecksher 2003).

A close look at the analyses and critiques raised by a variety of social movements during the 1980s and 1990s shows that these groups anticipated the types of economic crises that came to plague Mexico in 1994, Southeast Asia and Russia in the late 1990s, Argentina in 2001, and eventually the United States and Europe in 2008. Each of these successive crises had wider repercussions, of course, as the world's economies had become increasingly interconnected and interdependent. These movements also anticipated the global ecological crisis, which world leaders can no longer afford to ignore. Indeed, their work to focus leaders' attention on global environmental issues led corporate actors to begin lobbying at international meetings and engage in systematic efforts to obfuscate public debate about environmental problems and emphasize market-based responses to them (Smith 2008, chap. 4; McCright and Dunlap 2003; Bruno and Karliner 2002).

Sociologists in the United States have tended to understand these global conflicts in terms of the world political economy or through the lens of institutions.[2] The former approach is reflected mainly in the subfield of world-systems analysis, which views the modern capitalist economy in largely structural and world-historical terms. With this lens, global social change is seen as a function of the operation of capitalism on a global scale, which generates patterns that change in predictable ways over long periods of time. Such changes are driven largely by competition among economic and political actors operating within a system organized to facilitate the endless accumulation of capital (see, for example, Wallerstein 1976, 1980, 2004a; Chase-Dunn 1998).

In contrast, the world polity or world culture perspective emphasizes a much shorter time frame, highlighting the role of more recently established intergovernmental organizations, such as the United Nations, in shaping how states and other global actors interact, as well as how they define agendas and advance their respective interests. They identify the emergence of global norms, practices, and institutions as a world culture that is shaped more by institutional processes and organizational routines than by structural and material factors.

Our task in this book is to try to account for changes in the population of transnational organizations working for social and political change. This work originates from discussions and approaches in the field of social movement studies, which has tended to focus more on the proximate, organizational dynamics of social movement actors, often bounding these within the context of national polities. We seek to globalize social movement theories to help scholarship in this area better account for the ways global structures and processes affect the dynamics of conflict and mobilization, even in local and national settings. In this chapter, we discuss key ideas of each of these analytic and theoretical traditions and their contributions to our thinking about social movement transformation in a global context.

Theorizing Global Social Change

How does global social change happen? What advantage do we gain from embedding our consideration of movements and institutions within a world-systemic framework? Moreover, can such a perspective help us make sense of the changes we see in the population of transnational movement organizations in which we are interested? A world-systems perspective helps us contextualize the data we observe on transnational organizing, showing changes in the organizational population in relation to other economic, political, and social developments taking place over long periods. In particular, the world-system lens sensitizes us to the nature and the sources of vulnerabilities—or movement opportunities— in the prevailing world economic and political order.

A key advantage of a world-systems perspective is that it helps us break out of the conceptual prisons created by our state-centric paradigms. World polity and social movement theories, for the most part, take the interstate system as a starting point. They tend to treat states as (relatively) "homogeneous invariables" (Amin 2006, 6). For both approaches, conflicts taking place within particular states are largely independent of one another, even if, as for world polity theorists, they are shaped by the organizational structures and models emerging from the world polity. Although both perspectives help explain the emergence of modern states and account for the forces that have shaped their content and form, it is difficult within either framework to imagine or explain a fundamental transformation of the national state structure. In contrast, world-systems analysis conceptualizes the state as part of a much larger set of social relations, and can envisage a fundamental reordering of those relations in response to crisis and systemic transformation. Conflicts within states are thus understood in relation to this world-systemic context, in that they are not independent from the larger structures and competitive dynamics of globalized capitalism.

In all three perspectives we consider, states have changed over time in ways that affect the ongoing national and increasingly transnational conflicts. But in both world polity and social movements approaches, states are often assumed as existing actors, even as they are influenced by political contestation and organizational processes. Thus it is difficult within these frameworks to imagine even struggles aimed at ending global capitalism as moving beyond the national state as a principal unit of social organization. Yet, if globalized capitalism ceases to be the dominant model for organizing the economic life of humanity, as is anticipated by some in the world-systems perspective, then our familiar national state is likely to be fundamentally altered or to disappear altogether. A world-systems lens, in other words, allows us to consider possibilities for discontinuous change in the basic structures of the world economic and political order, opening new possibilities for articulating and imagining alternatives.

But there is much to explain between large-scale global structures and the sort of radical changes in states and societies anticipated by world-systems analysts. Many critics of this perspective argue that its structural emphasis prevents us from appreciating how the activities of institutions, groups, and other actors can affect political outcomes. This is where world polity and social movement theory are most helpful. Clearly, interstate institutions have come to assume important roles both in structuring and mediating conflict among states (and between states and capital) and in shaping the character and form of the social forces emerging to challenge the dominance of both capital and states. From world culture–polity theorists, then, we take important lessons about how institutions operate and how they condition interactions among diverse actors, including social movements. We emphasize especially the processes generating organizational isomorphism as well as the tendency for decoupling between norms and practices. Both processes help us account for and explain global conflict and social change.

Social movement theory informs our research most directly, and our research methods draw from and build on scholarship in this area. This theoretical tradition helps us understand the role of individual and organizational agency within this larger context of collective political struggle. In what follows, we demonstrate how we integrate these diverse frameworks in our analysis of transnational social movement organizations over the past half century.

Analysts of social movements have achieved considerable consensus that three basic factors affect social movement emergence and consequences (see, for example, Snow, Soule, and Kriesi 2004; Tarrow 2011). These three factors correspond to our argument that the contemporary period of hegemonic decline creates opportunities for antisystemic challenges, and that movements' capacity for transnational mobilization has grown in recent decades, at the same time as we have seen a shift in emphasis from coercive to normative forms of influence in world affairs. First, movements are most likely to form and expand when political and economic opportunities are present or constraints are low. The vulnerability of political targets, splits among elites, or the emergence of new powerful allies—through elections or through some other process that alters power relations—increases the possibility that social movements will mobilize around an issue (McAdam 1982; McAdam, McCarthy, and Zald 1996; Kriesi 1996, 2004; Tarrow 1996).

Second, collective action is most likely where conditions allow for or support popular mobilization. Strong civil societies and material resources allow the creation of associations that can serve as mobilizing structures for social movements (McCarthy 1996; Lewis 2002). Whether associations are specifically organized to promote social change is less important than the mere presence of social structures that facilitate some level of autonomous (that is, not state- or elite-controlled) communication and cooperation among people and groups. Such networks are essential for generating collective action on a large scale. Thus, we see that most social movements are made up not only of movement-specific associations such as social movement organizations or networks, but also of some mix of churches, recreational clubs, labor unions, and other structures that create routine connections among diverse and sometimes geographically dispersed people.

Third, the emergence and success of social movements depend on the ability of activists to frame, or communicate, their claims effectively to particular audiences. It also requires appropriate analyses of the sources of political grievances and of the mechanisms of social change. In other words, thinking about social movements requires attention not only to the broad political contexts and structures that condition opportunities for action or to the ways activists organize resources and create networks of potential supporters, but also to how movements and activists define issues and create systems of meaning that justify their claims and encourage sustained activism (Snow et al. 1986). We examine these three dimensions separately, but note that they are obviously interrelated. For instance, the likelihood that movement frames would find resonance in the larger population and that civil society networks and organizations could be mobilized against a common target (or set of targets) is related to the real or perceived vulnerability of a regime. And the capacity of movement mobilizing structures is related to factors like the unity among elites and the concentration of resources in a society, all of which are conditioned by the larger context of political opportunity.

Our main empirical emphasis in this book is on a particular set of international nongovernmental organizations and their interactions with intergovernmental bodies. By examining transnational social movement organizations—that is, formally organized actors explicitly engaged in collective efforts to promote global social change—we explore how the organizational forms, frames, and strategies adopted by transnational movement organizations, as well as the geographic patterns of participation within these organizations, reflect geopolitical tensions and divides within the world-system, such as those manifested during the long years of the Cold War. The world polity is also characterized by competition and efforts to overcome power asymmetries, often by combining diverse actors into alliances. We therefore interrogate the forces that both support or obstruct collaboration in a global context of inequality and conflict. Our study begins with an overview of the lessons and insights we bring from diverse analytic and theoretical perspectives on globalization and social movements.

Political Opportunities

Scholars have observed that though social structures and institutions influence the possibilities for social movements to mobilize and affect policy, the reverse is also true. For instance, John Markoff and Charles Tilly have documented how modern democratic institutions were shaped by interactions between political elites and social movement challengers over many decades (Markoff 1996; Tilly 1984, 1978). As states in Europe were consolidating, they needed to draw more resources from their populations so that they could defend territory and support the administrative structures necessary to support growing armies. Subjects facing growing demands from emerging state authorities for their crops and their bodies (needed to fill army ranks) insisted— at first through collective actions such as bread riots and attacks on tax collectors and later through petitions and public demonstrations—that they receive something in return. This came in the form of new protections and services as well as the gradual extension of rights to popular participation in political processes. Thus, the divine right of kings was gradually replaced with popular sovereignty, whereby rulers' authority emerged from their accountability to citizens. State legitimacy came to require demonstrations of popular support, which eventually encompassed periodic elections by ever-larger segments of the population. Modern states, and the interstate institutions they create, continue to depend on popular legitimacy for their authority, and it is this that gives social movements their power. Thus movements have influenced the forms and character of institutions, and these institutions in turn affect the opportunities and constraints that determine the mobilizing potential of movements. Over time, this competition between authorities and challengers has helped shape, however incrementally, our systems of representation and political participation, including regulations about public protests and association as well as the definitions and enforcement of citizens' rights (Tilly 2004; Markoff 1996; Clemens 1996; McAdam, Tarrow, and Tilly 2001).

From this understanding of social movement–state relationships, scholars of transnational activism have documented parallel relationships in the global political arena (see, for example, Smith 1995, 2008; Tarrow 2005; Keck and Sikkink 1998). Just as modern state structures were defined through interactions between authorities and challengers, we find the interstate system (as well as its actors) being shaped by these same types of interactions. Although transnational contention takes different forms from national contests, it is no less significant in the ongoing historical struggles to alter global structures of power and authority (for more on how social movements have engaged within the UN, see Smith, Chatfield, and Pagnucco 1997a; Willetts 1996a; Smith 2008; Friedman, Clark, and Hochstetler 2005).

The World-System and Political Opportunities.   Like social movement theorists, world-systems analysts also see movements as fundamentally connected to the emergence of modern states. However, this perspective emphasizes not the actions of political challengers but the ways world-scale economic and historical forces shape the conditions under which people organize in different parts of the world (see, for example, Amin et al. 1990; Arrighi, Hopkins, and Wallerstein 1989; Wallerstein 1990). Scholars working from this perspective emphasize the importance of large-scale world historical relationships as the source of the grievances that motivate movements and define the conditions in which challengers mobilize. In other words, they treat states and other global actors as fundamentally shaped and constrained by world-level structures and processes of interstate competition within a global capitalist order (Boswell and Chase-Dunn 2000). These structures and processes, moreover, have a long history that also must be taken into account, because a pattern of cycles and trends that affect a variety of political conflicts are evident only in this long-term perspective.

World-systems analysis emerged in the 1970s, building on earlier work by dependency theorists like Raul Prebisch who, working within the United Nations Economic Commission on Latin America, had argued that the development of countries of the global South was constrained by those countries' unequal relationships to the global political and economic order. Their colonial histories and international trade relationships were structured in ways that perpetuated inequality and undermined prospects for development, despite claims that they would lead to economic development and greater equity between the global North and South (Broad and Hecksher 2003; Chirot and Hall

1982; McMichael 2006). The key contribution of this approach was the argument that scholars needed to look at the world not as a constellation of multiple autonomous states, but rather as a system of interdependent economic relations organized on a global scale. The world-system is thus a single unit of analysis encompassing a hierarchical division of labor between core areas, which are engaged in the most profitable aspects of production and exchange, and peripheral areas, the value of whose labor and resources are defined by this systemic relationship and help fuel the system's expansion (for reviews see, for example, Wallerstein 2004; Chirot and Hall 1982). Analysts have identified multiple world-systems throughout history (for example, Chase-Dunn 1998), and most agree that the contemporary world-system emerged in the sixteenth century. The distinctive feature of this system is that it is a capitalist world economy—that is, an economy organized around the logic of endless accumulation.

World-systems embed various cyclical patterns and secular, or much longer-term trends that should be seen as creating opportunities for movement challenges. The dynamics of world-scale competition also place important constraints on social movements. The modern world-system has exhibited cycles of economic expansion and contraction, which extend across roughly fifty-year periods. There have also been hegemonic cycles, produced by competition among leading powers over the leadership of the system. The modern world-system has seen the rise and decline of at least three distinct hegemonic powers—the Dutch, sixteenth through the eighteenth century; the British, eighteenth through the early twentieth century; and the United States, late nineteenth through the twentieth century (Arrighi 2010; Wallerstein 2004). Each hegemonic state advanced and defended a unique "accumulation regime," or set of rules and practices that help ensure the sustained accumulation of capital and reinforce the competitive advantages of the hegemonic power (Arrighi and Silver 1999, 2001). Cycles of hegemonic rise and decline are linked to the cycles of economic expansion and contraction, and each contraction (or B-phase of the economic cycle) tends to be punctuated by crises that result from declines in the profitability of existing accumulation practices. Such accumulation crises invite challenges, and core powers try to innovate to restore profits, at least for a time. But ultimately they tend to generate increased financialization within the system—that is, a greater reliance on credit and debt—as capital seeks to enhance profits on a more restricted material base. As the financial crisis of 2007–2008 revealed, financialization increases the volatility and vulnerability of the hegemonic order, inviting new challenges to the existing leadership and contributing to adaptations and innovations that transform both the system and the actors within it.[3] Such crises open opportunities for movements to come together to challenge the basic logics and structures of the world economic and political system.

Whereas hegemonic cycles and other shorter-term dynamics help shape the openings or opportunities for movements to challenge dominant powers, long-term or secular trends within the world-system shape the capacities of less powerful groups to mount effective challenges. One important example of such a trend is proletarianization, or the mobilization of increasing numbers of people into the wage labor market. Proletarianization is encouraged by processes such as urbanization and the development of industrial manufacturing as well as through the integration of national economies into global markets. Proletarianization was fundamental to the rise of labor and socialism as antisystemic movements (Silver 2003). A related trend of depeasantization has pushed small farmers out of agricultural production by disrupting local food markets and land ownership patterns, contributing to the expansion of urban slums as well as to the growth of transnational agrarian activism (McMichael 2008; Davis 2006). The increased complexity and centralization of national states is another world-system trend that has shaped modern social movements, and the most influential movements are those that develop structures and tactics that relate to modern states (Tilly 1984). Formal organizations thus tend to be important elements of contemporary social movements (McCarthy and Zald (1987). An important feature of world-systems trends is that they have distinct limits, and when these limits are approached, the system faces new crises. For instance, as proletarianization reaches its limits, labor costs rise, limiting economic growth and profitability. Extensive depeasantization contributes to vulnerabilities in food supplies, generating social instability.

Many world-systems scholars and other analysts portray the contemporary period as one marked by increasingly frequent and intense crisis (as in our introduction). This is not the first period of crisis of the modern world-system, but it is arguably one of the most urgent. Earlier crises have tended to fall during times of economic contraction, when the ability of the system to ensure profits declined. These crises generate interstate competition, because other states seek to take advantage of the vulnerability of the hegemonic power and to redefine the rules of the system to better suit their interests. Such crises led to World War II and shaped the postwar consolidation of U.S. hegemony. The postwar period saw a greater centralization of capitalism under the Bretton Woods system that created the World Bank and International Monetary Fund. More recent crises began in the late 1960s and early 1970s, when the United States faced challenges in Vietnam as well as at home from domestic social movements,[4] coupled with rising energy costs, a large trade deficit, and growing inflation and militarization (Wallerstein 1993).

To restore stability and profitability following the 1970s energy crisis, the United States advanced what came to be known as neoliberalism, a form of globalized capitalism that limits governments' role to the regulation of monetary policy and the protection of private property, and that promotes economic growth through the expansion of international trade, the privatization of public entities and services, deregulation of business practices, and strict limits on government spending (Evans 1997; Harvey 2005; McMichael 2006). Neoliberalism served as a temporary fix and restored profitability to the system in the short term, but could not reconcile some of the basic contradictions of the system that grow from the fundamental limits to capital's ability to extract profits through continued exploitation of workers and the environment. In short, physical limitations mean that the system cannot continue to mobilize expanding human populations into the workforce, suppress wages, and maintain peace among a growing population of unemployed and underpaid workers. It also cannot maintain endless growth on a planet that has finite limits in its energy stores and its capacity to absorb pollutants.

Political Opportunities and World Culture–Polity.   In contrast to world-systems analysts, scholars using world polity or world cultural approaches argue that the global system is characterized by increasingly consequential institutions and norms that guide the behaviors of states and other actors. National governments are seen as principal players in international organizations and treaties defining the world polity, but are facing growing competition from other transnational actors whose roles are both defined and legitimated by global institutions and the world culture they articulate and reproduce. The world polity has thereby expanded opportunities for social movement challenges and indeed has itself been altered by movements' engagement with institutions. The capacities of transnational movements to mobilize antisystemic challenges has increased in recent decades, in part because of the accumulation of lessons, ideas, and organizing infrastructures from earlier civil society engagement with interstate processes.

The world culture–polity approach begins from the observation that, since the nineteenth century especially, national political elites have formed increasing numbers of intergovernmental organizations (IGOs) to regulate military competition among states and to otherwise manage issues that cross geopolitical boundaries.[5] The United Nations is a universal (global) example of this kind of organization, and its related agencies help coordinate national and regional policies around many issues, including development, public health, trade, environment, military and social policy. IGOs are often very specialized, such as the International Postal Union or the World Health Organization, but some are forums for the routine discussion of a variety of issues, such as the UN General Assembly. Regional organizations such as the European Union, the Organization of American States, or the African Union help countries within a particular geographic territory respond to common interests and problems. These regional groups have been gaining importance in more recent years (Farrell, Hettne, and Langenhove 2005), and help expand regions' influences in global bodies like the UN or the World Trade Organization.

In addition to IGOs, world culture–polity theorists see the growing numbers of international nongovernmental organizations (INGOs) as crucial to explaining global level change. INGOs—including groups like PEN International, the World Council of Churches, and Doctors Without Borders—are voluntary associations formed to bring people together around a wide variety of causes and interests. Some INGOs work for social and political change, and these would fit within our category of transnational social movement organizations, while others promote particular hobbies (like stamp-collecting or bird-watching), recreational activities (like chess or bicycling), identity (such as, linguistic, religious, or professional), or group interest (like industry lobbying). As politics and communications becomes increasingly global, world culture–polity theorists argue, citizens around the world face growing pressures and incentives to form transnational associations and embrace other elements of world culture. Although they find increasingly that they must organize transnationally to affect even local concerns, they also find that international arenas provide resources and potential allies that can advance their interests.

IGOs and INGOs thus have a symbiotic relationship, which John Boli and George Thomas refer to as a "mutual legitimation process" (1997, 179). IGOs help reinforce the tendency toward new INGO formation by identifying these groups as recognized and legitimate global actors, even establishing ground rules for their participation in intergovernmental negotiations. States find that, to be seen as legitimate and responsible players in the interstate system, they must acknowledge and accept the presence of international nongovernmental organizations. Thus Kim Reimann found that by hosting the 1997 review conference on the Convention on Climate Change—and reaping reputational and economic rewards from doing so—the Japanese government was forced to allow environmental NGOs in Japan new levels of access to national and intergovernmental policymaking processes (2002). Also, states rely on the government-monitoring work of INGOs as they wage political war on their counterparts within the world polity, as is seen in the U.S. attacks on China in the UN Human Rights Commission and Council.[6] Similarly, a growing body of research shows that governments more embedded in international treaty regimes face greater scrutiny on their practices, encouraging the formation of new NGOs as well as eventual changes in policy (for example, Ball 2000; Hafner-Burton and Tsutsui 2005; Tsutsui and Wotipka 2004; Economy 2004; Smith and Wiest 2005; Risse, Ropp, and Sikkink 1999).

States and other actors—including INGOs and the subset of transnational movement organizations we examine in this book—are embedded in networks of relationships structured by a growing array of organizations, associations, and treaties that affect their understandings of their roles and identities, interests, and opportunities for affecting social change. Culture is an increasingly global force that brings extra-local influences to bear on actor's perceptions and definitions of norms, values, and modes of action (Finnemore 1993; Hammack and Heydemann 2009). Thus, understanding social change processes requires attention to actors' embeddedness in global-level organizations and associational networks. Relationships between IGOs and INGOs helps explain how particular values and norms rise to prominence and how change in the cultural content of social movement agendas happens over time.

Although some scholars view the world polity and world culture as reproducing global inequality and hierarchy (see, for example, Beckfield 2003), less dominant actors in the world-system use the symbolic and organizational resources of the world polity to challenge political and economic inequalities. In other words, the world polity is not simply a space that reproduces the core-periphery hierarchy of nation-states and concentrates the most profitable production and exchange processes, and by extension political and military power, in the northern or core countries of the world economy. Nation-states of the global South have increased their participation and influence in the world polity in the twentieth century through the formation of the G77 and the Non-Aligned Movement, for instance, and more recently by forcing changes to World Bank and IMF weighted voting procedures, pressing the Group of Twenty (G20) to expand to the G20(+), and through the formation of regional blocs like BRICS (Brazil, Russia, India, China, and South Africa). The creation and restructuring of regional organizations such as Mercosur and the African Union also signal shifts in the relative influence of various states in the larger polity. As we will show, world polity and world cultural resources have not only shaped the form and substance of this interstate competition, they have also affected transnational movement networks.

Centuries of world integration through military conquest; trade, migration, and communication networks; cultural and educational exchange; intergovernmental bodies and international nongovernmental organizations have yielded efforts to create and enforce universal rules and regulations to organize human relations. Rather than a single authoritative body or institution, emphasis has been placed on the emergence, through social interactions, of cultural scripts and models—a world regulatory culture—to produce desired actions in all "sub-units of world society" ranging from subnational economic actors or educators to national governments (Meyer 2000, 263). With increased world integration, in both depth and breadth, cultural models for framing and organizing human action have been globalized (Meyer 2000; Finnemore 1996). The expansion of intergovernmental bodies and international nongovernmental bodies organized around the core concerns of a world society, such as economic regulation, rules of war, human rights, education, science, and environmental protection, is both an indication and a source of the globalization of cultural models for organizing human activity and authorizing political authority. The result is a social and cultural system that is self-managing and self-reinforcing, held together not only by codified principles and regulations but also by individual, corporate, government, and nongovernmental actors that enact, project, and hold each other accountable to global models.

Intensified world interaction and integration has produced a global consciousness that orients the self-perceptions and actions of actors at all levels. John Meyer (2007) describes a world of complexity and uncertainty in which any individual or collectivity seeking recognition and efficacy looks to approved models for defining their identity and purpose, and for orienting their actions. Through various forms of world integration (for example, membership in intergovernmental bodies or trade and finance networks) states are pressured not only by other states and international actors to conform to universal conceptions of modern statehood but also by subnational actors (corporations, individuals, civil society organizations) that emulate and structure their actions and expectations according to the same principles and models. This works in the other direction as well: states seeking recognition as modern and efficacious players on the world stage pressure domestic actors to conform to globally legitimated models of actorhood, either by structuring incentives or by force (Meyer 2007).

The increasing formalization of transnational economic and political relations has occurred during a time of rapid growth in the organization of all sorts of social relations within and across national boundaries. As governments have formed international organizations to coordinate policies and address transnational problems, private sector and civil society groups have developed similar structures in response to changing social environments. Thus, world polity analysts have documented a robust tendency of states and other collectivities, including INGOs, to mimic other entities in their environments, a phenomenon referred to as isomorphism (DiMaggio and Powell 1991; Jepperson and Meyer 1991).

This process can be seen in some of the earliest transnational mobilizations, formed around demands for an end to the slave trade, for peace, and a bit later for women's suffrage (Keck and Sikkink 1998). All these struggles aimed to define limits on state authority. Anti–slave trade and peace campaigners argued that states had to respect the human rights and dignity of all people, regardless of their race or geographic origin. Women's suffrage advocates demanded that a state's legitimacy be defined by its extension of the notion of citizenship rights to women as well as men. These struggles inspired the rise of additional claimants who worked to extend the franchise (for example, to landless citizens) and to further define the boundaries of state authority and responsibility.

Although the targets of many transnational social movement activists were states, the ideas about what constituted appropriate state behaviors flowed freely across national boundaries, shaping people's understandings about human rights and citizen-state relationships, and defining these norms in ways that transcended national identities (Markoff 2003, 2004, 1994; Jacobson and Ruffer 2003; Rupp 1997). As states established mechanisms to foster interstate communication and policy coordination, citizens mobilized these transnational linkages to extend discourses about rights to these emergent interstate arenas. Social movement action was thus crucial to the development of the laws of war (Finnemore 1996) and to the creation of interstate institutions that would make war between states less likely (Chatfield 1997; Evangelista 1995; Risse-Kappen 1994). Activists were present at the formation of the League of Nations as well as the United Nations, demanding that any agreement among states include the recognition of human rights as a key indicator of state legitimacy (Charnovitz 1997; Forsythe 1991; Robbins 1971). The gradual institutionalization of interstate relations both resulted from and further inspired transnational organizing around supranational targets (della Porta and Kriesi 1999; Smith 1995; Smith, Chatfield, and Pagnucco 1997b; Tarrow 2001).

Thus, a world culture–polity perspective offers conceptual tools for explaining changes in participation of activists from outside the core in transnational movement organizations over time, despite the material and political disadvantages of their world-system position. Where this approach is weak, though, is in accounting for power inequities and their reproduction in this world polity, as we discuss in more detail in the following section.

Mobilizing Structures

Within this global political context, advocates for social and political change must be able to muster resources and people if they are to take advantage of any political opportunities, whether national or international. And though globalization has helped reduce the costs of international travel and communication, it is clear that transnational organizing brings higher costs and other challenges to those attempting it. Social movement theory thus draws our attention to the mobilizing structures, or the social infrastructures that facilitate collective action. Early work in the tradition of resource mobilization theory highlighted the importance of formal organizations to social movement mobilization (McCarthy and Zald 1977; Zald and McCarthy 1980), whereas later work preferred the notion of mobilizing structures, to account for the fact that most movements were assemblages or networks of formal and informal organizations, including those specifically organized for social change (social movement organizations, or SMOs) as well as those organized for other purposes, such as religion or recreation.

As modern societies have become more bureaucratized and dispersed, formal organizations play increasingly important roles to maintain communications among citizens (Wuthnow 1989), leading to the expanding roles of professional SMOs (McCarthy and Zald 1977) and the development of a "social movement society" of permanently mobilized social movements (Meyer and Tarrow 1998; Smith and Fetner 2007; Zald 1987). Movement scholars working to understand how mobilizing structures contribute to social movement development speak increasingly of the importance of networks to movement processes (Diani 1995; Diani and McAdam 2003; Rosenthal et al. 1985), and the network concept may be even more prominent in work on transnational organizing (Keck and Sikkink 1998; Maney 2001; Moghadam 2005; Riles 2001; Rupp 1997; Wiest 2006; Risse 2000).

World-Systems And Mobilizing Structures.   For world-systems analysts, social movements' power results from their ability to withhold consent or participation from economic and political elites. This power, or ability to disrupt the functioning of capital, has increased over time in re-

sponse to economic restructuring and earlier challenges from organized labor and other social forces to the stability of the world-system
(Silver 2003; Silver and Arrighi 2005). Over time also, elite efforts to
curb political unrest and otherwise address challenges to the system
have helped fuel underlying threats to its longevity. Thus, one important trend that world-systems scholars have observed is the persistent
presence and expanding power of counter-hegemonic and antisystemic
movements.[7] As a result of ongoing processes of capital accumulation
and state consolidation, social forces have gained increasing ability to
mobilize populations and resources and to thereby challenge hegemony in the world-system. These forces have thus become increasingly
important to challenging successive hegemonies, according to analyses
by Arrighi and Silver (1999, 2010). Wallerstein concludes that antisystemic movements have "collectively grown stronger in the 20th century, despite failures and the cooptation of most individual movements" (1984, 53). At the same time, "the financial expansion and the
underlying restructuring of the global political economy [that is, neo-
liberalization] have undoubtedly succeeded in disorganizing the social
forces that were the bearers of these demands in the upheavals of the
late 1960s and 1970s. But the process is creating new social forces that
the decaying hegemonic order will have even greater difficulties ac-
commodating" (Arrighi and Silver 1999, 184–85). These new social
forces include the growing numbers of transnational alliances of people from both the core and periphery, joined in common struggle
around claims that extend beyond workplace demands to all areas of
life.

In addition to shaping the structural sources of power for social
movements, the world-system also helps define the character of social
movement organizing. In particular, world-level inequalities and the
international division of labor led earlier movements in the core countries of the world economy to take on organizing forms and frameworks that differ from those in the periphery and semiperiphery. The
structured inequalities of the world-system and their embeddedness
in ongoing political processes have thus reinforced divisions between
people in the core, periphery, and semiperiphery. Wallerstein argues
that the extension and deepening of global capitalism after World
War II contributed to greater polarization between core and periphery,
making it more difficult for movements to converge across the core-
periphery divide. Core-periphery political and economic differences,
in other words, "reduced even further the parallelism of the political
process in the various states," thereby diminishing likelihood of transnational alliances and enhancing capitalist control over labor (Wallerstein 1990, 26). Also, the expansion and deepening of capitalist pro-

cesses helped strengthen states and interstate institutions, making state power an attractive target for many movements. However, postindependence nationalist movements in the South and social democratic movements in the core states found that acquiring state power was a double-edged sword for social movements in both regions, whose aims for more democratic and equitable political systems were frustrated by the fact that national politics is inescapably shaped by world-system (Boswell and Chase-Dunn 2000).

Although controlling state power enabled movements for greater equality and democracy to challenge the practices of the dominant order, it also gave them a stake in supporting the interstate framework and the larger world-system of global capitalism it supported (Wallerstein 1990, 26–27). Because states cannot alter the basic structure of the world economy that constitutes them, workers movements were thus forced to develop worldwide organizations to cultivate the necessary power and resources to affect change in the larger system (Wallerstein 1984, 11). This realization led to internationalist efforts throughout history, although earlier socialist internationals did not generate robust transnational alliances. However, Immanuel Wallerstein observes a shift in movement organizing beginning in the 1980s toward greater unity and transnational cooperation among the "family" of movements he calls the antisystemic movements. Before 1945, the three main streams of antisystemic movements were the workers–social equity, women's, and ethnic nationalist streams. Despite some attempts to build bridges across these distinct movement segments, these were largely ineffective. But following World War II and the consolidation of U.S. hegemony, the rise of so-called new social movements such as student, environmental, and human rights helped expand the potential for today's antisystemic mobilization. Wallerstein notes that now, despite lingering suspicions, "the arrogances [of diverse movements] have been toned down, and the common heritage remembered. . . . The common heritage is that, when all is said and done, all these movements (as movements) emerged out of a rejection of the injustices of the existing world-system, the capitalist world economy. Each in its own way was seeking to fulfill the slogan of the French Revolution: more liberty, more equality, more fraternity" (1990, 45).

Analysts in the world-system tradition expect to see growth in transnational social movement organizing over time, in part in response to activists' experiences of working to advance change in national contexts. In the course of struggle, they often find that states are incapable of addressing problems rooted in the world-system. Thus more activists see organizing for world-systemic change as essential.

World-systems analysis also sensitizes us to the ways the world-system affects the character of states. Neoliberal globalization fundamentally transforms states by promoting deregulation, reductions in state spending, privatization, and increased foreign investment and trade (Robinson 2004; Evans 1997; Harvey 2005). This has effectively transferred power from the state and toward private sector actors and global markets. The gap in state capacities has resulted in reductions in education, health care, and public utilities in the global North as well as in the global South. To fill some of this gap in public services without contributing to government expansion, northern states have shifted much of their official development assistance to private, nongovernmental actors. The resulting "Western grant economy" (Aksartova 2009) has fueled tensions among civil society groups who see themselves as both competing for scarce resources and channeling energies of many groups into activities that support the existing neoliberal order (Ferguson 1990). The result of this neoliberalization of the state has been the disenfranchising of southern people, whose governments are rendered unable to provide many basic services, and conflict among civil society groups seeking to advance progressive global change (see, for example, Macdonald 1997; Bebbington, Hickey, and Mitlin 2008; Manji and O'Coill 2002). Official aid practices have, in short, contributed to a "political economy of civic rent-seeking" (Heydemann and Hammack 2009, 25) that channels civil society efforts in ways that serve the interests of core states.[8]

We can thus conclude from our reading of world-systems analysts that ongoing processes of capitalist expansion and deepening around the world affect the resources as well as the structures of the movements that have formed to resist capitalist exploitation in its various forms. At the same time, social movements help shape the competition among diverse global actors, thereby affecting the evolution of the world-system (Arrighi, Hopkins, and Wallerstein 1989). This conclusion mirrors arguments in the social movements literature about the need for attention to the dynamic processes of contention (see, for example, McAdam, Tarrow, and Tilly 2001), although the stress is on the centrality of world-historical forces to these conflict dynamics.

Organizational Theories in a World Polity. Although world-systems analysis and world culture–polity theory help sensitize us to the ways global-level forces shape the practices of states and nonstate actors, these approaches are less suited to helping us understand meso- and micro-level dynamics that affect individuals' and small groups' decision processes. Organizational and social movement theory are useful in helping identify how interactions among actors and operations within organizations both shape and reproduce particular mobilization patterns and outcomes.

Organizational theory is an important intellectual foundation for both social movement and world culture–polity approaches because it emphasizes the ways organizational structures affect social behaviors and social reproduction. This theoretical perspective draws analysts' attention to both the structures that define particular organizational forms, practices, and routines, and to the wider organizational fields in which organizations are embedded. Organizational fields help define the character and cultures of particular organizations as well as patterns of growth, decline, and change among organizations (see, for example, Davis et al. 2005; Campbell 2001, 2004; Powell and DiMaggio 1991). Thus, because world culture–polity theorists have noted the tendency toward isomorphism among world polity actors, we expect to find important parallels between the developments in the broader population of international organizations and changes in the population of transnational social movement organizations we are studying.

Organizational theorists are also attentive to the ways that cooperation and competition among organizations affect change in the population. Much of the research in this area is based on studies of private firms and the resulting observation that firms operating within particular industries will compete in some areas (for example, for market shares) and cooperate on others (such as in supporting prices or opposing regulation). These population dynamics affect organizational survival and success independently of other forces in the broader environment (Zald and McCarthy 1980). For instance, using organizational theory to study social movement organization and protest among civil rights and women's organizations, Debra Minkoff (1997) found that population dynamics such as population density and inter-organizational competition were important to explaining both the formation of new organizations as well as the timing of protest actions (see also Zald and Garner 1987). Erik Johnson and John McCarthy (2005) explore relationships between national and transnational organizational populations, arguing that transnational populations are shaped largely by bottom-up processes of organizational expansion and competition. Alternatively, David Frank and his colleagues found that top-down processes explain NGO formation in East Asia, where domestic, environmental nongovernmental organizations followed the emergence of chapters of international nongovernmental organizations, which provided the "key ingredients for NGO formation" (Frank, Longhofer, and Schofer 2007, 284). Changes in the broader institutional environment—including the expansion and formalization of regional intergovernmental organizations such as the European Union—as well as growth and competition among transnational social movement organizations themselves are thus key factors affecting the changing patterns of transnational association (see, for example, Tarrow 1995, 2001).

Organizational approaches are increasingly attentive to the role of networks in explaining patterns of social relations. Attention to social networks has intensified with globalization, perhaps because network forms of organization may be most appropriate for environments of wide geographic scale, complexity, and uncertainty (Barabási 2002; Castells 1998; della Porta, Peterson, and Reiter 2006; Wittel 2001). Network theorists and social movement scholars have shown that effective networks are those with dense ties and robust links that enhance communications across distance and social sectors (Barabási 2002). Network forms are most useful in environments characterized by uncertainty because they enable actors to adapt to change more quickly than other associational forms (Haas 1992; Podolny and Page 1998). They are also better able to withstand repression because information and authority tend to be more widely disseminated in networks than in more formal organizational structures (Escobar 2003). Research on transnational organizing suggests that network forms and networking activities are particularly relevant to this scale of organizing, even if the effects on social change are ambiguous (Juris 2008b; Keck and Sikkink 1998; Krut 1997; Riles 2001; Edelman 2005; Yanacopulos 2005).[9] Marisa Von Bülow's research, for instance, shows how new forms of organization were developed to facilitate transnational coalition-building and brokerage among anti–free-trade groups as activists learned strategies for working together on contentious issues (2010).

These theoretical approaches generate several important assumptions about the cooperative and competitive processes within the interorganizational fields in which social movements are embedded. Organizations compete for scarce resources and members, even as they pursue similar or complementary goals within the polity. Opponents of movements, moreover, have strong interests in encouraging such competition by pitting organizations against each other for funding, political access, or other privileges. Movement allies, which may include foundations and other entities that provide resources to movements, often unwittingly encourage competitive dynamics within movements. At the same time, the weakness of social movements relative to states and corporate actors requires them to build larger alliances to coordinate collective action and maximize their impacts (Zald and McCarthy 1980; Minkoff 1995, 1997; Bob 2005). Thus, within organizational fields are competing pressures and organizational imperatives that affect the character of organizational populations as well as movement outcomes.

As we discuss in greater detail in chapter 5, global political processes have encouraged competition and conflict among organizations advocating for social change, generating geographically segmented and single-issue-oriented organizing efforts that have for the most part not tended to cohere into durable transnational alliances that could sustain large-scale collective action (Edelman 2005; Tarrow 2005). International organizations like the World Bank have been seen to channel some advocacy organizations into what has been called "anti-politics" (Ferguson 2002) or the "development machine" (Manji and O'Coill 2002), which is driven largely by Western priorities and the interests of capital and reproduces colonial patterns of exploitation and domination (Rajagopal 2003; Macdonald 1997). Within the United Nations, organizations attempting to shape international policies and discourses are seen as becoming hopelessly enmeshed in a process of professionalization and de-radicalization that activists refer to in disparaging ways as "NGO-ization" (Alvarez 1998; Eshle 2005; Kamat 2002; Naples and Desai 2002). At the same time, IGOs provide common targets and discourses that can help transnational movements develop shared understandings and analyses of problems and their solutions while also creating spaces for activists to gather across national divides as they engage in struggles for social change (Amin 2006; Smith 2008; Rajagopal 2006; Khagram 2004).

Framing

Global changes also affect the ways movements frame conflicts, or how they assign meanings to symbols and events and package their claims in ways that resonate with large and politically influential audiences (see, for example, Snow et al. 1986; Snow and Benford 1988). Framing is important to helping groups expand their mobilizing capacity by attracting members and resources as well as fostering a sense among potential adherents that collective action can make a difference. Movements, in other words, must frame the political context in ways that highlight the degree to which a system is open to change or otherwise vulnerable to particular forms of pressure (Gamson and Meyer 1996; McAdam 1999). For transnational activists, this framing work can create particular challenges, as citizens in many countries lack familiarity with international negotiations in the World Trade Organization or the United Nations (McCarthy 1996). It can therefore be difficult for movements to make international issues relevant and urgent to people in local settings. But globalization brings with it the expectation that greater communications, stronger international institutions, and increasing awareness of transborder problems will enhance people's identification with communities beyond their national borders. Evidence from surveys of contemporary social movement participants signal the emergence of new forms of identity to correspond to global changes (della Porta 2005a, 2005b; Reese et al. 2008).

World-Systems and Framing.   World-systems analysis is better suited to help us account for the tensions or incompatibilities between world cultural values and principles. And although world-systems analysts don't tend to pay much attention to international institutions or cultural systems (for exceptions, see Boswell and Chase-Dunn 2000; King 1997), they do acknowledge the role of culture and ideas in the operation of hegemony. Whereas world culture–polity theorists speak of the decoupling of norms and practices, world-systems analysts speak of the tension arising from the fact that the modern world-system's legitimating ideology rests on norms of universalism—such as inclusion, equity, rights—that grew out of the French Revolution. These norms form what is known as the geoculture of the capitalist world-system, and the system's survival depends on the widespread and unquestioning acceptance of the contradictory norms that enable capital accumulation through inherently unequal practices. The system itself requires "active institutional discrimination against particular status-groups or identities" (Wallerstein 2004a, 39). Yet universalizing ideologies of equity and rights help legitimate the system and justify the (rationalized) inequalities inherent to it (see, for example, Wallerstein 2004a, chap. 4; 1991). The capitalist world-system thus "must profess universalism while practicing anti-universalism" (Wallerstein 2004a, 39). This tension between universalism and anti-universalism is "as important as the core-peripheral division of labor to the operation of the system" (Wallerstein 2004a, 41), and is a key driver of social change.

Another important notion that world-systems analysis brings to our thinking about transnational movement organizing is that the resonance that antisystemic frames will find in the general population varies over time, and is highest when the world-system is in crisis. At such times, it is easier for movements to challenge dominant ideologies and legitimating accounts that are part of the public discourses that help reinforce hegemony. Where hegemonic leadership is in decline and under threat from counter-hegemonic challengers, movements can more readily advance frames that are critical of the building blocks of the world economy and its institutions. For instance, Philip McMichael shows how peasant activists advanced a *food sovereignty* frame that taps popular concerns about rising food costs and scarcity, linking them to

the world economy: "The food sovereignty movement engages critically with the political infrastructure of neoliberal capitalism, denatu-
ralizing the market narrative as a precondition for elaborating an alternative narrative" (2008, 44). Thus, movement frames can challenge
concepts that are essential to the world-system and its supporting geoculture, such as markets and sovereignty, and can disrupt dominant
cultural logics that define collective identities, agendas, and priorities.
At times of transition, antisystemic claims move beyond the core networks of social movement activists and their "critical communities"
(Rochon 1998) to inform and inspire activism by a larger public (Wallerstein 2004a, 37).

Framing in the World Polity.   The concept of world polity incorporates
many contradictions. The term *polity* implies centralized authority, but
theorists of world culture–polity are quick to point out that there is not,
nor will there likely ever be, a world-level state (Meyer 2007). Nevertheless, we can speak of the presence of a world polity conceptualized
as a thick and globally expansive network of actors—international organizations, social movements, nation-states, and individuals—that
embed, reproduce, and project world culture. World culture is understood as a set of universal models for framing and interpreting human
purpose, and for organizing human activity in all areas of social life. It
shapes global, national and subnational discourses around issues like
human rights, environmental sustainability, democratization, and economic development. It orients, through various rewards and sanctions,
the worldviews and actions of large-scale actors, including national
governments and social movements toward global rather than particu-
laristic goals. It endows all individuals with certain rights, subjects
them to certain obligations, and empowers them to "seek rational solutions to social problems" (Boli and Thomas 1997, 182).

    But the very language that describes world culture betrays the spec-
ificity of its origins: certain rights, certain obligations, the rationalization of human purpose, and the agency of individuals. With globalization, the dominant powers of the rich, core countries project their own
local values, norms, and modes of thinking onto others, creating what
Boaventura de Sousa Santos (2006b) refers to as globalized localism.
Theorists of world polity concede the Western origins of world culture,
but insist that it is not strictly an imperialist force born of the interests
of powerful nation-states. After all, one of the most highly legitimated
and institutionalized movements of the world polity—human rights—
emerged despite the reluctance of leading states to support norms that
would restrict their own autonomy. The long-standing hesitance of the
United States to actively support international human rights law and to

ratify international human rights treaties has not prevented the development of an expansive and increasingly significant international human rights regime (Meyer 2007; Hafner-Burton and Tsutsui 2005; Risse, Ropp, and Sikkink 1999). World culture thus operates at least somewhat independently of the interests of powerful actors, and therefore plays an authoritative role in coalescing interests, identities, and purposes around its core principles and values. In this regard, it is a powerful force of world integration and stability, producing surprising institutional similarities across nation-states and societies, regardless of very real differences in resources, interests, and capabilities.

Although macro-level state policies and institutional forms may be increasingly similar worldwide, these are often merely shells, given that actual practices and experiences differ markedly from global models. As Meyer writes, there is "great inconsistency between high models of complete, rational actorhood and the practical capabilities and resources of actual putative actors" (2000, 244). This decoupling of norms and practices is itself a critical source of social change, as actors discover and articulate "new problems" and agendas for reform in the space between policy and action, ideal and circumstance (Friedland and Alford 1991). New models born from these contradictions also globalize rapidly, perpetuating the decoupled nature of a system that is "in a kind of permanent crisis" (Meyer 2000, 244).

In addition to a decoupling between world-cultural norms and practices, we also see that actors' embeddedness or participation in the world polity—an integral site for the production, reproduction, and dissemination of world culture—remains uneven. This is a point that world polity theorists acknowledge but which remains unexamined in much of the literature. This contradiction in both the conceptualization and empirical reality of world polity has not gone unnoticed in sociological scholarship, and indeed it has been a central element in world-systems analysis, as we discuss. Relative to the developing countries of the global South, wealthy democracies of the global North have more extensive ties to the world polity via memberships in intergovernmental and international nongovernmental organizations (Smith and Wiest 2005; Beckfield 2003). This makes sense, given that they tend to have more influence in these institutions because of their ability to use their economic and coercive advantages to shape policy outcomes. It also reflects the fact that these institutions tend to be based in the global North and to privilege the languages and cultural practices of this region. Also, the motivations for connecting to the world polity differ across states. Many global South countries join international treaty regimes to gain legitimacy in the world community, with little intention (at least initially) of complying with their prescriptions.

Northern countries, in contrast, are less likely to sign treaties they do not intend, at the time of signing, to follow (Hafner-Burton and Tsutsui 2005; Risse, Ropp and Sikkink 1999). However, as institutional theorists argue, states' decisions of whether to join a treaty regime affect the subsequent choices available to them. So, for instance, the 2002 U.S. decision to withdraw from the International Criminal Court constrained (though it could not fully thwart) its ability to affect the course of negotiations by state parties to the convention. The ways a state relates to institutions and other actors also affect its ongoing process of identity formation. So, when a state takes on the identity of a party to a human rights convention, it moves down a path that will reinforce pressures on it to conform with human rights principles.

These observations regarding the unequal structure of world polity ties raise questions about the effects of inequality and power. What forces shape and reproduce uneven patterns of world integration? How is the cultural content of globally dominant models for framing and acting on social problems determined? In addition to the opportunities for social action provided by world culture and its institutional manifestation, we must also ask how the world polity and the operation of power within it restricts discourse and action around important global problems.

Contestation over the cultural content of world polity is thus an enduring feature of world relations, although the conflictual nature of the world polity is not emphasized in the world culture–polity perspective. One of the earliest challenges in the post–World War II era of world polity development, demarcated by the founding of the United Nations in 1945, was presented by the Nonaligned Movement, which rejected the power bloc politics of the Cold War era and sought to reorient world political priorities toward the global South's concerns for national liberation, national sovereignty, and equity in world economic relations. Later, governments and civil society actors of the global South challenged the globally dominant frame of environmental protection as a response to growing evidence of worldwide environmental degradation, pushing more inclusive frames—such as sustainable development and, more recently, ecological debt or food sovereignty. Such frames advance claims in terms of rights and also acknowledge the central place of natural resources for communal livelihood and economic development in the global South. More recently, the World Social Forums have provided space outside the governmental realm of world polity to develop and articulate challenges to elite-led, neoliberal globalization.

The contradictions between global norms or templates with on-the-ground circumstances of daily life are the sources of conflicts that manifest in both violent and nonviolent social movements. These range from popular protests against neoliberal globalization (Walton and Ragin 1990), to the rise of informal markets and criminal networks (for example, Chabal 2009; Nordstrom 2007), to international migration and transnational terrorism (Moghadam 2008). The principles, values, and norms privileged in the world polity are given concrete form in national development projects and related policies. At the same time, world culture authorizes and empowers individuals and other social actors to act in ways that challenge national and world cultural authorities. Challenges to world culture and the social, cultural, political, and economic forces that it supports thus reflect an essential dialectic arising from the inequities of power and differences in interests across a range of global actors. Hence world culture in the world polity produces contradictory effects, setting the stage for contestation.

Conclusion

If we are to understand the variable opportunities and constraints available to actors in the world polity, we need a world-historical and systemic approach that accounts for variations in power among global actors as well as for changing power dynamics over time. The primary actors in world polity—including nation-states, intergovernmental organizations, and social movement and other nongovernmental actors including for-profit corporations—operate under different organizational logics, practices, and priorities, even as they compete within a shared system. Institutions and global governance are not the domain of any one of these actors, but of all of them in combination and competition with each other. The participation and interventions of each is legitimized under the authority of world culture and shaped by a highly stratified global division of power and resources. Interactions among them have significant consequences for the overall world-system, given the global reach and impact—both symbolic and material—of policy scripts and issue regimes constructed within and disseminated via the networks of world polity.

The perspectives that help orient this volume emphasize the role of competitive and cooperative interactions between states and other actors in the world political system in shaping global change. State structures developed in response to movement challenges, and movements continue to affect the evolving character of modern states. Social movement research has recently emphasized the need to focus on the interactions between challengers and elites, or the "dynamics of contention," to fully appreciate the sources and implications of social movements (McAdam, Tarrow, and Tilly 2001). World culture–polity theorists have shown how state preferences and practices are shaped by their interactions with other states and with international organizations and nongovernmental organizations. The system may be constrained by the needs of globalized capitalism, but capitalists and their agents have become increasingly enmeshed in webs of institutionalized relations that alter their options for pursuing their interest in maximizing profits. These shifting institutional arrangements reflect changes in the operation of capitalism and affect the strength and capacities of antisystemic movements, as well as the playing field on which the struggle between capital and popular forces takes place. As Arrighi and his colleagues argued,

> the relational networks forming the trunk lines of the circuits of capital have been so structurally transformed that the very workings of the accumulation process appear to be historically altered. It is this ongoing transformation that has continually remade the relational conditions both of the organizing agencies of accumulation . . . and of those in fundamental struggle with them, the antisystemic movements; and so have continually remade as well the relational character of the struggle itself and hence the nature of the movements defined by it. (1989, 41–42, emphasis added)

With this larger context in mind, we proceed in our examination of the transnational organizations that populate the movements that might be seen to be converging over time around a struggle to transform the global economic and political order. Regardless of whether they are antisystemic in their collective vision, it is clear that this population of organizations is expanding globally and converging into more coherent and integrated networks (Byrd and Jasny forthcoming; Katz 2007). More activists and organizations are indeed framing their struggles in relation to the unfolding global crises, even a "crisis of civilizations," a theme that has come to prominence in activist circles since the 2009 World Social Forum.

In chapter 2, we describe the overall changes in the population of transnational social movement organizations over the last decades of the twentieth century in relation to these analytic and theoretical perspectives.

= Chapter 2 =

Changing Patterns of Transnational Social Movement Organizing

TRANSNATIONAL social movements have always shadowed states and other powerful actors in the world political economy (Chatfield 1997; Finnemore 1996), but over time they have become more formally organized and more connected transnationally (Smith 2008). Following the theoretical logics outlined in the previous chapter, we summarize this trajectory of social movement development, which is happening alongside other global trends such as the growth and increasing bureaucratization of states, the proliferation of intergovernmental institutions, and the expansion of the world economy.

In this chapter we situate the evidence we have on developments in the population of transnational social movement organizations within the evolving geopolitical context of the mid-twentieth to early twenty-first centuries. This context has shaped opportunities and constraints for social movements through the policy priorities of states, the patterns of alliance and division among states and between states and other actors, and the global distribution of symbolic, economic, and political resources. Globalization is characterized by expanding international interactions, stronger and more elaborated international institutions, and changing perspectives and cultural understandings, all of which affect the ways people organize to advance social and political goals. Because we see transnational social movements as both products and drivers of global integration, it is important to account for this larger global context to uncover lessons about the prospects for broader social transformation.

Transnational activism and advocacy work takes many forms. Some research has emphasized formal transnational associations (for example, Boli and Thomas 1997; Smith 1997; Clark 2003), whereas other work focuses on transnational networks (Beckfield 2007; Katz 2007; Keck and Sikkink 1998; Moghadam 2005; von Bülow 2010), campaigns (Rothman and Oliver 1999; Sikkink 1993; Smith 1999), coalitions (Bandy and Smith 2005; Brown and Fox 1998; Chilton 1995; Murphy 2005), and protest events (Imig and Tarrow 2001; Podobnik 2005; Friedman, Clark, and Hochstetler 2005). As summarized earlier, world-systems scholarship has tended to take a broader perspective on antisystemic movements, emphasizing the commonalities in the sources and grievances of movements organized around diverse issue areas. The study of transnational advocacy work is complicated by the many different units of analysis or focal points one might choose, and by the blurred boundaries between concepts such as networks, campaigns, coalitions, and movements.

We do not pretend to resolve these conceptual challenges here. However, we hold that behind the most important and durable political campaigns, fueling the most powerful transnational networks and coalitions, and supporting the largest protest events are strong organizations that help bring steady flows of resources—including personnel as well as ideas and money—to support transnational change initiatives (compare McCarthy and Zald 1977). By identifying these key "mobilizing structures" (McCarthy 1996), we can better understand the broad contours of transnational collective action, including its causes and long-term effects. Thus we pay particular attention to the changing population of transnational social movement organizations, understanding such changes as part of larger struggles to define the world political and economic system.

Methods

The main source of systematic data we use for this study come from the *Yearbook of International Organizations*, which has been published annually by the Union of International Associations since the early 1950s.[1] The numbers of active transnationally organized citizens' groups, known as international nongovernmental organizations (INGOs),[2] grew from fewer than 1,000 in the 1950s to nearly 20,000 by the end of the twentieth century (Union of International Associations 2004). Because only some INGOs are explicitly involved in work to change the dominant political and social order, we focus on a smaller subset of INGOs, which we refer to as transnational social movement organizations, because such groups are formed explicitly to advance social change, and thus are more likely than other groups to be routinely involved in social change work. This is not to say that other groups are not involved in change initiatives, sometimes in important ways. In fact, many groups without explicit movement purposes—such as the World Council of Churches, professional associations of various kinds, and social clubs—become regular participants in social movements (McCarthy 1996). Nevertheless, existing research suggests that it is those groups

Figure 2.1   Types of Nongovernmental Organizations

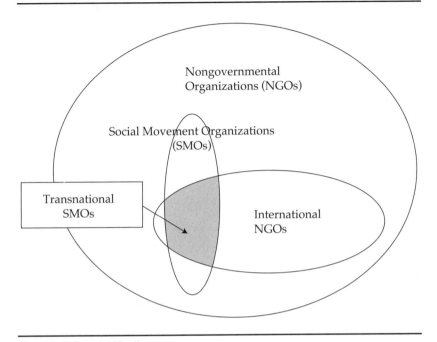

Nongovernmental
Organizations (NGOs)

Social Movement Organizations
(SMOs)

Transnational
SMOs

International
NGOs

Source: Kriesberg (1997, 13).

specifically focused on movement goals that are most likely to play consistent roles in mobilizing and introducing innovations into social movements as well as in sustaining movement networks during periods of movement abeyance (Taylor 1989; Staggenborg and Taylor 2005). Thus we focus on those groups we expect to be most involved in transnational social change activity. Figure 2.1 presents a typology of nongovernmental organizations, showing how transnational social movement organizations compare with other organizational types.

To identify groups that can be classified as transnational social movement organizations, we reviewed each yearbook edition for oddnumbered years between 1953 and 2003.[3] One of us reviewed each page of yearbook entries to identify organizations whose primary purpose is the pursuit of social change goals (broadly defined). To be included, an organization must be nongovernmental, autonomous (that is, not directed or led by a government or international agency), and not-for-profit. Selection decisions were based on reviews of organizations' name, aims, structure, membership, and founding. Occasionally, the organization's affiliations with other groups—or for newer groups, a look at the group's website—helped us make the final decision about whether a group's aims centered on social change (see appendix 2.A1 for further details on selection criteria). Each of us reviewed the other's selections for accuracy, and we consulted in cases that proved difficult to categorize. In most cases we could very easily distinguish between groups that fit our category of transnational social movement organization or not (see appendix 2.A2 for a sample list of organizations in the database).

However, a small but significant number evaded easy classification. These tended to be groups providing services to underprivileged populations, with no clear indication that they advocated for changes that would eliminate the need for their services. They also included groups working on economic claims, which can involve work that advances the national development and globalization projects discussed earlier or at challenging these elite projects. Given the considerable official funding for development, many civil society and social movement groups participate in government- and international agency-sponsored or supported projects. Many seek to maintain an autonomous, critical perspective on the larger development enterprise while accepting government funds to mitigate human suffering or to help address the needs of a minority group. Many develop a more critical perspective in the course of their work (Smith, Pagnucco, and Romeril 1994; Marullo, Pagnucco, and Smith 1996; Nelson 2002). This makes it difficult at times to determine from the yearbook entries whether a group is simply carrying out work sanctioned by elites or mobilizing critical opposition to this, and our methods attempt to account for this complex reality.

Also complicating the work of defining a category of transnational social change organizations is that, over this time of major change, we find that some groups are working on projects that may have at one point been clear examples of movement activity—such as microfinance—but which have more recently been appropriated by dominant institutions such as the World Bank and private lending institutions, thereby reducing or eliminating their socially transformative elements. In more recent years, for instance, public-private partnerships to work in controversial areas have proliferated and generated popular mobilization and critique. Such partnerships are excluded from our database, given their privileging of financial and government power over civil society voices (Martens 2007; Martens 2003; Beausang 2003).

We also excluded from the database religious bodies or groups whose primary purpose was to promote a particular religious or spiritual identity, as well as foundations and research institutes primarily engaged in research rather than active public promotion and mobilization around research findings. However, religious or faith-based organizations whose formal organizational mission was to engage in social change work are included. We coded transnational labor unions separately, and we present analyses of these organizations separately. Nevertheless, many groups included in our category of transnational social movement organizations are working for labor rights. These organizations are not trade unions, however, and tend to focus on issues such as economic human rights, immigrant worker and unemployed worker rights, and other labor-based claims that do not fit conventional trade union organizing models. This decision to separate trade unions from the larger collection of transnational social movement organizations stems from a number of observations. First, trade unions have developed particular organizational structures that distinguish them from other social movements. They tend to be structured as collective bargaining entities designed primarily to serve members rather than having some broader social or political change as their main organizational objective. Also, because of trade unions' particular relations to states and business owners, known as *business unionism*, it becomes difficult with this data source to discern the autonomy of labor associations in some countries. Our coding decision follows the treatment in the social movements literature, which has separated analyses of social movements from the study of labor organizing during much of the latter part of the twentieth century (Fantasia and Stepan-Norris 2004).[4]

The yearbook's comprehensiveness in mapping the population of transnational associations obviously improved with time as the Internet became more widely available and as transnational networks became denser. Thus we found that the average time between an organization's founding date and its first appearance in the yearbook declined from 15.6 years in the 1960s to 10.1 years by the 2000s. This figure, however, overstates the extent to which new transnational groups might be excluded from this annual census, because many transnational organizations are formed as national or binational entities before becoming formally transnational, and therefore may not be eligible for inclusion in the yearbook when they are founded.

The predominance of progressive organizations in our dataset reflects their far greater representation in this population, and that many nationalist and right-wing organizations may be less inclined to be publicizing their work in this particular arena. But it is also due in part to the systematic underreporting of organizations using violence as a political tactic. The illicit nature of some of these groups' activities, and the exclusionary nature of their organizing work make them less likely to either respond to yearbook requests for information or to be tied to international networks that increase the chance that their presence will be known to other international groups. Nevertheless, yearbook editions—particularly in later years—include records of such groups, and the Internet allows yearbook editors to identify more of them. Thus these groups are included in the dataset, but their numbers are small.

In addition to organizational goals, each yearbook entry includes information on organizations' founding year, headquarter locations, membership type (such as individual or organizational), contacts with intergovernmental and international nongovernmental organizations,[5] and countries with membership. All of these data were collected for the analyses presented in this volume. Thus, for each organization we have an updated record or entry for every year it is deemed active and therefore present in the yearbook listing. To classify countries as either global North or South, we used the membership in the Organisation for Economic Co-operation and Development (OECD) before 1975, after which the organization expanded to include more traditionally lower-income countries (that is, Mexico). OECD members are considered part of the global North—that is, among the wealthiest countries that have tended to be most influential in the global political economy. Southern countries are those outside pre-1975 OECD membership. Throughout the book, we use different years and periods to examine the data in ways appropriate to the questions we are asking. The details of each analysis are provided in the following chapters to clarify how we aggregated or disaggregated the data.

The dataset we draw from has several important advantages. It provides us with a historical record of formal transnational movement organizing going back more than five decades. It also helps show the patterns of transnational linkages by indicating which countries are reflected in a given organization's membership as well as the ties these groups have with intergovernmental organizations. It also helps us track changes in things like how activists have framed their struggles and the structure of their alliances.

As with any data source, however, there are limits to what we can know from these data. The yearbook entries are based on groups' self-reporting in response to annual surveys issued by the Union of International Associations, as well as research done by yearbook editors. The yearbook's purpose is to provide an overview of information about these groups, leaving us relatively little information about the actual content of transnational association within the groups. When a group indicates that it has members in a country, we don't know whether this means a single individual member or a hundred individuals or organizational affiliates. We also don't know what membership means for a given organization, such as whether it involves extensive interpersonal meetings and exchanges, regular organizational activities, or simple one-way transfers of information such as email alerts or newsletters. We also cannot rely on yearbook records for reliable comparisons of the resources available to different organizations, because data on this was not collected for every year, and, when it was collected, reporting was often inconsistent or missing.

Finally, our focus on formally organized transnational associations misses a growing number of associations that are part of transnational social movements but are not formal and may not be effectively transnational, according to the criteria for inclusion in the yearbook.[6] With the expansion of low-cost communications technologies, it has become increasingly possible for national and local groups to engage directly in the transnational political sphere, reducing the need for formal secretariats and organizational routines to facilitate transnational coordination and exchange (see von Bülow 2010; Edelman 2001). This reality became evident especially at the first major global United Nations conference, the UN Conference on Environment and Development in 1992, after which the UN began granting consultative status to national organizations. We are thus certain that our dataset understates the levels of transnational activity since the 1990s.[7]

With these caveats in mind, we note that the data do provide a baseline indicator of changes in the strength of the social infrastructures for social movements operating across national borders. Although these formal transnational organizations are not the only entities that comprise social movements, they do provide long-term continuity and resources that help sustain movements over the long periods required for most social change initiatives. They serve as the incubators of what Thomas Rochon calls "critical communities," generating ideas and transnational mobilizing frames for activist groups (1998). Like their national counterparts, they serve as "abeyance structures," sustaining and supporting movements and activists during times when large-scale protest and activism is absent or suppressed (Taylor 1989; Staggenborg and Taylor 2005). By looking at this particular organizational population, we contend that we can learn about the relationships between transnational social movements and larger global processes.

Our interpretations of these bird's-eye level data on the population of transnational social movement organizations are informed by a rich collection of qualitative data on transnational campaigns, alliances, and internal organizational dynamics. This work includes a growing body of published research in this field as well as original research on transnational global justice activism within the United States and World Social Forum processes (Smith 2001, 2004, 2008; Smith et al. 2011; Smith, Karides et al. 2007). Thus, though we acknowledge important limitations to our quantitative data source, we argue that by combining it with the primary and secondary evidence we have about the activities that take place within these formal organizations and informal networks, we can indeed learn a great deal about the opportunities and constraints faced by transnational activists in the contemporary world.

To help embed our discussion of large-scale organizational change within its historical context, we start with a brief overview of some important developments in recent history that are likely to affect changes in transnational organizations.

Key Historical Developments in the Contemporary World Polity

Our empirical study extends over a time of important social and political change. Clearly there are overlapping processes with multiple forces at work throughout the time frame of our study, affecting the politics of transnational organizing. For instance, in the 1950s and 1960s, decolonization was the major development in the international arena. But later years of that period (that is, the early 1970s) saw the collapse of the Bretton Woods financial system and the rise of neoliberal globalization. The Cold War had taken shape well before the 1970s and affected the process of decolonization and postwar realignment. The end of the Cold War aided the spread of global trade and expanded markets, generating dramatic economic growth in many parts of the world. But serious inequities have persisted and fueled tensions within and between countries, and shape the opportunities and constraints on transnational organizing.

The early post–World War II period saw rapid decolonization as Western imperialist states relinquished colonial territories in response to resource demands as well as to changing interstate norms that had become less tolerant of colonialism. Importantly, this period marked the rise of the United States as global hegemon, which had significant implications for the organization of interstate relations as well as for transnational organizing, a topic we examine more closely in chapter 3. Demands for national self-determination encouraged nationalist, anti-colonial movements within many colonized countries and fostered ties of solidarity between people from the global North and South (Arrighi, Hopkins, and Wallerstein 1989; Keck and Sikkink 1998). This period also saw the rise of what Philip McMichael calls the "national development project" (2006), which entailed a shift from nationally to globally defined development strategies with more deliberate application of modern technology and social engineering to economic development policy and planning (see also Scott 1998). Newly created international institutions like the World Bank and the International Monetary Fund both enabled countries to expand international trade and carry out large-scale, capital-intensive development projects such as dams and roads and helped centralize economic power within national states. These institutions contributed to the emergence of national economic development as an international concern. Newly independent states of the global South were expected to play more active roles in orchestrating the economic development of their countries than rising Western states had, and northern governments became more deeply entrenched in the global management of economic planning and development during this era. As they did so they invited new challenges from both the states of the global South as well as social movements.

As national development strategies were implemented in the countries of the global South, government leaders and analysts from those countries began to articulate important critiques of development ideology and practice. These critiques contributed to the emergence of dependency theory (see, for example, So 1990; Amin 1994; Broad and Hecksher 2003; Chirot and Hall 1982) and helped fuel calls by governments and movements of the south for a New International Economic Order (NIEO). This in turn inspired the development of the Nonaligned Movement of southern governments, and later the Group of 77, which pressed for reforms to the global system to ensure better terms of trade for countries of the south and to otherwise expand the economic power of these countries (Krasner 1985; Prashad 2007; Silver 2003). These early efforts of the south to unite in an effort to strengthen its hand in the world economy were, however, undermined by Cold War politics, competition among southern governments, superpower intervention in countries of the global South, the debt crisis of the 1980s, and ultimately by the rise of global neoliberalism (McMichael 2006; Harvey 2005; Bello 1999).

The Cold War, which developed as the new post–World War II global order unfolded, structured global conflict around two major blocs led by the United States and the Soviet Union. This framing of conflict privileged dualistic debates over whether free-market capitalism or state-controlled socialism was the better model for organizing society. Conflicts within either bloc tended to be constrained by this larger geopolitical debate because the two superpowers competed by supporting their respective allies in various countries. These relations encouraged transnational contacts outside the governmental sector, expanding the variety of webs of transnational ties across national boundaries. The Cold War affected social movement mobilization within states by situating many national struggles within a broader context of superpower rivalry (see, for example, Kolb 2005; Anderson-Sherman and McAdam

1982; Wallerstein 1990). Not only did some domestic challengers gain access to significant outside resources with which to oppose a particular government, but also groups that were critical of their governments' foreign or domestic policies could be delegitimized or otherwise undermined by opponents pointing to their real or imagined ties to a rival superpower. Global human rights discourse was one casualty of the Cold War, and the superpower rivalry became articulated as a struggle between political and civil rights as advanced by the United States and economic and social rights as defended by the USSR (O'Brien 2000; Rajagopal 2006; Steiner 1991). Separate treaty bodies defined civil and political rights as separable and distinct from economic, social, and cultural rights. Organizations tended to form to advance one or the other set of rights and to relate to particular treaty bodies, undermining efforts of some to demand a more holistic and integrated human rights regime (Lynch 1998; Steiner 1991; Smith, Pagnucco, and Lopez 1998). Globally, the Cold War shifted interstate agendas toward issues of arms control and military security at the expense of other concerns.

If the Cold War constrained the global issue agenda, its end helped open new possibilities for global dialogue and cooperation. As the Soviet Union dissolved and newly democratic states replaced it, a new optimism emerged that the United Nations and other institutions could become more effective tools for addressing a growing array of concerns that transcended national boundaries. Freed from the politics of superpower stalemate, the UN Security Council became more proactive in addressing global and regional conflicts and in expanding its agenda beyond the realm of traditional, military security concerns. The United Nations launched a series of high-profile global conferences to address issues ranging from children's rights to environmental protection to poverty reduction. Although UN global conferences had been held before this era, they had not been organized in such rapid succession and had not mobilized such extensive public participation. UN and even some national government officials expanded their efforts to engage with civil society actors to benefit from the analyses and organizational support that nongovernmental organizations could provide (Willetts 1989, 1996a, 1996b; Wiseberg 1992).[8] The sequencing of conferences coupled with new links between governmental and nongovernmental actors facilitated the expansion of transnational networks and helped foster awareness of the complex relationships among issues that governments prefer to treat as distinct (Krut 1997; Friedman, Clark, and Hochstetler 2005).

The rise and decline of the *Washington Consensus*[9] also had significant implications for transnational organizing. Beginning in the mid-1980s, the United States and global financial institutions promoted an alternative to the national development project of the decolonization era, which was no longer effective at promoting the profitability of capital (Harvey 2005; McMichael 2006). This new development model, known as neoliberalism, responded to the needs of a more globally integrated version of capitalism and for greater and more predictable access to national markets and financial opportunities. The "globalization project," as McMichael calls it, responded to this need by integrating into the lending policies of the World Bank and International Monetary Fund conditions that required national governments to open their markets and deregulate their national economies to encourage global trade and investment. The creation of the World Trade Organization in 1994 was also designed to expand global markets by limiting governments' ability to restrict flows of goods and services across their borders.

The globalization project met early on with challenges from a variety of places. During the 1980s and early 1990s many countries of the global South experienced what were referred to as IMF riots in response to the austerity measures, known as structural adjustment programs, imposed by the IMF and later by the World Bank as conditions on loans (Walton and Seddon 1994). By the mid- to late 1990s, the failures of this development model to address basic human needs and protect the environment were widely apparent (Broad and Cavanagh 1999; Khagram 2004), and a growing number of organizations began protesting at the meetings of global institutions, including the G7, G8, World Bank, or IMF meetings (Foster 1999; Pianta and Marchetti 2007; Gerhards and Rucht 1992). As protests grew, in 1990 the UN Development Program began publishing its annual Human Development Report, which highlighted the gaps between measures of national economic growth and indicators of human well-being (see, for example, ul Haq 1989).

The World Trade Organization ministerial meeting in Seattle in 1999 marked a critical turning point for the globalization project as large numbers of activists from the global North joined their counterparts from the global South in opposing the global economic order. Not only did this protest help overcome geographic divides, it also brought together activists working in many issue areas—including, for instance, human rights, environmental justice, labor, peace, women's rights, and environmental conservation. At the same time, southern governments and elite insiders—such as the former chief economist of the World Bank Joseph Stiglitz and the prominent financier George Soros—also began raising questions about the viability of the market-driven model of global integration that had guided policy making since the 1970s (for example, Soros 2002; Stiglitz 2000, 2003). Since then, negotiations to further liberalize global trade have been stymied, and critics of economic globalization have mobilized to advance ideas for more equitable, humane and sustainable forms of global integration.[10]

This very brief historical overview highlights major shifts in the global political arena that impact the organizational patterns we explore in this book. The constellation of interstate relations and patterns of dominance, the rise and decline of U.S. hegemony, the variable strength of multilateral institutions, and the major issues and crises that occupy the global agenda shape possibilities for challengers to form and mobilize members and other resources across national borders. Also, although the historical and institutional contexts affect the dynamics of organizational populations, transnational movement organizations help set the historical stage on which they act. For instance, transnational human rights organizations contributed to the demise of the Soviet Union and the rise of democracy movements in Eastern Europe (Chilton 1995; Evangelista 1995; Thomas 2001; Meyer 1999; Marullo and Lofland 1990). They also helped construct a multilateral human rights regime that could define limits on the legitimate uses of state power (Chatfield 1997; Finnemore 1996; Keck and Sikkink 1998; Smith 1995). Social movement mobilizations around the United Nations global conferences contributed further to public awareness of global interdependence and to the cultivation of networks that could challenge the globalization project (Smith 2008; Alvarez 1998; Moghadam 2005).

This relationship is partially expressed in figure 2.2, which shows the growth in number of both international governmental and transnational social movement organizations. Before the late 1980s, the numbers of both types of organizations rose together. In the early 1990s, however, patterns for the two began to diverge, the number of transnational social movement organizations increasing sharply and that of intergovernmental organizations declining, perhaps due to a saturation effect. The divergence in later years suggests that the changing security needs and interests of states at the end of the Cold War led to a reorganization of multilateral organizational entities. It also increased opportunities and incentives for forming international nongovernmental organizations, in part by creating space for the diffusion of the pro–NGO norm in global institutions during the early post–Cold War years. Subsequent chapters explore further the evidence we have about the mutual influences between global institutions and transnational social change organizing.

In the next section, we present additional data on transnational social movement organizations to illustrate how patterns of participation within and across world-system divisions, issue framing, and patterns

**Figure 2.2   Changes in Numbers of Transnational Social Movement
Organizations and Intergovernmental Organizations**

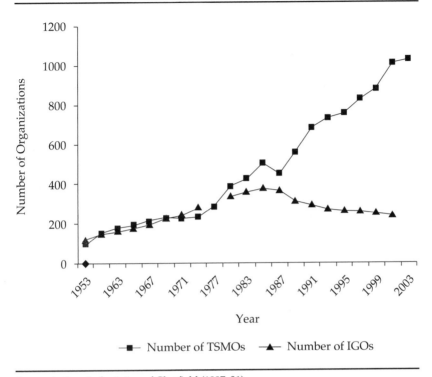

Source: Authors' adaptation of Chatfield (1997, 21).

of engagement with intergovernmental organizations have changed over time.

Changing Patterns of Transnational Social Movement Organizing

As discussed earlier, world-systems analysts have argued that changes in the world economy over the second half of the twentieth century have both consolidated economic power globally in transnational corporations and leading core states and expanded the ability of antisystemic social forces to disrupt the system (see, for example, Silver 2003). Most analyses of social movements, however, tend to examine them within particular national or historic periods, thereby missing their connections to broader world-systemic dynamics. World-systems analysts have argued that opportunities for antisystemic movements expand in times of hegemonic decline, and that the current period of U.S. hegemonic decline has encouraged growth in antisystemic activism. If this were the case, we should expect to find consistent growth in the population of transnational social movement organizations, as more activists and movements see connections between their local grievances and global forces. These new organizations help respond to the proliferation of constituencies that have emerged to contest the forces of neoliberal globalization (Arrighi and Silver 1999; Silver 2003). Over time, we would expect dynamics of organizational competition and cooperation and institutional processes to contribute to the increasing coherence or consolidation of movement energies around a smaller number of issues.

Since the founding of the United Nations, the population of transnational social movement organizations has risen sharply, from around 120 organizations in the 1950s to more than 1,000 in 2000 (see table 2.1). We also see divergent patterns of transnational labor and social movement organizing. Labor groups tend to be older, more than 75 percent of them formed before 1980 and 40 percent before 1960. In contrast, more than 50 percent of all other transnational social movement organizations active in more recent years were established after 1980, and nearly 25 percent after 1990. Moreover, although these groups have been growing rapidly in recent decades, labor groups have seen very slow growth. This trajectory suggests that antisystemic movements have over recent decades shifted the emphasis of struggle from the workplace and labor-based identities to encompass a wider range of social policies and identities. It also reflects more restricted opportunities for labor and workplace-based organizing that have marked the neoliberal period.[11]

Issue Composition

From the early years of contemporary world polity development to the post–Cold War era, transnational mobilization agendas have become more consolidated around particular issues. Changes parallel the development and expansion of intergovernmental bodies, reflecting the extent to which the institutional realm of the world polity exerts pressure on activists to frame their grievances in legitimate, or institutionally sanctioned, ways. Figure 2.3 illustrates changes in the percentage of all organizations mobilized around specific issue agendas.

Over the time frame of our study, human rights and environment grew in their representation on transnational mobilizing agendas and

Table 2.1   Transnational Social Movement Organizations and Labor Unions[a]

	Movement Organizations		Labor Unions	
	Active	Percentage Founded Each Decade	Active	Percentage Founded Each Decade
Before 1950		12		33
1950s	127	7	39	11
1960s	205	11	59	26
1970s	250	20	80	12
1980s	467	26	104	8
1990s	777	23	85	9
2000s	1022	1	87	1
Total	1660[b]	100	184	100

Source: Authors' compilation based on their Transnational Social Movement Organizations Dataset.
[a] Counts are the average number of organizations identified in the *Yearbook* as active over the years in each of the decades listed.
[b] Counts over each decade do not add to the figure in the total cell because an organization could have been active over more than one decade and is included in the count for each decade in which it was active.

labor unions and groups working on issues not presented in the figure saw the most dramatic declines in representation. The falling percentage of labor union organizations reflects the relative weakening of workers in the labor force and the decline and mergers of trade unions since the 1970s. Human rights and peace were predominant foci in the early years of the United Nations, and the fastest growth has been among transnational environmental groups, which grew nearly tenfold in the study period. More movement organizations began focusing on environmental issues following the 1972 and especially the 1992 UN Conference on Environment and Development. This growth also reflects the emergence in the early 1970s of many national environmental movements in the global North (Johnson and McCarthy 2005; Roberts et al. 2003).

That transnational movement organizations have tended to adopt more multi-issue organizing frames in recent years is likely due to more frequent intermovement interactions facilitated by both greater transnational organizational development and UN global conferences. It also reflects activists' greater attention to the links between the global economy and other concerns. In the course of their efforts to affect global politics and to build transnational connections, organizers have

Figure 2.3   Percentage of Transnational Social Movement Organizations in the Poplulation by Issue-Focus[a]

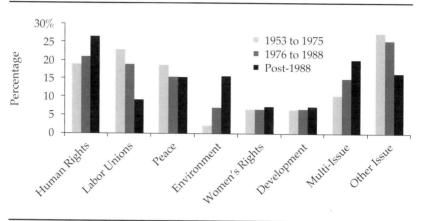

Source: Authors' compilation based on their Transnational Social Movement Organizations Dataset.

[a] For all groups except labor unions, the categories depicted above are not mutually exclusive. Figures are based on the number of organizations active in each issue area as a percentage of all organizations active at any time during the period. The denominator includes every occurrence of an organization during each of the years covered in the time period.

learned new ways of thinking about their grievances. Transnational links between organizers in the global North and South especially have encouraged activists to embrace more systemic, structural understandings of problems ranging from environmental concerns and labor and women's rights to the experiences of small-scale farmers (see, for example, Rothman and Oliver 1999; Hertel 2006; Moody 1997; Martínez-Torres and Rosset 2008). As we discuss in chapter 4, these global conferences highlighted the interdependencies among many global concerns. For instance, peace groups have long pointed to the trade-offs between military and social spending (Atwood 1997), and critics of the globalization of trade and finance emphasize the contradictions between social and environmental concerns and global markets (Cavanagh and Mander 2004; Daly 1999; Porter 2005).

The decline in representation of other issues—such as international integration, Esperanto, and ethnic unity—suggests a more consolidated world polity agenda in later years. Typical of other multi-organizational fields, including national polities, the isomorphic pressures of the world polity produce convergence around a more limited set of issues and policy agendas and adaption to predominant organizational models and strategies (see Garner and Zald 1988; Zald and

Garner 1987). For instance, the expansion of international human rights instruments has led many ethnic separatists and militant ethnic groups to shift their strategies to take advantage of opportunities in this expanding regime (Olzak and Tsustui 1998). Also, in international institutions, debates related to peace and security are highly centralized or framed in highly technical terms, offering relatively few opportunities for substantial popular participation and deliberation. Thus, growth in some areas, such as environmentalism and human rights, reflects expanding institutional opportunities for mobilization, whereas lack of growth in other areas, such as peace and demilitarization, reflects institutional constraints.

Moreover, in the earliest period, just 65 percent of all organizations fit within the six most prominent issue areas, but more than 80 percent did so in later years. This pattern reflects both the channeling of social movements into institutional discourses and frames, and a more dialectical process whereby movements seek to take advantage of opportunities in institutions as well as to shape interstate discourses and priorities. The pattern we see is consistent with the notion that transnational social movement issue agendas are more consolidated around the same issues that drive interstate politics.

Geographic Composition

Most analysts anticipate that the richest countries will be home to the most organizations, given the relative access to resources needed for advocacy work. Poor countries may have more grievances motivating organizational growth, but fewer resources with which to pursue social movement organizing, especially transnational organizing. But if anti-systemic movements are indeed growing and expanding their potential to challenge existing hierarchies in the world economic order, then they should demonstrate a capacity for mobilization outside the core countries of the world-system and for integrating groups across world-system divides.[12] As many would expect, the richer countries in the world are highly overrepresented within transnational associations. Over all years, the United States averaged participation in around 80 percent of the transnational social movement organizations that did not restrict membership to specific regions. Western European countries have been prominent in an even larger percentage of transnational social movement organizations: for example, 75 percent of nonregional movement organizations had representation from at least two western European countries in 2003, compared with an average of around 40 percent that had representation from at least two countries in Africa, Asia, or Latin America. Over time, however, the percentage of move-

Table 2.2   Percentage of Transnational Social Movement Organizations
with Headquarters in Various Geographic Locations

	1953 to 1977	1976 to 1988	Post-1988
Western Europe	77%	64%	56%
U.S. and Canada	10	13	15
Africa	2	4	6
Asia	3	6	8
Eastern Europe	4	4	4
Latin America	1	3	5
Middle East	2	4	3
Global North	88	80	75
Global South	12	20	25

Source: Authors' compilation based on their Transnational Social Movement Organization Dataset.

ment organizations with members in the global South has increased. For instance, in 1953, roughly 28 percent of transnational social movement organizations had members in more than two African countries, versus 43 percent in 2003. The proportion of organizations with headquarters outside of the global North has also increased, as we show in table 2.2. The geographic distribution of labor organizations' headquarters, while somewhat distinct from that of TSMOs, remained fairly stable over this same time frame. Roughly a third of transnational labor organizations were based in the global South throughout the time frame of our study, and the population of organizations doubled between the 1950s and 2000s from thirty-seven to eighty-eight organizations. Notable differences between labor and other TSMOs were that a smaller percentage of labor headquarters are in North America and a larger percentage are in Latin America. Over time, the percentage of labor organization headquarters in Latin America declined from 24 percent in the 1950s to 14 percent in the early 2000s.

What table 2.2 reveals is the growth in the numbers of headquarters in the global South, which grew from just 10 percent of the population in 1953 to roughly 25 percent of all transnational movement organizations in 2003—a nearly tenfold increase.[13] But even as participation from the global South has risen, more than 75 percent of all organizational headquarters were still based in the core countries of the world economy in the post–Cold War period. These figures reflect a very rapid proliferation of new organizations in Europe, many of which were founded as the European Union consolidated its reach and instituted a common currency. In fact, 32 percent of all transnational social

Table 2.3   Disbanding of Transnational Social Movement Organizations

	1953 to 1977	1976 to 1988	Post-1988
Number of disbanded organizations	60	191	378
Percentage of disbanded organizations that were based in the global South	17	25	33
Percentage of disbanded organizations that were based in the global North	83	75	67
Percentage of all organizations based in the global South that disbanded	29	30	34
Percentage of all organizations based in the global North that disbanded	19	26	24
Total number of observations	1537	2625	5930
Total number of unique organizations	294	716	1409

Source: Authors' compilation based on their Transnational Social Movement Organization Dataset.

movement organizations in our data that were founded after 1990 were European regional organizations, versus 16 percent of those founded before 1990.

Moreover, transnational social movement organizations based in the global South were also less likely to survive than those based in the global North, as revealed in table 2.3. Different rates of organizational disbanding reflect differences in access to resources, but also indicate important differences in the structures of civil societies in the north and south. The prevalence of inter-national donor influence in the south, though perhaps expanding short-term opportunities for transnational organizing, may be limiting the longevity of donor-dependent organizations lacking strong grassroots ties (Heydemann and Hammack 2009; Aksartova 2009). Clearly, the 1970s and 1980s saw rapid growth and volatility for transnational movement organizational populations in both the north and south, as well as high rates of disbanding. As southern organizational populations expand, they also see greater volatility and higher rates of disbanding than their northern counterparts.

Thus, although geopolitical changes, democratization, and world culture have facilitated the growth of an internationalized nongovernmental sector in the global South, transnational associations are relative newcomers outside Western democratic countries. Particularly in the latter half of the twentieth century, international nongovernmental organizations based in the global North expanded their reach into the developing countries of the global South by establishing projects or offices and partnering with south-founded organizations (Bob 2005). Political liberalization opened the door to this expansion, but the growth has also been fueled by funding opportunities from private (Ford Foundation, Soros Foundation) and public sources (official development assistance from advanced economies) supportive of nongovernmental efforts in areas such as poverty relief, humanitarian assistance, and technical assistance, particularly in countries where government capacities are perceived as nonconforming to global standards of "good governance" (Weiss and Gordenker 1996; Weiss 1998). At least discursively, the neoliberal turn that began in the 1970s shifted the burden of "bringing development to the people" from governments to nongovernmental organizations and ultimately to the people (Manji and O'Coill 2002; Ferguson 2006). By the 1980s, because of democratization, a facilitative ideological and funding environment, and increased capacities of southern civil societies, the number of nongovernmental organizations in many regions of the global South increased impressively (Foster and Anand 1999; Fisher 1993).

The logic that led southern NGOs to engage in transnational alliances was similar to that of northern NGOs: to influence national and intergovernmental political processes, to gain supportive allies in multilateral arenas, and to gain access to resources needed to organize. As Thomas Dichter observed, "many southern NGOs came into being because they wanted to address genuine needs and were thus demand driven. But many came into being because they were aware that foundations, northern NGOs, and bilateral funders were looking for local partners" (1999, 52). Because private funding sources are scarce in the global South, links with north-based international nongovernmental organizations remain an important source of resources and support among south-based nongovernmental organizations.[14] However, actual practices of transnational associations in the global South challenge the assumption that power and influence flows from the core countries of the world economy to the semiperiphery and periphery. Although resource advantages have tended to be concentrated in the north, southern organizers have brought their own organizing priorities and imperatives to their work, sometimes adapting their organizing frames to take advantage of resources and opportunities (see, for example, Bob 2005) and at other times challenging and transforming understandings and agendas of northern activists and networks (see Rothman and Oliver 2002; Hertel 2006; Brooks 2005; Stewart 2004;

Sperling, Ferree, and Risman 2001; Edelman 1999; Borras, Edelman, and Kay 2008).

Comparing transnational social movement organizations with transnational labor unions, we find some important differences. Labor groups have tended to have greater representation from the global South—in terms of both their locations and their membership bases. Nevertheless, core countries are still overrepresented in labor associations, with more than half of all labor groups' headquarters based in western Europe. Latin America has seen much stronger transnational labor activism than other regions outside of Western Europe, with nearly one-quarter of all labor groups between 1976 and 1988 based in the region. Moreover, a considerably larger percentage of transnational labor unions than other transnational movement organizations are headquartered in the region, a topic we explore in chapter 3.

Decentralization and Regionalization

Beyond their numbers and geographic makeup, we must consider changes in these organizations' structures. Movement strength depends on development of effective mechanisms for managing diversity in the organization as well as strong networks of connections to other actors in the same environments. Theories of organizations and networks anticipate that a context like the rapidly changing global economic order would require organizational structures that can readily adapt to changing and uncertain environments. This typically means that organizations in uncertain environments will be less centralized and have more ties to other organizations. Table 2.4 displays organizational features of transnational social movement organizations, including their structures, age, and their ties with intergovernmental organizations (IGOs) and other INGOs. It also shows the number of organizations that disbanded in each period, the percentages of these that were south- and north-based, and the proportion of organizations based in the south and north that disbanded in each period.

Looking at organizational structures, we find a consistent pattern of decentralization over the study period. This is evident in the growing percentage of groups that have autonomous organizations as their members (coalitions) and the declining percentage organized around a more centralized structure of nationally organized sections that manage communications and exchanges between international secretariats and members based within countries. An example of the latter type of organization is Amnesty International, within which national sections are generally required to adhere to particular practices and to use a

Table 2.4   Characteristics of Transnational Social Movement Organizations

	1953 to 1977	1976 to 1988	Post-1988
Organizational structure			
Coalition	28%	28%	40%
Federation	30%	30%	21%
Any individual members	22%	29%	41%
Regionally organized	22%	29%	36%
Average age (median in parentheses)			
All TSMOs	29 (20)	29 (22)	25 (18)
North-based TSMOs	30 (21)	31 (24)	27 (19)
South-based TSMOs	24 (16)	21 (15)	20 (15)
Networks			
Average number of ties to IGOs	1.4	1.5	2.4
North	1.4	1.5	2.5
South	1.0	1.3	2.0
Average number of ties to INGOs	1.1	1.8	4.9
North	1.1	1.8	5.0
South	1.3	1.8	4.4

Source: Authors' compilation based on authors' Transnational Social Movement Organization Dataset.

common organizational name and organizing framework. Coalitions, by contrast, allow participating organizations more discretion in how they engage in the association, allowing more direct communication and participation by groups in the work of the international and generally allowing groups to maintain their own set of organizational priorities and frames. As we see decentralization in the organizational structures used to coordinate transnational association, we also see that these organizations are integrating larger percentages of individual members. Clearly the expansion of the Internet and other means of communication have enabled individuals to join transnational campaigns in ways that were not possible in the past, and transnational movement organizations have adapted to these changing possibilities for individual activism across borders.[15]

Another trend we see in this population that reflects its decentralization, or the increase in more local forms of autonomy, is the distinct trend toward more regional forms of organizing in more recent years. The collapse of the Soviet Union brought an end to the bipolar system that defined world relations for more than half a century. The emergence of a multipolar system, characterized by the dispersion of global power and influence, is also a consequence of declining U.S. hegemony since the 1970s and the crises and competition that hegemonic instability instigates. As we discuss in chapter 3, the rise of new forms of interstate regionalism throughout the world is a by-product of such changes in the larger world-system. Our data show that these changes have also been accompanied by growth in the number of regionally organized transnational social movement organizations. At the same time as the overall population of transnational social movement organizations grew more than fourfold, the percentage of those groups organized within a single world region expanded from less than 25 percent to about 30 percent of all transnational organizations. Although more than half of the regional movement organizations are based in Europe, developing in response to expanding opportunities and institutional changes in that region, the number of regional movement organizations in Africa, Asia, and Latin America has doubled since the 1980s. In the last decades of the twentieth century, the growth of regional sectors, the substance of regional organizing, and relations between regional transnational social movement organizations and regional intergovernmental bodies have been shaped by the dynamics of crisis and hegemonic decline in the world-system as well as by the institutions of the world polity. We discuss these changes in chapter 3.

Connections to Other Actors

Another clear and consistent pattern in these data is that transnational social movement organizations are embedded in more extensive networks, or connections with other organizations, including both intergovernmental organizations and other international NGOs.[17] These patterns hold for groups based in the north as well as in the south. Ties to intergovernmental organizations and to other nongovernmental actors in the world polity confer resources and legitimacy that enhance organizations' chances of survival and success (Edwards and Marullo 1995; Minkoff 1993).[18] Indeed, connections to other international actors can help reduce north-south inequalities in world polity representation over time by redistributing resources and opportunities to participate in international meetings and other transnational activist work. Over the years we examine, north-based organizations had, on average, more ties to IGOs than their southern counterparts did, a pattern that likely results from these groups' age, their greater access to resources, and their geographic proximity to IGO offices.

For both south- and north-based groups, the mean number of international nongovernmental organizations with which they had ties increased over the three periods, from an average of just one to nearly five, reflecting the dramatic growth in the number of INGOs as well as the increasing importance of network politics in the global political arena. As with IGO ties, links to INGOs correlates with organizational survival: surviving organizations, regardless of where they were based, had higher average INGO ties than disbanded organizations did.

Interestingly, south-based organizations reported only slightly fewer ties to INGOs than north-based groups did despite their relative youth (the association between the numbers of ties a group has and its age is statistically significant). This may reflect a strong need for the organizing resources provided by these groups, but also a particular strategic orientation of south-based groups, which stresses the building of relationships over the emphasis on particular policy-oriented campaigns. Such an interpretation is supported by case study research and other evidence on the activities of movement organizations in global conferences. Observers and participants noted a relatively greater interest among many southern groups in networking over engaging in the formal aspects of negotiations (Krut 1997; Friedman, Clark, and Hochstetler 2005). This emphasis on networking has certainly contributed to the discourses and strategic emphases in the World Social Forum, which grows out of south-based transnational organizing work (Santos 2006a; Smith, Karides et al. 2007; Whitaker 2009).[19]

Conclusion

Geopolitical changes opened new opportunities for social movement organizing and enhanced the ability of transnational organizations to mobilize across world-system divisions, which in turn has helped generate new and shared understandings of global problems. One of the most important features of the time period since the end of World War II is the expanding numbers and significance of international governmental and nongovernmental organizations, including their more rapid expansion during the more recent period of U.S. hegemonic decline. Although the majority of these organizations are based in the global North, growth in participation from countries of the global South has also been considerable, a trend that enhances the capacities of social movements to operate on a global scale. Consistent with our expectations that transnational mobilizing capacity would become stronger over time, we find that organizational structures have become more decentralized, with greater inclusion of individual members and more decentralized decision making. Transnational social movement organizations have also expanded network ties to both governmental and nongovernmental organizations, enhancing their ability for communication and coordinated action. Finally, as the world polity has become more densely interconnected, transnational movement organizations have mobilized around an increasingly consolidated set of political issues or frames. The patterns support our contention that the infrastructures and capacities of transnational social movements have become stronger over the study period, as well as more able to mobilize diverse sets of people from outside the core countries of the world economy.

We saw too that an increasing percentage of transnational movement groups are organized within world regions. In the next chapter we link this change to the dynamics of U.S. hegemonic ascendance and decline and to the shifting geopolitical conditions of the post-Cold War era. Intersecting with these changes was the rise and diffusion of world culture and the embedding of world cultural principles and norms in a growing number of international organizations, including regionally based intergovernmental bodies. The symbolic resources of world culture enhanced possibilities for transnational collective action during a time of crisis and change in the world-system, facilitating the rise of transnational social movement organizing within and beyond world regions.

Appendix

Appendix 2.A1: Identifying Entries for Selection

To identify groups for inclusion in our dataset, senior members of our research team carefully reviewed each page of the odd-numbered years of the *Yearbook of International Organizations* 1953 and 2009, with the exception of 1961, 1975, and 1979 because no English-language edition was published in those years. Data for 1987 through 1989 was collected from the 1986–1987 and 1987–1988 editions , which had been collected before our decision to code the entire time series.

The organization's name, aims, structure, membership, and founding details were used to determine whether the group should be included in the dataset. Occasionally, the organization's affiliations with other groups helped us make the final decision. The main criterion for inclusion is that the primary purpose of the organization is the pursuit of social change goals, broadly defined. The group should be not-for-profit and autonomous (that is, should not directed or led by a government or international agency).

To bound the dataset and strengthen its validity, we set the following selection rules to exclude the following types of organizations:

- intergovernmental organizations
- foundations, trusts, and funds
- institutes and organizations primarily devoted to research
- organizations whose purpose is primarily religious
- sections or committees of other international organizations
- organizations whose primary work is education, individual transformation or spirituality, or providing services.
- nongovernmental organizations or hybrid NGO-IGO organizations founded by or initiated at the request of the United Nations or other intergovernmental body

The *Yearbook*'s criteria for inclusion are as follows:

- Aims of the organization must be truly international.
- Individual or collective voting participation from at least three countries is required; membership must be open to any qualified individual or entity in the organization's area of operations; voting power must not permit one national group to control the organization.

- A formal constitution, permanent headquarters, and procedures for the election of a governing body are required.

- Officers might, for management purposes, all be of the same nationality, but are included in the *Yearbook* only if a rotation at designated intervals is required of headquarters and officers among the various member countries.

- "Substantial" contributions to the budget must come from at least three countries, and no profits may be made for distribution to members.

- Organizations must not be subsidiaries of other organizations, or at least must maintain their own independent decision structures and officers.

- Evidence of the organization's current activity must exist.

Inter-Coder Reliability   Once a senior researcher reviewed *Yearbook* entries and selected cases for inclusion, a second researcher—usually the principal investigator—reviewed this list and checked any questionable cases. Researchers discussed cases when no agreement could be reached on whether a group should be included. Often aims that seem at one point to be clearly about social change become institutionalized or appropriated by elite actors, and we wanted to be certain that the dataset included only groups working to advocate for social and political change.

Once cases were selected, a team of coders entered data from the organizational entries using our coding scheme. A random selection of cases was coded by two coders to ensure inter-coder reliability.

Appendix 2.A2: Examples of Transnational Social Movement Organizations in Dataset

Asian Peoples' Anti-Communist League

Campaign Against Military Prostitution International

EC Migrants Forum

Europe-Third World Association

Anti Slavery Society for the Protection of Human Rights

Central European Federalists

Christian Peace Conference

Environmental Development In The Third World

European Health Network Against Racism

European Union Of Women

Friends Of The Earth International

Green Belt Movement

Inclusion International

International Abolitionist Federation

International Association Against Noise

International Catholic Migration Commission

International Commission for the Protection of Alpine Regions

International League of Religious Socialists

International Organization of Journalists

International Registry of World Citizens

International Union of Local Authorities

International Youth Federation for Environmental Studies and Conservation

Nordic Council for the Protection of Animals

Pan American Women's Association

Peoples' Global Action Against Free Trade and the WTO

Permanent Peoples' Tribunal

Pesticide Action Network

Pugwash Conference on Science and World Affairs

Quaker Esperanto Society

Regional Council of Indigenous People

Solidar

Trickle Up Program

Union of Resistance Veterans for a United Europe

Unrepresented Nations and Peoples' Organization

War Resisters' International

Women's Global Network on Reproductive Rights

Womens World Banking

World Council of Indigenous Peoples

World Peace Through Law Center

= Chapter 3 =

Regionalisms and Counter-Hegemony in the World-System

L IKE OTHER interstate bodies, regional intergovernmental organizations (IGOs) such as the African Union, the European Council, and the Association of Southeast Asian Nations assume important roles in structuring cooperation and mediating conflict among states and between states and other actors. The mandates of many of these organizations have expanded since the 1990s, facilitating cooperation around myriad economic, political, and social goals. In the process, regions have become important arenas for interactions between political elites and social movement challengers seeking influence over domestic and international policies. Most often, regional projects represent efforts by groups of states to advance their interests within the existing system of globalized capitalism. But to the extent that they help bring unity among diverse state and nonstate actors wishing to challenge and expose the contradictions of the dominant world-system, they are counter-hegemonic projects that can support and nurture antisystemic movements.

The shifting scope of regional governance worldwide, partly expressed through the enlargement of governance mandates to include human rights, environmental protection, and other issues not directly related to economic cooperation and integration, has been accelerated by geopolitical changes in the world-system since the end of the Cold War. Regionalism throughout the Cold War was shaped by the dynamics of the superpower rivalry and U.S. hegemony in the world-system (see, for example, Amin 2006). Although some hailed the demise of the Soviet Union as signaling the "end of history" and the triumph of Western capitalism, in reality the collapse of the bipolar world order destabilized U.S. hegemony. This opened space for counter-hegemonic rivals, who challenged the leadership of the dominant state in the world-system, as well as for antisystemic forces, which include social movements challenging the fundamentals of the world-system itself (Wallerstein 1993; Moghadam 2008). These changes have also refashioned earlier forms of counter-hegemonic, global South-based regionalisms. Regional organizations created during the Cold

War, such as the Organization of African Unity and the Association of Southeast Asian Nations, prioritized security as well as economic and political autonomy. Counter-hegemony also found expression in cultural and institutional projects such as pan-Arabism and pan-Africanism and in the liberation movements that seized state power after decolonization.

The end of the Cold War undermined the bases on which these regional projects were established. However, it was but one of several interrelated destabilizing forces in the modern world-system. The crisis of profitability and related financial strains of the 1970s also challenged U.S. dominance, and it generated important shifts in global economic strategies to restore economic expansion and profitability. These neoliberal economic policies emphasized reduction of government regulation and spending, elimination of barriers to international trade and investment, and privatization of public assets. This strategic shift to a neoliberal accumulation regime also affected the nature of regionalism and its counter-hegemonic potential. Neoliberalism was promoted as an alternative to Keynesian, national development projects, and was characterized by a set of policy prescriptions aimed at harmonizing national economic policies in ways that would enhance capital's profitability by expanding international markets for trade and financial investment.

But this "solution" to the accumulation crisis weakened numerous foundations upon which the system's stability was based, including the notion that global integration would generate sustained economic growth in poor countries and continued advances for northern workers (Silver 2003). Neoliberal policies quickly produced debt crises in many poor countries which fueled popular protests against global financial institutions and policies. Moreover, persistent and rising inequality, social displacement, and increased concentration of wealth in much of the world helped give rise to new and potent challenges to the system of globalized capitalism. In response to the debt crises, the World Bank and International Monetary Fund imposed structural adjustment policies and other austerity measures, forcing the world's poorest countries and people to bear the costs of the system's volatility (Babb 2003, 2005; Babones and Turner 2003; World Commission on the Social Dimensions of Globalization 2004; UNDP 2005). As they were squeezed financially, low-income countries were being pressed by the World Trade Organization to further open their borders to international trade and financial investment. It is in this context, in response to the pressures of globalized capitalism, that many states turned to new forms of regional cooperation and integration to assert and protect their interests.

Although declining U.S. hegemony and changes in the accumulation regime of globalized capitalism has conditioned the rise of new regionalisms, the global cultural and institutional context has shaped the nature of these challenges, providing important material and symbolic resources for both counter-hegemonic and antisystemic challengers. Regionalism is embedded in a larger world polity, and thus reflects and draws on prevailing institutional logics and normative arrangements. We therefore find growing isomorphism in the organizations and agencies, as well as in normative, discursive, and legal architecture that undergirds regionalism throughout the world. For instance, most of the major regional polities have adopted a human rights charter and also provide some legal mechanism for the participation of civil society in regional political forums. These are found, as well as in the European Union, within the context of the Association of Southeast Asian Nations, the Arab League, the African Union, and the Organization of American States.

Within the broader context of hegemonic decline in the world-system, regional institutional changes have facilitated efforts to build transnational social movement alliances. The rise of counter-hegemonic competition has created opportunities for antisystemic mobilization, including the converging interests between counter-hegemonic multistates (for example, the European Union and the BRICs) and social movements. As regional institutions exert more influence in domestic and global political arenas, they grow in relevance as targets of contention and collaboration and as arenas for securing resources and allies for social movements. Table 3.1 presents the growth in number of regionally organized transnational social movement organizations in four world regions from the period of U.S. hegemonic stability and extending through the post–Cold War years.

The end of the Cold War marked a new period of hegemonic transition as the bipolar world order collapsed. As table 3.1 suggests, this created new opportunities for transnational social movement mobilization. The number of these organizations rose between 1975 and 1988, during a period of systemic crisis when the United States and global financial institutions increasingly promoted neoliberalism as an antidote to the accumulation crisis and the perceived failures of national development policies.

The table also shows that regional, transnational movement mobilization has been most pronounced in Europe. The difference between Europe and other regions is a consequence both of its location in the core of the world economy and its related approach to regionalism built on the principles of social democracy and interstate governance

Table 3.1   Active Regional Transnational Social Movement Organizations
with Ties to Regional Institutions

	1953 to 1975	1976 to 1988	Post-1988
Africa			
Total	5	34	83
Percentage IGO ties	7%	29%	39%
Americas			
Total	9	41	76
Percentage IGO ties	12%	6%	21%
Asia			
Total	5	33	81
Percentage IGO ties	0%	5%	10%
Europe			
Total	54	117	308
Percentage IGO ties	27%	34%	45%

Source: Authors' compilation based on their Transnational Social Movement Organization Dataset.

(Held and McGrew 2007; George 2005; Amin 2006). It also reflects the relative advantages a united Europe has within the existing world-system in terms of both collective counter-hegemonic potential and exercise of state sovereignty. In contrast to Europe, states in the global South have been reluctant to cede their hard-won sovereignty and autonomy to regional institutions, and slow to adopt provisions for civil society participation in regional governance (Acharya 2002). The supranational character of European regionalism over a growing range of policy domains coupled with expanding institutional opportunities for civil society participation facilitated the growth of a transnational social movement sector on the continent.

Further revealed in table 3.1 is an important difference between the American regional sector and others. Ties between transnational social movement organizations and regional intergovernmental bodies increased between the decades of U.S. hegemonic stability to the first period of hegemonic decline for all regional sectors *except* for the Americas.[1] There the percentage of organizations with ties to the regional intergovernmental realm declined by 50 percent. Moreover, the percentage of American regional organizations with participation from activists in the United States also declined over this period—from 57 percent of organizations active through 1975 to 15 percent of the organizations active between 1976 and 1988.

Interestingly enough, this is the same period when case study research shows that transnational movement activism was expanding in Latin America. For instance, liberation theology animated autonomous local mobilizations for social justice and led to the widespread development of Christian base communities throughout the region, despite opposition from various Church authorities. Liberation theology first emerged in the late 1960s and its emphasis on the realities of the poor in Latin America in relation to Catholic social teaching provided fertile ground for activism. The ideas and organizing networks spread throughout Latin America through church-based infrastructures and personnel, and also fueled ties to faith-based activist networks in the global North. Liberation theology thus provided a basis for more formal political organizing as repression eased (Cavendish 1994; An-Na'im 2002).[2] Liberation theology ideas and networks have been key in supporting transnational movements, including most recently the World Social Forums (Smith 1996; Shor 2010; Nepstad 2002; Grzybowski 2006). Feminist groups began regular transnational gatherings known as "encuentros" in 1981 in Bogota (Sternbach et al. 1992; Vargas 1992). Also at this time, under pressure from structural adjustment policies, Latin American peasant groups began transnational conversations aimed at addressing the common sources of their problems. Their encuentros were precursors to La Vía Campesina, one of the key transnational organizations involved with the World Social Forums (Martínez-Torres and Rosset 2008, 2010).

Over the years of superpower rivalry, distrust among Latin American activists toward U.S. civil society and U.S. institutions developed in response to the U.S. government's Cold War policies and interventions in Latin America (von Bülow 2010). This dampened the extent to which U.S. activists developed formal and lasting ties with activist groups in the region, and is evident, for instance, in the limited role of U.S. groups in early tri-national activism surrounding the North American Free Trade Agreement, or NAFTA (Ayres 1998; Macdonald 2005; Foster 2005). With the end of the Cold War, ties between American regional movement organizations and regional interstate bodies increased to around 20 percent, and the percentage of movement organizations that included participation from U.S.-based activists also rose slightly. However, as we discuss shortly, movement momentum shifted to extra-institutional and contentious forms of collaboration and mobilization as the United States stepped up efforts to control the regional political economy through a series of trade agreements, including the

North American Free Trade Agreement, the Central American Free Trade Agreement, the Free Trade Agreement of the Americas, and numerous bilateral treaties.

The timing and uneven growth in regional sectors coupled with different patterns of relations between regional movement sectors and regional IGOs is the puzzle we sort out in the remainder of this chapter. U.S. hegemony and the superpower rivalry had significant implications for all world regions through the course of the Cold War, shaping priorities as well as patterns of cooperation and conflict. Over time, movement capacities and infrastructures for challenging the world-system increased, because the end of the Cold War brought new opportunities for counter-hegemonic regional governance and for the mobilization of regional, transnational civil society. The experiences of neoliberalism also helped refashion regionalism in the form of new regional intergovernmental arrangements, such as Mercosur in South America, and the reconfiguration of older regional bodies such as the European Union and the Organization of African Unity. These global shifts in regionalism are counter-hegemonic to the degree that they challenge U.S. dominance in the world-system. To the extent that they intersect with the mobilization of social movements they can also nurture antisystemic challenges. In this way, world-system dynamics of hegemonic decline and economic contraction help set the stage for the emergence of both counter-hegemonic regional projects and antisystemic social forces, as we discuss in the next section.

Regionalism During the Cold War

The era of U.S. hegemony began with the establishment of the Bretton Woods institutions and the United Nations following World War II. A monetary system based on the U.S. dollar and global financial institutions built from the perspective of U.S. development needs and priorities helped consolidate U.S. power and dominance of the world economy. Over the subsequent decades of the Cold War, the U.S. strengthened its hegemonic position in the world-system by cultivating trade and aid ties with European and Third World countries. U.S. hegemony was further strengthened by the strategic placement of American military power throughout the world, the dispersal of military aid, economic assistance to the countries destroyed during World War II, and political linkages established through security pacts, the United Nations, and other international agencies (Arrighi 1999b).

Over the course of the Cold War, the global accumulation regime defined by the development priorities of the global North and an international agenda dominated by the superpower rivalry was challenged by various forms of south-south cooperation. The Organization of African Unity was built around the ideals of African socialism and, like Latin American regionalism, embraced a critique of international political economy informed by dependency theory. The Group of 77, a coalition of southern countries, presented a unified front at the UN Conference on Trade and Development (UNCTAD) in 1964 and placed the economic interests and concerns of the global South at the center of international negotiations (Amin 2006). The Nonaligned Movement, promoted at the Bandung Conference in 1955 and established in Belgrade in 1961, generated calls for a New International Economic Order, a proposal that challenged existing global economic arrangements and was adopted by the UN General Assembly in 1974 (Jain and Chacko 2009; Prashad 2007; Bello 1999).

Through organizations such as the Nonaligned Movement and coalitions such as the Group of 77, the Third World presented an occasionally unified and potent political-ideological challenge to domination by core powers. Moreover, the growing cohesion and influence of Third World countries occurred during a time of their rapid industrialization, when the terms of trade began to turn in their favor, and when the economic gap between rich and poor countries appeared to be narrowing somewhat (Silver and Arrighi 2001). The Organization of Petroleum Exporting Countries (OPEC), founded in 1965, was also an important form of emergent south-south cooperation, as its goal was to strengthen the position of member countries in international trade by regulating oil prices. The petroleum cartel became more overtly political when, in 1967, the Organization of Arab Petroleum Exporting Nations was formed within OPEC to exert pressure over Western powers for their support of Israel.

Sovereignty and autonomy were central to these regional projects. Regional institutions were created to deflect superpower intervention in state affairs and the economic dependence of southern states on the business cycles of core states (Amin 2006; Shaw 2002). Further, regionalism was a mechanism for establishing economic and political self-reliance and for challenging the global division of labor and hierarchy of authority in the world-system (Acharya 2002; Phillips 2004). In Southeast Asia, for example, state leaders were concerned that the United States and other foreign powers would use the communist threat to manipulate politics within the region (Hussey 1991). This concern impelled the formation of the Association of Southeast Asian Nations (ASEAN) in 1967. Also central to the ASEAN mandate was the principle of noninterference in governance, which blocked interference from foreign actors in the affairs of ASEAN member-states (this included interference of ASEAN member-states in each other's affairs).

Hence, although earlier attempts at regional cooperation in Southeast Asia had failed, Cold War dynamics helped condition the rise of ASEAN as a security-based organization that prioritized state sovereignty, self-directed economic development, and regional stability. Through the 1980s, by denouncing the participation of the United States and other Western states in the Asia Pacific Economic Community (APEC), ASEAN remained a source of resistance against outside influence in Asia.

But superpower interference did affect the nature of interstate relations within regions. In northeast Asia, for example, the security and economic interests of the United States played a central role. With the rising threat of communist China in the early 1950s, the United States successfully pressed other northeast Asian leaders, particularly in Japan and Korea, to adopt a bilateral over a multilateral approach to security and trade. This system enabled the United States to play a central role in security and development within the region, preventing the emergence of a regional bloc that could pose a significant challenge to its leadership. The result was a hub-and-spoke system of regional relations, with the United States at the center and shallow integration among countries of the region (Calder and Fukuyama 2008).

Other attempts at regional unity, such as pan-Arabism and pan-Africanism, were stymied by superpower interference. In the Middle East, for instance, the two superpowers attempted to create client states that would act as local proxies for superpower competition within the region (Milton-Edwards and Hinchcliff 2004). In 1958, for instance, the United States joined the military committee of the Baghdad Pact, which was a security agreement between Iran, Iraq, Pakistan, Turkey, and the United Kingdom, in an unsuccessful attempt to prevent Soviet expansion into the Middle East. The Soviet Union strengthened its position in the region throughout the 1950s and 1960s, establishing military and political relationships with several states, including Egypt, Iraq, Yemen, and Libya. Superpower rivalry also played out in Africa. As the United States and its Western allies supported anticommunist governments in Rhodesia, South Africa, and Zaire, the Soviet Union provided direct and indirect forms of military aid to socialist governments and to liberation movements throughout southern Africa.

The United States played a highly interventionist role in Latin America throughout the Cold War, undermining, and sometimes overthrowing, governments in countries thought to be transitioning to communism (Dominguez 1999). Socialists had gained influence in the region, both in the political realm through militarized challenges as well as in the popular realm through the expansion of liberation theology. The U.S. government targeted pro-communist, populist, and nationalist governments and acted to prevent antisystemic movements from gaining power. It intervened directly through the CIA, overthrowing procommunist governments throughout the region, including Guatemala in 1954, Ecuador in 1961, Dominican Republic in 1963, and Brazil in 1964, and indirectly by providing military assistance to anticommunist forces, such as in Nicaragua.

Indeed, U.S. interventionism in Latin America has been a key part of its hegemonic strategy, allowing it access to the region's material resources and economic opportunities and limiting interstate competition within the hemisphere. Toward this end, the U.S. government mobilized trade unions in the Cold War struggle, and U.S. labor organizations promoted U.S. aims in Latin America (Herod 2001; Scipes 2005; Fletcher and Gapasín 2008). In its effort to establish its dominance in the Western Hemisphere, the U.S. government sought to manipulate and control the formation of trade unions in Latin America. It engaged in what workers of the region came to refer to as "monroismo obrero," or worker Monroism. In response, however, critical Latin American organizers formed their own Confederacion de Trabajadores de America Latina in 1938 to counter the U.S.-sponsored Pan-American Federation of Labor (Herod 2001, 141). And as we discuss, the Cartegena Agreement that created the Andean Community in 1969 further conditioned the emergence of autonomous regional labor unions in Latin America.

Although hemispheric regionalism was driven by the U.S. ambition to strengthen its political leadership in the region, subregionalism—in this case, regional cooperation among South American or Central American countries—had the goal of protecting state sovereignty and autonomy in matters of economic development. Subregional forms of cooperation and integration were motivated by the twin goals of reducing dependence on Europe and the United States and sparking self-reliant economic development through import substitution industrialization (Phillips 2004; von Bülow 2010). Developed within and promoted by the UN Economic Commission for Latin America and the Caribbean (ECLAC), this model of regionalism was grounded in dependency theory, which understood the development challenges of the south, or periphery, as directly related to their subordinate position in the world-system hierarchy.[3] An important piece of this regionalist strategy was to create common markets among sets of Latin American countries to reduce dependence on core states (Phillips 2004). Initiatives included the Latin American Free Trade Association (LAFTA) and the Central American Common Market, both established in 1960; the Andean Pact in 1969; and the Caribbean Community and Common Market in 1973.

In Africa, Cold War–era regionalism was driven largely by a quest for unity and liberation from colonial rule, efforts enhanced in southern Africa through Soviet Union patronage. These objectives were institutionalized with the founding of the Organization of African Unity (OAU) in 1963. Soon after founding, the OAU established a liberation committee to provide funding, logistic support, training, and other resources to liberation movements officially recognized by the regional organization. Related goals of sovereignty and state autonomy in political, social, cultural, and economic development were also driving principles of African regionalism. The Lagos Plan of Action, proposed by the Organization of African Unity in 1980 to address poverty and economic stagnation, asserted the primary role of African states in the economy; national-based strategies and prescriptions were proposed on issues ranging from food security to women and development, and both economic growth and income redistribution were prioritized (Owusu 2003).

In the mid-1980s, however, African regionalism collapsed under the weight of debt burdens and an urgency to attract development assistance. In the Lagos Plan and other African initiatives, African leaders had blamed global political and economic forces for the dismal state of development throughout sub-Saharan Africa. But in its 1981 Berg Report on African development, the World Bank blamed domestic factors such as failed policies, corruption, and mismanagement, and it proposed market-based solutions to Africa's problems (Owusu 2003). In line with neoliberalism, the Berg Report also called for a significant reduction in the role of the state in African development. To secure assistance from the World Bank and other international lenders, African leaders abandoned the Lagos Plan and adopted structural adjustment policies, signaling a break with homegrown development agendas and a turn toward the neoliberal model.

The accumulation crisis of the 1970s and the neoliberal response spelled the end of the period of south-south cooperation and resistance that emerged in the post–World War II years and after decolonization, resulting in what Silver and Arrighi refer to as the "strange death of the Third World" (2001; see also McMichael 2006; Escobar 2004b). In 1971, the United States replaced the Bretton Woods monetary system with a floating-exchange rate system, and it liberalized capital flows in 1974. This period also marked important shifts in development thinking and policy. Whereas the earlier period was marked by Keynesian national development strategies that emphasized the state's role in the economy, the neoliberal globalization project deemphasized the state and linked southern countries' development to their integration into the global economy (McMichael 2006;

Hahn 2008; Harvey 2005). These changes helped focus social movements on world-systemic sources of grievances, laying a foundation for new counter-hegemonic regionalisms.

The shift to a global floating currency regime was meant to jump-start profitability after a long period of stagnation by enhancing global investment opportunities and reducing investor risks. When the U.S. Federal Reserve increased interest rates in 1979, the debt burden of low-income countries increased as well, marking the beginning of the Third World debt crisis (Duménil and Lévy 2005). Massive financial flows in the form of interest payments signified a reversal of global development financing, which flowed from north to south during the post–World War II Bretton Woods development era and from south to north during the neoliberal era (McMichael 2006). Together, these changes put an end to the overt calls for a new international economic order as states in the global South were forced to find their footing in the new neoliberal order (McMichael 2006; Bello 1999).

The collapse of the Soviet Union brought an end to some of the ideological divisions that were the source of significant tensions within world regions. But it also brought an end to superpower competition, which had been a stabilizing force in the world-system. The end of Cold War–related ideological divisions was a boon for various counter-hegemonic forces, including renewed forms of interstate regionalism. The openings it created provided new spaces for transnational popular groups to collaborate across former geopolitical divisions around a variety of issues.

Hegemonic Transition and Regionalism After the Cold War

By the end of the1990s, several regional initiatives that developed over the course of the Cold War had stalled or failed, and many were being retooled in response to a new global reality (Grugel 2006, 209). In Latin America, for instance, although the Latin American Free Trade Association helped to increase trade between member-countries and the rest of the world, it had failed to increase intraregional trade to any significant degree or to transition countries from reliance on primary to more profitable secondary goods exports (Phillips 2004). In East Asia, largely as a result of its apparent mishandling of the financial and environmental crises of the 1990s, ASEAN's "narrow elite-centered and sovereignty-bound framework" came under increasing attack from its own member-states, the international community, and regional civil society (Acharya 2003, 380; see also Ahmad and Ghoshal 1999; Chandra 2004). The Pan-Africanism and national liberation framework of the Organization of African Unity gave way in 2002 to the African Union (AU). The European Union turned its attention to repositioning itself in the global political economy by pursuing deeper integration and harmonization through currency and enlargement policies, and by establishing partnerships with emergent regional polities, such as with Mercosur (Grugel 2004).

The United States began to pursue regionalism through economic reengagement with its own hemisphere (Grugel 2004). The turn to hemispheric regionalism signaled a shift in policy partly in response to the difficulties the United States faced in advancing its agenda in the World Trade Organization following its 1999 ministerial. As global trade negotiations stalled following the refusal by a bloc of global South countries to adopt new liberalization agreements without concessions from the U.S. and Europe, the United States shifted its efforts to advance bilateral and regional trade agreements where it could wield greater coercive power (compare Arrighi and Silver 1999). Beginning with NAFTA in 1994, CAFTA in 2005, the ongoing negotiations around the Free Trade Area of the Americas (FTAA), and a series of bilateral trade agreements, the United States has sought to create a stable model of regional economic governance that "reinforces the parameters of a neoliberal political economy in the Americas. . . [and] consolidate[s] the foundations of U.S. hegemony itself in the global and regional contexts" (Phillips 2005, 5; see also Grugel 2004). Phillips describes the U.S. approach to regionalism in the Americas as a project of economic governance "defined by U.S. power in the region and oriented toward distinctively U.S. interests and preferences" (2004, 4). South American leaders have responded to the increasingly coercive measures used by the United States to advance its preferred, neoliberal model of regional integration by promoting new forms of subregional cooperation and integration. In 1999, Mercosur and the Andean Community began negotiating a merger that would ultimately facilitate the creation of a South American Free Trade Area.[4] In 2004, a cooperative agreement was signed between the two regional blocs, which led to a 2008 treaty that lays the foundation for a Union of South American Nations.

With the end of the Cold War, regionalism throughout the world began to expand beyond the set of relatively narrow security and economic goals that defined earlier regionalisms to become a much more comprehensive and multidimensional project of governance (Acharya 2002; Grugel 2006). Neoliberalism itself provided an important ideological foundation for governance by an enlarged range of actors participating in activities formerly restricted to states. Civil society organizations were increasingly mobilized into development projects through official aid policies, which used international financial assistance to reduce the role and capacities of southern states. Western governments channeled official development assistance and other international aid directly to civil society groups rather than government agencies. As we discuss in chapter 5, this reflected a process some analysts have called the "neoliberalization of civil society" (Ferguson 2006; Goldman 2005). Although it helped to harness or co-opt social forces, it also reflected a projection of global institutional logics that northern powers could not fully control (Swidler 2009; Macdonald 1997).

Ironically, as neoliberal policies sought to open space for market forces, they restrained the capacities of the state during a time when demands on states to adhere to world cultural norms such as human rights, environmental protection, and transparent and democratic governance have increased. Neoliberal policies thus helped expand the incentives for southern governments to engage in regional cooperation as a way of easing the transition to new governance models and of increasing regional leverage in global politics. However, world cultural norms could also serve as mechanisms through which dominant powers reinforce their position in trade and politics by increasing pressures on noncore states to conform to human rights and environmental standards. But when states adopt and institutionalize world cultural norms, they signal an intention to comply with global norms and subject their practices to scrutiny by other states and nonstate actors. The existence of world cultural norms has inspired and legitimated movements against states and corporations, and against the contradictions and hypocrisies of the system of globalized capitalism itself. In a global context in which there has been a shift from power or authority based on coercion to that based on norms, world culture empowers challengers to hegemony and to the world-system, whose resistance may take the form of pointing to gaps between world cultural norms and the practices of more powerful states.

Many regional organizations have some provision for civil society participation in regional governance, reflecting the global pro-NGO norm that proliferated more broadly in United Nations politics beginning in the mid-1980s (Reimann 2006). The norm of citizens' participation has been diffused worldwide via donor agencies, Western governments, IGOs, and nonstate actors including NGOs, all of which "actively advocat[ed] the inclusion of NGOs in policy-making processes at the national, local, and regional levels" (Reimann 2006, 62). As the pro-NGO norm gained prominence internationally, the international donor community (for example, the U.S. government, the World Bank, OSCE, and the Council of Europe) directly pressed states to relax legal and fiscal restrictions that had curtailed civil society growth in the past (Reimann 2006). The norm's institutionalization along with funding opportunities from sources such as the United Nations has fueled the expansion of both service-oriented and political advocacy NGOs in a variety of areas, including human rights, environment, peace-building, and women's rights (Boli and Thomas 1999; Paris 2003).[5]

The pro-NGO norm strengthened the neoliberal project to the degree that it helped advance particular understandings of democracy and rights that favor the expansion of global capitalism. Changes in regional governance mandates reflect the projection of governance models advanced through neoliberalism, and institutional openings may channel popular resistance into "acceptable" forms that pose no fundamental challenge to the neoliberal project. At the same time, however, once civil society actors are accorded a greater voice in governance, their own authority stems from the larger set of world cultural norms that contradict neoliberal practices.

The institutional and cultural dynamics of the world polity have helped define the paths different actors took in response to opportunities created by the end of the Cold War. The embeddedness of regional polities in wider institutional processes has led to growing isomorphism in the scope and substance of regional agendas and treaties and in the types of regional-level agencies established to enforce compliance with regional treaties. As regions expanded their mandates to increase participation from civil society groups, non-state actors began to play an increasingly prominent role in influencing the trajectory of change. Contemporary activists increasingly point out the hypocrisies between global human rights norms and the actual practices of states and international institutions. For instance, Jackie Smith documented the efforts of transnational human rights activists to challenge the "institutional contradictions" between the UN human rights machinery and the practices of the World Bank and other international development bodies (2008, chap. 9). World culture and global institutions provide symbolic and material resources for activists striving to shape the substance and scope of regional governance and to bring these bodies into alignment with world-cultural norms. Table 3.2 compares the four regions on timing of the adoption of treaties in the areas of human rights, women's rights, and the environment; the institutionalization of mechanisms for civil society participation; and the establishment of representative and constitutive bodies.

Comparing these regional treaties (or charters, as in the case of the ASEAN Human Rights Charter) around general human rights and women's rights, we see that European institutions and the Organization of American States (OAS) were very early adopters. However, two differences between the two regions are crucial. Although the OAS was an early adopter, it was much slower than the EU (or even ASEAN) to

Table 3.2   Comparison of Regional Institutions

	European Union and the Council of Europe	Organization of American States	Association of Southeast Asian Nations	African Union/ Organization of African Unity
Regional treaties				
Human rights[a]	1953[b]	1948	*2010[c]*	1986
Women	1953	1954	2004	2005
Environment	1982	—	1985	1968
Civil society participation				
Formal mechanisms in place	1957	1999	1986	1990
Representative or constitutive bodies				
Parliament	1957	—	—	*2004[c]*
Principal court	1952	—	—	*2003[c]*
Human rights court	1950	1979	—	2004

Source: Authors' compilation based on multilateral treaties deposited with the secretary general (United Nations n.d.).
[a] The list of treaty areas included here is not exhaustive. We include only three of the major noneconomic treaty areas for illustrative purposes.
[b] ASEAN does not have a regional human rights treaty but adopted a human rights charter in 2010. For treaties, years represent the date the first treaty in the area of human rights, women's rights, or environmental protection was first adopted by the regional institution. For civil society participation and representative-constitutive bodies, the year included is the start date of a functioning body or protocol.
[c] An italicized date indicates that the treaty, body, or protocol is not yet ratified or operational.

adopt mechanisms for the participation of civil society groups in regional policy processes. Further, unlike either the European Union or the African Union,[6] the OAS has not established representative or constitutive bodies. These discrepancies between regional treaty adoption and both democratization (civil society participation and representative bodies) and the establishment of oversight and enforcement mechanisms (courts to adjudicate treaty violations) indicate a high degree of hypocrisy within the OAS, suggesting that in the world-system, decoupling between normative commitments and actual practice is greatest where hegemonic influence is stronger. The OAS helps the United States maintain its hegemony in the region by, on one hand, embedding world cultural norms of human rights and democracy through treaty mechanisms and the creation of agencies such as Inter-American

Council for Integrated Development, which lend legitimacy to the dominant hegemonic order. At the same time, regional arrangements provide few institutionalized mechanisms through which states and social movements can hold the United States accountable to the norms that justify and legitimate its authority. By contrast, in Europe, where the distribution of state power and capacity in the region is comparatively more equitable, the effort within institutions to build unity among states and between states and social forces, and to project the European social-democratic model as a challenge to U.S. dominance in the world-system and in the American hemisphere, has been much greater (see Grugel 2004; George 2005). For instance, the European Union has become increasingly involved with the development of Mercosur over the years, challenging U.S. leadership in Latin America through attempts to steer the subregion toward social-democratic regionalism and away from the liberal-capitalist variant favored by the United States (Grugel 2004). And though the African Union adopted rights treaties much later, it has moved ahead of the OAS in terms of institutionalizing world cultural norms around citizen participation as well as in the creation of a parliament and regional courts. We now trace changes in regional institutional mandates in conjunction with the emergence of regional, transnational social movement sectors to illustrate the extent to which counter-hegemonic state interests and social movement interests coincide in regional polities.

Over the years of European institutionalization, legal changes have expanded channels for civil society participation in the European polity. The Council of Europe, the Court of Human Rights, the European Parliament, and the European Commission were all active by the end of the 1950s. The treaties that established the Council of Europe and the European Parliament mandated guidelines for civil society participation. Since 1952, NGOs have been allowed consultative status with the Council of Europe, an independent institution established by the Treaty of London in 1949 that produces European treaties covering subjects such as human rights, environment, and migrant workers. A further step was taken in 1976 when the Liaison Committee of INGOs (international non-governmental organizations) was formed, providing participatory status and a permanent structural link between INGOs and the Council of Europe. This encouraged and facilitated the development of regional transnational associations (see, for example, Cullen 2005). The Council of Europe also hosts the European Court of Human Rights, one of the main mechanisms for enforcing the obligations of states that have ratified the various rights treaties. In addition to contracting states, individuals, groups, and NGOs are eligible to enter complaints to the court. Further, as a result of civil society pressure for a more transparent European Commission, the Amsterdam Treaty, signed in 1997, provides a legal framework for civil society consultation with the commission.

Since the breakdown of the bipolar world order, other government leaders have adopted some aspects of the European model in efforts to build regional polities. These efforts increasingly coincide with the interests of social movements and potentially strengthen the antisystemic potential of movements. The Organization of African Unity adopted the Charter for Popular Participation in 1990, which complemented the African Charter on Human and People's Rights that entered into force in 1986, paving the way for increased citizen participation in regional governance. In 2000, the African Union replaced the Organization of African Unity with the primary aim of accelerating economic integration while addressing the social, economic, and political problems that African states faced and that were aggravated by neoliberal globalization. Three important institutions were established four years after the AU Charter was adopted. First, the Pan-African Parliament (PAP) was inaugurated in 2004. Although it initially extended only consultative and advisory powers, the parliament was expected to achieve full legislative authority like the European Parliament upon which it was based. Second, the protocol establishing an African Human Rights Court went into full force in January 2004 after it was ratified by fifteen states. However, the Human Rights Court has not yet been established, partly because of delays caused by negotiations around a recent protocol to merge the Human Rights Court with the also yet-to-be-established African Court of Justice. In consultation with civil society groups, the African Union further created a legal framework for facilitating civil society engagement with the institution through the 2002 protocol that established the African Economic, Social and Cultural Council. This protocol includes an accreditation criteria and a code of ethics to be applied to all civil society groups hoping to engage with the AU. The provisions in the protocol were developed through the combined efforts of a large gathering of civil society groups and representatives of the AU in 2002.

Although much slower than the African Union and certainly the European Union to expand its mandate, the Association of Southeast Asian Nations (ASEAN) has also undergone significant changes since the mid-1980s that have altered the infrastructure for and strengthened the antisystemic potential of transnational social movements. ASEAN established a formal protocol for limited civil society participation in 1986 during the fifth meeting of the nineteenth ASEAN Standing Committee in Manila. Along with democratization in several member-countries beginning in the late 1980s, this protocol facilitated a shift in ASEAN's elite-centered and sovereignty-bound framework as member-governments and civil society groups began to openly challenge ASEAN's founding principle of noninterference (Ahmad and Ghoshal 1999; Acharya 2003). For example, the governments of Singapore and Malaysia challenged this principle when they reached out to the international community and to domestic NGOs for help in pressing the Indonesian government to act more forcibly in constraining the activities of businesses responsible for the deadly pollution haze that engulfed the region in 1997 (Cotton 1999).

The environmental and the financial crises of the late 1990s led to restructuring and the enlargement of ASEAN's scope to include social development and environmental goals. In 2002, several important regional policies were implemented: the Plan of Action on Rural Development and Poverty Eradication, the Plan on Social Safety Nets, and the Agreement on Transboundary Haze Pollution. During that same year, the ASEAN Sub-Committee on Women, formed in 1981, began discussions on a work plan for women's advancement and gender equality in the region, and declarations and commitments around SARS, HIV/AIDS, youth, education, and industrial relations were adopted. In 2007, ASEAN leaders adopted a new charter that established the institution as a rules-based organization and a binding legal entity. This change is significant because, since its creation in 1967, ASEAN's founding principle of noninterference in the affairs of member states stood in the way of a more bureaucratized structure with legal power over the activities of members. The charter also provides for a human rights body and a multilateral dispute-settlement mechanism—changes that came about through a ten-year effort on the part of Southeast Asian civil society networks and coalitions.

Turning once again to American regionalism, since the mid-1990s, the Organization of American States has taken several steps to accommodate civil society organizations seeking to engage with the institution. For example, Resolution 759, adopted in 1999, outlines rules for the participation of civil society organizations in OAS activities. Accommodations offered to civil society groups registering with the OAS include entry into public and closed meetings of the Permanent Council (PC) and the Inter-American Council for Integrated Development (CIDI); the right to distribute written documents and to present statements in OAS meetings; and access to virtual consultations, restricted OAS websites, and the calendar of public meetings. The OAS reports that since 1999, 218 NGOs have registered with the institution.

But despite the multifaceted nature OAS governance—with formal commissions in place to govern human rights, democratization, children's rights, gender equality, development, trade, and other policy areas—and the establishment of channels for the participation of civil society groups, the United States has steered regionalism according to its own security interests and economic priorities, curtailing meaningful civil society participation in regional hemispheric governance. Therefore, ties between regional social movement organizations and the hemispheric regional body have not increased as much as in other regions (see table 3.1). Regarding trade agreements since the 1990s, government leaders in the Americas have deliberately created two distinct policy negotiation tracks, one focused on regional economic integration and the other on political integration. Although it is the economic agenda of regionalism that has inspired the most visible and vocal opposition, social movements and NGOs seeking to influence the policy agenda of region-building have been channeled towards the summit process—considered the lesser of the two available negotiating forums—where the United States has kept formal discussions of the economic agenda off the table (Grugel 2004, 2006; Korzeniewicz and Smith 2001). The economic-political dichotomy institutionalized in hemispheric regionalism has resulted in two types of civil society engagement with the summit process: insider groups engaging in nonbinding consultative relations with the summit, and outsider groups organizing counter-summits to demonstrate their rejection of the liberal political economy and promotion of a "political economy based on rights and community" (Grugel 2006, 219).

Regionalism and Antisystemic Movements

Contention around hemispheric trade negotiations grew into the 2000s, with state leaders such as Hugo Chavez and social movements challenging U.S. efforts to consolidate its domination over the American regional political economy through the Free Trade Area of the Americas. Subregional counter-hegemonic efforts such as the Andean Community, a free trade area established by Cartegena Agreement in 1969, and the negotiations around the establishment of Mercosur in 1991 helped mobilize the antisystemic forces that have arisen to challenge U.S. hegemony in Latin America and the world-system more generally. In this regard, counter-hegemonic regionalisms and antisystemic social movement are mutually supportive and coevolving. Transnational labor in South America, which is a significant element of the antisystemic social movement emergent in the region, emerged in the context of counter-hegemonic, subregional projects such as the Andean Community and Mercosur. Our data show that the formation of transnational labor unions in Latin America peaked in 1969, coinciding with the Cartegena Agreement. This subregional effort thus helped lay the foundation for subsequent labor mobilizations around hemispheric and subregional integration efforts, including efforts to influence the course of regionalism in the Southern Cone.

Although labor unions were marginal to trade negotiations between Mercosur member-countries before 1991, they strengthened their attempts to influence subregionalism in South America throughout the 1990s. They did so by participation through newly opened formal institutional channels within Mercosur and in parallel civil society meetings alongside Mercosur intergovernmental negotiations (Phillips 2004). By the late 1990s, transnational labor efforts had helped procure important gains within Mercosur, including the adoption of the Mercosur Multilateral Agreement on Social Security in 1997 and the Mercosur Social and Labor Declaration, both of which require that International Labor Organization (ILO) conventions form the basis for regional labor legislation and standards (Phillips 2004). The adoption of these agreements illustrates how social movements shape the trajectory of regionalism by appealing to world-level institutions and norms.

Certainly, as in other regions, neoliberalism has curtailed the power of labor to an important degree. But regionalism has created space for transnational linkages among labor groups and lent legitimacy to their claims. The ability to appeal to ILO norms and legal standards was significant both in creating a source of legitimacy and leverage for labor groups and in providing a transnational focal point and frame. As the United States stepped up its efforts through the 1990s to establish a FTAA, Southern Cone labor unions, invigorated by victories within Mercosur, began to collaborate more broadly with social movements throughout South America. Communication among these groups affected their understandings of conflicts and their ability to connect material demands to larger rights and environmental claims (Phillips 2004; von Bülow 2010; Rothman and Oliver 1999). In the American regional context, labor and cross-movement activism has been especially visible and contentious, and we believe this is largely in response to the persistent and often coercive U.S. efforts to strengthen its grip on the regional political economy. These challenges gain legitimacy and momentum through the high degree of hypocrisy between the norms formally espoused by the Organization of American States and the behavior of the United States as regional hegemon. In this context, the decoupling between norms and state practice has enhanced the mobilizing potential of antisystemic forces.

Reflecting the subregional struggles against hegemonic power in the region is a comparatively high proportion of transnational labor unions relative to other types of transnational social movement organizations. Here we compare the number of transnational labor unions with the

Figure 3.1   Regional Transnational Labor Unions as Percentage of Social Movement Organizations

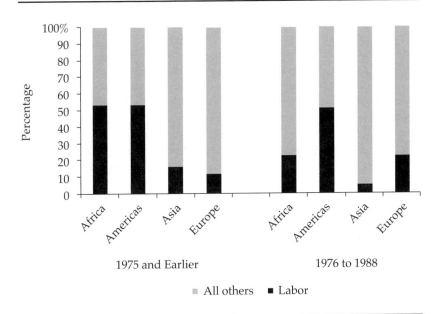

Source: Authors' compilation based on their Transnational Social Movement Organizations Dataset.

number of other transnational movement organizations as a percentage of all transnational movement organizations in each of the regional sectors over two periods, global U.S. hegemonic stability (through 1975) and its destabilization to the end of the Cold War (1976 through 1988). This analysis is presented in figure 3.1.

During the first period under consideration, in Europe and in Asia, transnational organizations mobilized around issues such as human rights or environmental protection made up a greater percentage of the population of regional transnational social movement organizations than transnational labor unions did. For Africa and the Americas, the opposite held true: the percentage of transnational labor unions was higher than the percentage of transnational groups organized around other issues. With world-systemic crisis, declining U.S. hegemony, and the globalization of neoliberalism as a response to the accumulation crisis of the early 1970s, the percentage of transnational labor unions relative to other transnational movement organizations decreased by 43 percent for Africa and by 31 percent for Asia. But in the Americas this figure remained stable at just 50 percent, whereas in Europe it increased to 22 percent. Despite its declining representation within the American regional sector in more recent years, transnational labor unions constituted over 20 percent of the total population of regional movement organizations into the post–Cold War era (figures not shown in table). This was double the figure for Europe and Africa, and triple that for Asia. In this regard, the American sector revealed a decidedly different pattern of regional transnational mobilization.

As discussed in reference to table 3.1, ties between regional transnational social movement organizations and regional IGOs in the Americas declined between 1976 and 1988, a period characterized by intensive U.S. intervention in Latin American states, such as in Nicaragua, El Salvador, and Guatemala. The decline reflects a trend that accelerated through the Cold War when, in addition to U.S. intervention in the form of military invasion and assistance to anticommunist forces through the CIA, the United States persisted in efforts to subvert autonomous and socialist-oriented movements for workers' rights in Latin America. As Washington sought to suppress communist movements at its borders and bolster pro-U.S. or anticommunist forces, it encouraged transnational alliances among labor activists who otherwise might have remained more nationally focused. The signing of the Cartagena Agreement in 1969 facilitated the rise of Latin American labor transnationalism. Also, following the establishment of Mercosur in 1991, transnational labor grew in significance as a social movement force in the post–Cold War era. Despite neoliberal globalization's harmful consequences for labor movements in much of the world, transnational labor unions in Latin America that emerged in the context of counter-hegemonic regionalism provided a foundation for the development of networks among labor and other social movements that have supported subsequent collective actions around the FTAA process (von Bülow 2010; Foster 2005).

The United Nations and Regional Social Movements

World culture and global institutions provide important sources of leverage for social movements seeking to challenge the practices of states and regional bodies. Similar to what Margaret Keck and Kathryn Sikkink refer to as the boomerang strategy of transnational activists, whereby activists marginalized in national polities appeal to international norms and allies to gain leverage in national contexts, transnational organizations make appeals to UN agencies and world-level norms to bring pressure on and gain leverage over regional authorities.[7] To what extent, then, are links to global institutions helping activists shape the course of regionalism and challenge inequality and injustice in regions and the world-system more broadly? We would expect position within the world-system, particularly in relation to hegemonic power, to influence connections between transnational activists and intergovernmental bodies. This is so because, as we outlined, regional trajectories over the course of the twentieth century were shaped significantly by the dynamics of the Cold War. The United States and the Soviet Union used their power to influence relations within regions according to their own security and economic interests. This dynamic influenced the nature and course of regionalism until the breakdown of the bipolar world order.

But even as the end of the Cold War and the destabilization of U.S. hegemony facilitated the rise of regions as counter-hegemonic forces in the world-system, the legacy of Cold War geopolitics remains embedded in regional politics. Global South states have been reluctant to cede authority and sovereignty to regional bodies and to create mechanisms for the participation of civil society in regional policy negotiations. Where regional bodies have not developed resource, normative, and legal capacities for participatory governance, global institutions—particularly UN agencies—play a significant role in bolstering regional, transnational civil society. As regional institutions expand their governance capacities and mechanisms for the participation of civil society groups, and as they channel more resources into civil society development, we would expect activist organizations to increase ties to regional bodies relative to UN agencies. Figure 3.2 illustrates change over time in the density of activist ties to regional versus UN bodies for four world regions.

The figure illustrates that the relative density of ties between regional transnational social movement organizations and regional institutions versus UN bodies is much higher in the European sector than elsewhere. That is, in Europe, regional transnational social movement organizations are much more likely to have ties to European intergovernmental bodies than they are to the United Nations. This pattern not only reflects EU-based funding opportunities and the social-democratic nature of European regionalism, it also suggests the relative unity of political elites and social movements around European regionalism as a means of challenging U.S. hegemony. The projection of the European model and its adaptation in other regional contexts has been very uneven, but our data suggest that even though the number of organizations with ties to regional institutions relative to the United Nations is very low outside Europe, social forces are increasingly connecting to regional polities, potentially shaping the ongoing course of regionalism. What is also striking is that despite the multifaceted nature of the

Figure 3.2   Social Movement Organizations with Ties to Interstate Bodies Relative to UN Agencies

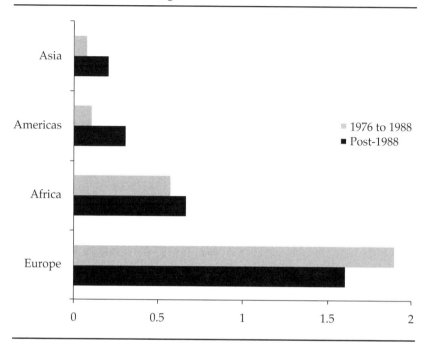

Source: Authors' compilation based on their Transnational Social Movement Organizations Dataset.

Note: The figures were calculated by dividing the number of organizations with ties to regional IGOs by the number with ties to UN agencies in each period. Longer bars indicate a higher proportion of transnational social movement organizations with ties to regional IGOs relative to those with ties to the United Nations. For example, between 1976 and 1988, the ratio of European transnational social movement organizations with ties to European regional IGOs relative to those with ties to UN agencies was nearly 2:1. This chart includes only the 1976-to-1988 and post-1988 periods because very few regional transnational social movement organizations outside Europe had ties to regional bodies before 1976.

OAS's governance mandate, the early adoption of regional treaties such as in human rights and women's rights, and the opening of channels for civil society participation in the early 1990s, the density of ties between regional movement organizations and regional IGOs versus UN agencies is lower than we might expect. That is, Latin American transnational social movement organizations are much more likely to link with UN agencies than they are with those of the OAS. The Asian regional sector also exhibits a greater preponderance of ties to the UN relative to the ASEAN, the only Asian regional organization with which any of the organizations in our dataset had established relations.

What these data suggest, then, is that where activists find little opportunity or few allies in regional institutions, ties to the United Nations—which can bring funding, allies, and informational resources—are instrumental in the development of regional transnational civil society. These ties are critical to the development of counter-hegemonic regional polities and antisystemic movements because they help embed world culture and international legal norms into regional contexts, granting legitimacy and resources to efforts by social movements and political elites to defend alternative models of social and economic development against the forces of neoliberal globalization and hegemonic power (see, for example, Amin 2006).

Conclusion

Since the end of the Cold War, the mandates of regional interstate institutions have expanded to cover a broad range of policy issues and to include provisions for the participation of civil society. Such developments have been very uneven around the world because they reflect the differential positions of states and regions in the world-system and in relation to the superpowers that competed for dominance over the course of the Cold War. The superpower rivalry shaped regionalism in the post–World War II years and into the late twentieth century as states responded to potential or real Soviet and U.S. interventions. Outside of the world-system's core, regional institutions were established to defend states against foreign intrusion and to protect their hard-won sovereignty and autonomy over political and economic matters. Cross-regional forms of south-south cooperation such as the Nonaligned Movement and the G77 were further intended to protect and assert the interests of states seeking better terms of trade and, in general, more equitable inclusion in international economic and political relationships.

Into the 1980s, declining U.S. hegemony and changes in the accumulation regime of globalized capitalism conditioned the rise of new forms of regional cooperation and integration as states responded to the growing pressures of neoliberalism and to economic and financial crises. In this context, more demands from international financial institutions and the United States were being placed on government leaders to not only open more space for market forces by reducing the role of the state in various domains, such as financial regulation, but also adhere to world cultural norms such as human rights and transparent and democratic governance. Such demands expanded the incentives for regional cooperation as states sought to comply with global models while defending and asserting their interests in global political and economic forums. In this regard, as a state-protective mechanism, re-gionalism is a counter-hegemonic force that has enabled distinct na-tional capitalist social formations to flourish—for example, the social democratic mixed economies in Europe and the development states of East Asia—against pressures to adopt the neoliberal model preferred by the United States (Held and McGrew 2007). The breakdown of the bipolar world order, which destabilized the bases of U.S. hegemony, opened spaces for such regional challenges to U.S. leadership and dominance in the global political economy.

One of the important differences between the regionalisms that have emerged since the end of the Cold War and those that were established in the post–World War II years and in the wake of decolonization is the scope of governance mandates. As regional institutions have enlarged their mandates to encompass a wider variety of policy domains, they have also adopted mechanisms allowing the formal—and in most cases limited—participation of civil society actors in regional policy pro-cesses. As our data on transnational social movement organizations show, in response to these openings, social movements have increas-ingly mobilized within regions to influence the direction and scope of regional governance. But the extensiveness of channels for civil society participation and opportunities to establish formal relations with re-gional IGOs vary across regions and, as a result, outside Europe, trans-national social movement organizations are much more likely to have ties with UN agencies than with regional institutions. Such ties provide critical resources and embed global institutional logics and norms into regional polities. This provides legitimacy and leverage that enhances counter-hegemonic and antisystemic challenges to power and resource asymmetries in the world-system.

In the case of Latin American resistance to U.S. regional dominance, counter-hegemonic regionalism can provide an important foundation for antisystemic challenges. The Cartagena Agreement and Mercosur, both subregional efforts at interstate cooperation and economic inte-gration, helped propel Latin American labor transnationalism. Even as neoliberalism weakened the foundations of organized labor globally through the 1980s and 1990s, including on the American hemisphere, Latin American labor unions have played a significant role in mobiliz-ing a range of social forces against U.S. hegemony on the continent and in the world-system more generally. And to the extent that social forces continue to converge around transversal demands for greater partici-pation and equity, and as they deepen and extend their networks within and across regions, they constitute a significant antisystemic force in the world-system.

The UN conference process, which picked up momentum in the

early years of the post–Cold War period, further contributed to growth in and strengthening of transnational civil society, both globally and within regions. Conference processes advanced networking across movement and geographic divides, helping facilitate the rise of contemporary antisystemic movements. We turn to an examination of the impact of UN conferences on transnational social movements in the next chapter.

= Chapter 4 =

Global Conferences and Movement Sectors

THE GLOBAL conferences hosted by the United Nations during the 1990s were a significant driver of the three trends we see as shaping the possibilities for world-system transformation. The conferences changed opportunities for organizing transnational activism, helping both increase the organizing capacities of transnational movements and introduce activists to new ways of understanding and framing global problems. High-level global conferences became possible because the end of the Cold War allowed new issues to gain priority on international agendas and generated optimism that new and more cooperative approaches to global problems were possible. Conferences became organizing opportunities for social movements, creating global focal points that encouraged and supported transnational organizing. The conferences provided resources to help overcome inequities in participation from the global South, encouraging the creation of stronger networks across the global North and South. As they participated in conferences, activists developed new analyses of global problems and learned to articulate claims in relation to global norms. They also developed skills and models for organizing across cultural, linguistic, and other differences.

The United Nations has been charged with the task of ending the scourge of war, and a key aspect of its work is providing spaces where government leaders can come together to discuss problems that can engender violence and to develop consensus around joint solutions to these problems. In addition to the regular meetings of the United Nations General Assembly and other more specialized organs of the UN System, the UN has convened ad hoc conferences that focus on a particular problem and develop a framework that structures international cooperation by setting policy targets and timetables and that establishes periodic reviews to assess relevant scientific evidence and government progress in addressing the problem.

UN-sponsored global conferences are high-level meetings of government officials that help governments assess emerging scientific evidence regarding a particular problem and ways of addressing it (for example, ozone depletion, climate change, or urbanization) or review progress or failures in an area to focus attention on it (for example, the rights and status of women). The UN's technical staff contributes expertise and background research to help define the state of scientific knowledge and to provide recommendations of negotiating targets. As such, the conferences are spaces for consensus-building among states (Willetts 1996a; Friedman, Clark, and Hochstetler 2005). Governments engage in preparatory meetings to develop their approaches to the problem, and the conference itself is devoted to interstate negotiations on a final plan of action.

By all accounts, these global conferences have also served as key sites of civil society mobilization and engagement with the world polity. The rapid sequencing of large-scale global conferences that began in the early 1990s was aided by the end of the Cold War, when we saw dramatic growth in the numbers of transnational social change organizations (see chapter 2, this volume). The conferences encouraged many new transnational groups to form, and many more groups defined their agendas and organizing strategies in relation to the conferences (Foster and Anand 1999; Friedman, Clark, and Hochstetler 2005; Willetts 1989, 1996a; Alger 2002).

At global conferences, activist groups scrutinize the negotiating positions of government delegations, lobby official delegates to adopt particular positions or approaches, and work to influence the negotiating process by bringing pressure and sometimes privileged or strategic information or proposals into the process. Examples of the latter types of intervention include the efforts of groups supporting nuclear disarmament or opposing free trade agreements to serve on government delegations of states sympathetic with their goals. Governments, some of which lack resources to retain expert staff to work on all of the many technical issues under international negotiation, are often grateful for the technical and political assistance provided by advocacy groups. Activist interventions in interstate politics can bring information and leverage to less powerful states, obstructing the efforts of dominant powers to affect negotiations. For instance, Jackie Smith (2000) shows how Parliamentarians for Global Action introduced and built multistate support for an unusual idea to amend the Partial Nuclear Test Ban Treaty, thereby pressing nuclear states to make progress on nuclear disarmament. Marisa von Bülow (2010, 184) refers to this process of disrupting the negotiating strategies of dominant states as "monkey-wrenching" (for more on UN global conferences and how they affect movement strategies, see Smith 2008, chap. 3).

Case studies of global conferences have shown that nonstate actors often help advance the policy objectives of conferences, complementing the efforts of some states and UN officials. Many activists hoping to improve national human rights practices or to strengthen local and national environmental protections seek to do so by promoting multilateral norms and institutions (Kaldor 2003; Keck and Sikkink 1998; Smith 2008). At global conferences, activists both learn about and work to influence international legal texts, and they press national governments to adopt international conventions and otherwise to conform to actual or emergent international norms, thereby helping "domesticate" international law (Tarrow 2005). They also generate common understandings of global problems and build support for common principles through their ongoing organizational and public campaigning work. One ironic testament to their impact in these arenas is that, since the late 1990s, governments and corporate actors have reduced civil society groups' access to the United Nations and stepped up efforts to challenge the legitimacy of civil society groups in global forums (Alger 2002; Willetts 2006; Jaeger 2007; Gray and Bebbington 2006). Since 2001, governments' counterterrorist efforts have also further undermined civil society engagement in global policy arenas (Howell et al. 2008).

Why might we expect these conferences to affect the character of transnational organizing, from the formation of new transnational organizations to the relationships between such organizations and intergovernmental bodies? A number of factors are at work. First, global conferences are official responses to urgent global problems that are already the focus of many social movements. Matters such as human rights, equitable economic development, environment, and peace are examples of such "problems without passports." Often it is pressure from social movements that helps bring these concerns onto national and international public and government agendas in the first place (McCarthy 1996; Haney 2005). UN conference processes provide focal points and opportunities for cross-national dialogue that encourage activists working on particular issues to consider the global forces shaping that issue, as well as the diversity of perspectives offered by people from different national contexts and sectors. Governments and private foundations have provided major financial support for activist engagement with the global conference processes, particularly from low-income countries, and the UN and its agencies have also advocated and supported expanded civil society engagement (Friedman, Clark, and Hochstetler 2005; McKeon 2009; Prügl and Meyer 1999; Willetts 1996a; United Nations 2004).

Second, officials within the United Nations or other specialized international agencies promote global conferences to advance public engagement and action on a problem on which governments have been unwilling to act. For instance, Maurice Strong used his role as secretary-general of the UN Conference on Environment and Development (UNCED) to mobilize civil society and business actors in support of a global environmental agenda (Willetts 1996b). It is not uncommon for intergovernmental officials—particularly those in the specialized agencies addressing major global problems—to have come from earlier careers in advocacy organizations. Such individuals understand the workings of civil society, and they also have detailed, specialized knowledge about global problems and international negotiating histories and processes. In their official roles, they can mobilize and inform movement networks and otherwise apply movement-related skills to advancing the UN's work.

Third, global conferences seek to enhance the geographic representativeness of global institutions, affecting the structures and organizing agendas of activist groups. In particular, they encourage greater representation from the global South as well as enhanced regional cooperation in transnational movement organizations. This need for greater representativeness is heightened by the context of hegemonic decline, as new actors—including multistate alliances—aim to strengthen their influence on global policies and as core powers seek to use multilateral institutions to preserve the existing distribution of power.

To enhance regional representation in the conferences, regional preparatory committee meetings are held in advance of the main conference. Conference secretariats and other UN agencies as well as governments provide funding to assist civil society groups—particularly those from the global South—to participate in these regional meetings, known as PrepComs. These regional conferences facilitated civil society networking within regions, providing activists with sometimes first-of-a-kind opportunities to discuss regional perspectives on major global issues. In this way, global conferences were important drivers of the increased regionalization of transnational civil society ties in the post–Cold War years, a period during which states were also beginning to engage in new forms of regional cooperation around transborder issues, as we showed in chapter 3.

Between 1961 and 1985, 147 global conferences were held, providing opportunities for taking stock, agenda-setting, and technical coordination among governments and for encounters between governments and representatives of civil society (Anand 1999, 77). Most of these conferences were highly specialized meetings of technical experts working to coordinate and share information about national policies in regard to public health, agriculture, aviation and transport, and other practical matters. Some, however, were designed to advance political dialogues, bringing together diverse actors and fostering communication and greater international understanding. As a result, "a generation of NGO leadership heard the articulation of Southern [governments'] frustration and took on many elements of the eclectic vision of the NIEO [New International Economic Order]" being advanced by southern governments (Anand 1999, 73).[1] By the early 1990s, even as northern governments resisted southern demands, many social movement leaders and activists were sympathetic to the systemic grievances southern governments brought to the international arena. This transnational discourse helped shape the agendas and mission statements of new groups and socialized new activists, who became skilled at mobilizing around the more frequent and larger-scale UN conferences of the 1990s. Table 4.1 lists the major UN global conferences, their themes, and levels of civil society participation.

What is clear from this table is that civil society engagement with UN conferences has been expanding over time. Whereas just a few dozen civil society organizations participated in the 1968 UN Conference on Human Rights, hundreds of civil society groups—including many transnational social movement organizations— participated in conferences during the 1970s, and by the early 1990s multiple thousands attended. This is in addition to a similarly large pool of individual civil society participants. Also apparent is that the level of civil society engagement with global conferences varies across issues. It seems that where national social movement activity has been strongest—such as around women's issues, on peace issues in the late 1980s, and on environmental issues beginning in the early 1990s—civil society participation in UN conferences has been similarly robust.[2] This suggests important connections between domestic and global politics.

In this chapter, we explore the impact of global conferences on world polity dynamics, specifically with regard to conference effects on transnational social movement organizations. Recognizing the simultaneity of the increases in the population of these organizations and the rising frequency and scale of global conferences, it bears considering whether a cause-effect relationship is in play. Also, what differences are there between various issue areas? Some issues, such as peace and security and international trade, are highly centralized or are framed in highly technical terms, offering relatively few opportunities for substantial popular participation and deliberation. For instance, nations' foreign policy processes typically limit public scrutiny and participation, privileging the executive branch of government over the legislative and the judicial (Pagnucco and Smith 1993). Thus peace movements targeting policy arenas often find themselves mired in highly technical debates about weapons systems and arms control agreements, rather than in broader dialogues about the conditions that would foster multilateral-

Table 4.1 Major UN Global Conferences

Conference	Place	Year	Civil Society Participation
UN Conference on Human Rights	Tehran, Iran	1968	53 NGOs with consultative status, plus 4 additional invited NGOs
UN Conference on the Human Environment	Stockholm, Sweden	1972	255 to 298 NGO observers
First World Conference on Women	Mexico City, Mexico	1975	6,000 individuals 114 NGOs
World Food Summit	Rome, Italy	1976	400 NGOs
UN Special Session on Disarmament-I	New York	1978	236 NGOs 800 individuals
Second World Conference on Women	Copenhagen, Denmark	1980	8,000 individuals
UN Special Session on Disarmament-II	New York	1982	3,391 representatives of 450 NGOs
Third World Conference on Women	Nairobi, Kenya	1985	15,000 individuals (including 3,000 Kenyans—many rural) 163 NGOs
UN Special Session on Disarmament-III	New York	1988	2,000 NGOs
World Summit for Children	New York	1990	45 NGOs
UN Conference on Environment and Development	Rio de Janeiro, Brazil	1992	Over 650 NGOs 2,400 representatives from NGOs participated in the formal event; 17,000 people attended the parallel NGO forum

(Table continued on p. 106.)

Table 4.1 (*Continued*)

Conference	Place	Year	Civil Society Participation
World Conference on Human Rights	Vienna, Austria	1993	1,400 to 1,500 NGOs Representatives of more than 800 NGOs attended the conference[6]
International Conference on Population and Development	Cairo, Egypt	1994	15,000 individuals 1,500 NGOs
World Summit on Social Development	Copenhagen, Denmark	1995	2,315 representatives from 811 NGOs attended conference
Fourth World Conference on Women	Beijing, China	1995	30,000 individuals [attended independent NGO forum] 5,000 representatives from 2,100 NGOs attended summit
Earth Summit-II	New York	1997	First conference to allow NGO representatives to speak in plenaries
Habitat	Istanbul, Turkey	1996	8,000 representatives from 2,400 organizations attended parallel NGO forum
World Conference Against Racism	South Africa	2001	8,000 individuals from 3,000 NGOs attended parallel forum
World Summit on Sustainable Development	South Africa	2002	Over 8,000 individuals attended summit

Source: Authors' compilation based on Clark, Friedman, and Hochstetler (1998); Morphet (1996); Van Roov (1997); Atwood (1997); and Pianta and Silva (2003).

ism and reduce states' reliance on militarized notions of security (Cooper forthcoming; Cortright and Pagnucco 1997; Lynch 1998). Other issues, such as the environment and development, are more broad and less consolidated institutionally, thus offering more openings for local and national social movement challenges.[3]

Global Conferences and Transnational Organizing

We noted in earlier chapters that the population of transnational movement organizations has grown most dramatically since the 1980s. This leads us to consider the extent to which the global conferences can be seen as shaping this population. Determining a causal relationship is difficult, however, given the many other important changes happening at the same time. The 1980s saw the beginning of the end of the Soviet Union, and Gorbachev's mid-decade introduction of perestroika created openings that allowed activists in Eastern Europe expanded connections to the West. Also significant was the introduction of new technologies, such as fax machines, personal computers, and the Internet, which meant increasingly cheap and rapid communication. Growth in international trade also helped spur more travel and exchanges across diverse societies, advancing new forms of transnational association and drawing attention to new transnational problems. Global conferences provided concrete spaces and focal points for activists from different countries to mobilize transnationally and discuss specific concerns and strategies with their international counterparts. It is not surprising, therefore, that many case studies link global conferences to the formal establishment of new transnational organizations (Anand 1999; Ferree and Mueller 2004; Friedman, Clark, and Hochstetler 2005; Keck and Sikkink 1998; Pianta and Silva 2003; Riles 2001; Willetts 1996a).

The early 1990s were an important turning point in the dynamics of world polity. In 1992, and after two years of preparatory meetings, the largest intergovernmental meeting in UN history took place in Rio de Janeiro, Brazil. More than 1,400 NGOs were accredited to participate in official meetings at the Rio conference, the largest number to ever be granted such access (Haney 2005). As mentioned, the conference cycle that began in the early 1990s represented a political response to the opening of opportunities for transnational cooperation with the end of the Cold War. The conferences took advantage of new technologies that could facilitate international dialogue and exchange and advance international understandings of global problems. They also helped institutionalize processes for intergovernmental negotiation and policy implementation that expanded opportunities for movements to mobilize around global agendas and policies (Krut 1997).

To begin to decipher the varying factors that shape the organizational dimension of world polity, we compared transnational movement organizations formed before the 1990s with those formed in 1990 or after. We found that transnational social movement organizations formed during the post–Cold War period were significantly more likely than pre-1990 groups to be based in the global South (25.4 percent versus 18.8 percent), to have a larger average number of ties to other INGOs (4.20 versus 3.40), and to be regional in structure (43.7 percent versus 23.6 percent). These patterns all reflect the organizing logics of the global conferences, and we argue that these overall changes in the population of transnational movement organizations are at least in part a result of activist interactions with global conference processes. Whereas the end of the Cold War helped create a context for expansions of both intergovernmental cooperation and transnational citizens associations, as discussed in chapter 3, the conferences were an intervening factor accounting for many of the important changes in the transnational movement mobilization we have seen in recent years. The geopolitical openings provided space for governments to host the conferences, which, once convened, shaped more generalized organizing practices. Table 4.2 compares organizational features of TSMOs formed during conference years and after 1990 with the overall population of organizations to see whether the major impetus of change is the post–Cold War geopolitical context or the (related) global conference processes. The results suggest that the conference processes have additional influence on TSMO characteristics.

A larger percentage of TSMOs tended to be founded in the years surrounding UN global conferences than in other years, and this remains true even after the end of the Cold War. Also, compared to groups formed after 1990, TSMOs formed during conference intervals tended to have somewhat greater representation from the global South and—for environmental and women's groups—more ties to INGOs than other groups formed in more recent years. In other words, changes in geopolitics and technology alone do not account fully for the patterns we see here. Institutional dynamics appear to be affecting how people organize transnationally.

This conclusion is reinforced by the findings we show in table 4.3. For the four sectors we consider here—human rights, peace, environment, and women's rights—modal founding years clustered within conference intervals.[4] For each sector, the highest numbers of organizations were founded within the five years surrounding a global conference.

Before the 1985 Nairobi Third World Conference on Women, the si-

Table 4.2 Comparing Founding Effects on Organizational Features for TSMOs Formed in Conference Years and After 1990[a]

	Human Rights N = 2803[b]		Peace N = 1886		Environment N = 1289		Women N = 827	
	Conference	Post-1990	Conference	Post-1990	Conference	Post-1990	Conference	Post-1990
Percentage Founded	13.6%	8.2%	20.8%	7.1%	27.5%	17.0%	38.0%	9.8%
Headquarters in global South	21.3% ***(+)[c]	**(+)	17.8% ***(+)	n.s.(−)	24.0% ***(+)	n.s.(+)	31.2% ***(+)	n.s.(+)
Ratio of south to north countries	2.11 **(+)	n.s.(−)	2.43 f(+)	n.s.(−)	2.37 **(+)	n.s.(−)	2.39 ***(+)	**(−)
Regional structure	25.0% **(+)	***(+)	17.4% ***(+)	***(+)	27.7% n.s.(+)	***(+)	27.1% ***(+)	***(+)
Average number of IGO ties	2.66 **(−)	***(−)	2.40 ***(−)	***(−)	2.28 n.s.(+)	*(−)	2.16 ***(−)	**(−)
Average number of INGO ties	3.87 n.s.(+)	n.s.(+)	3.67 **(−)	***(+)	4.49 *(+)	n.s.(+)	4.01 ***(+)	n.s.(−)

Source: Authors' compilation based on their Transnational Social Movement Organization Database.

[a] The table shows: a) the percentage of organizations in each sector founded during conference years and after 1990 (top row of table); b) the overall percentage, ratio, or average for transnational social movement organizations in each sector irrespective of founding period; and c) the results of statistical tests comparing organizations founded in conference years with those founded in other years ("Conference") and comparing organizations founded after 1990 with those founded in 1990 or earlier ("Post-1990").

[b] All figures in the table were calculated from the total number of organizations active over all years (organization-year spells). In other words, an individual organization is included in the count for each year that it is active.

[c] For the nominal variables "Headquarters in global South" and "Regional structure," Chi-square tests were used to assess the difference between the percentage of organizations founded during conference years and the percentage founded in other years, and the difference between the percentage of organizations founded after 1990 and the percentage founded in 1990 or earlier. Independent sample t-tests were used for comparisons of the scale variables "Ratio of south to north countries," "Average IGO ties," and "Average INGO ties." + and − signs indicate that the percentage/ratio/mean for organizations founded during conference years or after 1990 was significantly higher or lower than the percentage/ratio/mean for the relevant comparison group; n.s. indicates no statistical difference. The p-values associated with the comparisons are: * $p \leq .05$; ** $p \leq .01$; *** $p \leq .001$; f $p \leq .10$.

Table 4.3 Conference Intervals and Modal Founding Years for Transnational Social Movement Organizations[a]

Conference	Conference Interval	Human Rights	Peace	Environment	Women
UN Conference on Human Rights	1966 to 1970				
UN Conference on the Human Environment	1970 to 1974				
First World Conference on Women	1973 to 1977				South
World Food Summit	1974 to 1978				South
UN Special Session on Disarmament-I	1976 to 1980	North		North	North
Second World Conference on Women	1978 to 1982	North		North	North
UN Special Session on Disarmament-II	1980 to 1984	North	North		
Third World Conference on Women	1983 to 1987	North and south	North		North and south
UN Special Session on Disarmament-III	1986 to 1990	North and south	North and south	North	
World Summit for Children	1988 to 1992	North and south	South	North and south	North
UN Conference Environment and Development	1990 to 1994	North and south	North	North and south	North
World Conference on Human Rights	1991 to 1995	North and south	North	North and south	North
International Conference on Population and Development	1992 to 1996	North and south	North	North and south	North
World Summit on Social Development	1993 to 1997	North and south	North	South	
Fourth World Conference on Women	1993 to 1997	North and south	North	South	

Source: Authors' compilation based on their Transnational Social Movement Organizations Dataset.

[a] The chart indicates whether the modal year(s) for foundings of transnational movement organizations in the four sectors occurred within a conference interval. North indicates that modal years for north-based organizations correspond with conference cycles; south for south-based organizations; and north and south indicates that modal years for both north- and south-based organizations correspond with conference cycles.

multaneity of conferences and organizational founding was most evident for north-based organizations, for which foundings all spiked during the interval stretching from the First to the Second UN Special Sessions on Disarmament in 1978 and 1982. But during the Nairobi Third World Conference on Women interval and especially during the conference cycle marking the beginning of the post–Cold War era, we find that organizational foundings corresponded with conference intervals across both the global North and South. We also find more organizational foundings for global South–based human rights and environmental organizations in this later period. Thus we see that the expansion of participatory opportunities within the UN conference system intersected with post–Cold War geopolitical changes to facilitate transnational organizing not only within specific movement sectors but also across the global South.

Although these analyses suggest that, regardless of the specific conference theme, conference cycles encouraged transnational organizational foundings across sectors, there are also reasons to expect that conferences provided some sectors unique opportunities for mobilization. Environmental and women's issues, for instance, have been especially prominent among UN conferences. The four World Conferences on Women provided feminist activists with a long series of linked opportunities to mobilize transnationally around the needs of women. Case studies of these conferences showed that organizations and individuals communicated across these meetings to develop and learn ways of organizing in the global political arena. Although environmental conferences were less frequent, the 1992 UN Conference on Environment and Development was one of the first major UN conferences to attract large-scale citizen mobilization from around the world. It created the Commission on Sustainable Development, which has sustained annual gatherings of states and nonstate actors to discuss global environmental problems. And though other conferences attracted large civil society contingents and popular mobilizations, UNCED's timing during a period of optimism about possibilities for post–Cold War multilateral cooperation on the environment and organizers' strategy of actively working to mobilize civil society made it a watershed event in the UN's history.

Given this history, we would expect transnational movement organizations working on women's rights or environmental issues to be most affected by conferences specific to their aims. At the same time, however, global conferences are expected to have defined the broader organizational fields of which all transnational movement organizations are part. Thus, we should see some similar patterns and practices across all movement sectors. Global conferences shape discourses and

framings of problems and their solutions. They also structure the opportunities for political influence as well as the logics of political access
to both governments and intergovernmental organizations. The need
to mobilize at strategic times in the conference process (usually well
before the global conference actually convenes), the need for broad
geographic representation in a group's membership, and the need to
cultivate ties to other groups that can enhance one's access to information and other resources result from and are reinforced by global conference processes. A question we explore in the next section is whether
and how these institutional pressures affected the character of transnational social movement organizations, and whether these effects vary
across issue areas.

The World Conferences on Women and Transnational Feminism

Any reading of the history of the transnational women's movement
shows that this movement is intimately linked to the expansion and
strengthening of feminist agendas in intergovernmental organizations.
Many women were leaders in the antislavery and peace movements of
the nineteenth and twentieth centuries, and they advocated for the creation of international norms and institutions such as the League of Nations and the United Nations as a means of limiting the arbitrary use of
violence by states (Chatfield 1997; Rupp 1997; Taylor and Rupp 2002;
Wittner 1993). This strategy of forming transnational alliances to advocate for supranational norms reflects the classic boomerang strategy as
portrayed by Keck and Sikkink (1998).

Women and feminist activists also helped strengthen regional international organizations. For instance, Mary Meyer (1999) documents
how feminists in Latin America helped establish the Inter-American
Commission of Women in the Organization of American States in
he early 1920s. The Inter-American Commission of Women and the
women who staffed it helped press for changes in the League of Nations to reflect women's concerns. They also were important to the effort to establish the United Nations and to include women's concerns
in its charter (Prügl and Meyer 1999; West 1999). Through the Inter-
American Commission of Women, feminist activists brought women's
issues onto the agenda of the United Nations, leading to the campaign
to create the International Women's Year, the UN Decade for Women,
and the series of World Conferences on Women.

The four United Nations World Conferences on Women, the 1993
World Conference on Human Rights, and the 1994 International Conference on Population and Development helped focus the attention of

women and governments around the world on the experiences of women. They also facilitated the development of networks of activists and organizations and helped foster learning about global politics and institutions. The first of the World Conferences on Women was in 1975 in Mexico City, coinciding with the rise of what has been called second-wave feminism. The conference marked the beginning of a continuing conversation about how to alter the operations of politics and markets so that the needs of women are better addressed. The Mexico City conference led to the launch of a United Nations Decade for Women, which was punctuated by the 1980 midterm Second World Conference on Women in Copenhagen and the 1985 Third World Conference on Women in Nairobi. A Fourth World Conference on Women came in 1995 in Beijing. But the momentum of transnational women's organizing would not be contained within the women's conference track alone, and women organizers were major players in all of the major global conferences, including the UN Conference on Environment and Development in 1992 in Rio, and the 1993 World Conference on Human Rights in Vienna.

Once feminist activists opened space on the global intergovernmental stage for discussing concerns of women, the United Nations global conferences, and in particular the four World Conferences on Women, exerted profound influences on transnational feminist organizing in the late twentieth century. Global conferences and the intergovernmental agreements that resulted from them helped give legitimacy to feminists' claims and encouraged feminist organizing in multiple spaces at global and national levels (Sternbach et al. 1992). Thus, the population of transnational feminist organizations expanded and changed as activists used the conferences to further develop and strengthen the transnational women's movement. For instance, Elisabeth Friedman and her colleagues noted how the Latin American feminist *encuentros* of the 1980s and '90s were shaped by discussions started in earlier UN conference settings (Friedman, Clark, and Hochstetler 2005, 86). Moreover, feminists formed women's caucuses at UN conferences on issues other than women's rights to coordinate activist agendas, develop their organizing strategies, and maintain pressure on governments to advance women's interests in multiple policy areas. The experiences, practices, and networks that emerged from the UN conference process helped generate the new forms of transnational women's activism that have been articulated most recently in the World March for Women and the World Social Forums (Dufour and Giroud 2007; Hewitt and Karides 2011).

As was apparent in table 4.1, civil society has always been actively engaged in women's conferences, but this participation grew dramatically over the late twentieth century. Whereas only 6,000 individuals participated in the first conference in 1975, just twenty years later, 30,000 did so.[5] In addition to those attending global forums, many more activists are involved in national and local contexts pressing authorities on issues related to global meetings and helping ensure that governments follow up on their conference commitments (Riles 2001; Smith 1997).

Because the global women's conferences were among the earliest of the major global conferences to generate significant mobilization by civil society groups, they were sites where the tactic of staging parallel nongovernmental forums emerged and developed. This tactic is now a firmly established part of the transnational social movement "repertoire of contention" (Tilly 1995, 1978). For instance, as discussed in chapter 3, South American labor unions engaged in forums parallel to meetings of Mercosur member states beginning in 1991. The forums represent a form of "counterpolitics" (West 1999) that allow social movement actors to broaden the agendas and expand consideration of solutions beyond the typically very narrow range of debates allowed in official interstate negotiations. They also provide spaces for strategic networking between civil society groups and state- and intergovernmental officials who may share their aims. In this sense, they can help relatively weak actors in the interstate system enhance their leverage in relation to more powerful states and blocs of states.

NGO forums have become a routine part of UN politics, and may in fact be among the most important sources of dynamism for the organization. This is so because the forums help mobilize new constituents into global policy arenas, generate pressure on world leaders to confront the structural causes of problems rather than just the symptoms, and bring new resources to the table in the form of ideas, public pressure, and tools for monitoring international agreements (for example, Smith, Chatfield and Pagnucco 1997a; Willetts 1989, 1996a). They are part of and contribute to what Alvarez speaks of as the "multiplication of spaces in which [activists] can act and circulate feminist discourses" (1998, 294–95).

The conferences thus created opportunities for movement learning, debate, growth, and collaboration. The First World Conference on Women, for instance, was characterized by major divisions between northern and southern activists over whether discrimination against women or economic development should be the main focus of activism, with many women from the global North wanting to prioritize a single-issue women's rights agenda and many in the global South emphasizing more expansive, material concerns of economic development. Many women in the north were hearing alternative perspectives on feminism for the first time, and the conference provided valuable opportunities for listening and reflection that helped define contemporary transnational feminism (Riles 2001, 182; Rupp 1997).[6]

After the early conferences helped gain momentum for women's organizing and for the expansion of formal rights, antifeminist forces began to combine to create a backlash against earlier feminist gains. Doris Buss and Didi Herman refer to the 1994 Cairo Conference on Population as the "birthplace of conservative Christian global politics" (2003, 44–45).[7] This backlash was still noteworthy at the 1995 Fourth World Conference on Women, but achievements in establishing better mechanisms throughout the UN system to assess the effects of gender on human welfare were an important gain in terms of improving women's lives.

Overall, however, it is clear that transnational women's activism has redefined global agendas and transformed discourses about women (Alvarez 1998). The establishment, for instance, following the First World Conference on Women of the Convention on the Elimination of all Forms of Discrimination Against Women (CEDAW), marked a turning point. Despite the failure of many states to fully implement its principles, this document continues to shape discourse and policy in the global arena and to focus activist attention on some common goals and targets. The treaty helped overcome some of the challenges feminist organizers faced because it "gave women the free space to adopt what was essentially a feminist document without ever using the term 'feminist'" (West 1999, 180). That, after concerted work by women's rights organizations to press states to ratify the treaty, CEDAW has gained nearly universal accession signals the widespread official legitimacy of its basic norms and amplifies the moral force with which feminist activists can speak.[8]

Although we would expect global conference processes overall to contribute to the mobilization of activists from the global South, there is reason to believe that this might be particularly true for women's organizations. Because they are responding to the long-standing and nearly universal social and political exclusion of half the world's people, the transnational women's movement may be better able than movements working on other issues to integrate marginalized groups such as activists from the global South. In particular, the social marginalization of women requires them to rely more heavily than other groups on building broad networks with resourceful or otherwise powerful allies, and this undoubtedly has shaped feminist organizing practices (see, for example, Snyder 2003; Polletta 2002). In the following section, we consider how the global conferences on the environment compare with the world conferences on women, including the ways social movement actors have engaged with the conference processes.

Global Environmental Conferences and Environmental Movements

There was very little in the way of formal international negotiations around environmental issues prior to the early 1970s. The UN Conference on the Human Environment, held in Stockholm in 1972, was a turning point in global environmental politics. As Ken Conca observed, "Before the Stockholm conference, environmental organisations played only a limited role within the United Nations, just as the world organisation itself played only a limited role in environmental matters. The conservation of natural resources was made part of the constitutional mandate of the Food and Agriculture Organization (FAO), although its emphasis on natural resource production and extraction severely curtailed its environmental focus" (1995, 442).

Government delegates in Stockholm agreed to a program of action that established the UN Environment Program (UNEP) as the UN's official coordinating body for environmental issues (Thacher 1991). The Stockholm Conference thus generated more long-term institutionalized work on the environment within the UN system, and the data collected and disseminated as a result has helped shape global policy agendas since UNEP's formation. Another crucial shift in the environmental movement became apparent at this first global conference on the environment. Observers at the time noted a "transition from [an environmental] movement dominated by relatively depoliticised conservation groups to one heavily influenced by the 'new environmentalism' of the 1960s" (Conca 1995, 443; see also Morphet 1996, 124).

In 1982, UNEP hosted a follow-up meeting to the Stockholm conference, bringing government delegates together to assess their progress toward implementing the agreements made in 1972.[9] They concluded that governments had done little to move forward on their commitments at Stockholm, and so urged the UN General Assembly to establish the World Commission on Environment and Development, which would begin a process of dialogue about the relationships between the natural environment and economic development. This responded to concerns from the governments of the global South, which argued that environmental concerns were secondary to the aim of reducing poverty and securing the basic needs of their populations (Seyfang 2003; Willetts 1996b). The commission's report, *Our Common Future*, helped define and popularize the notion of sustainable development as a focus of international environmental negotiations. Thus the second major global conference on the environment, held twenty years after the first

conference in Stockholm, was named the UN Conference on Environment and Development (UNCED).

UNCED took place in 1992, as the Cold War's demise created new spaces and hopes for greater international cooperation on the environment. Sometimes dubbed the Earth Summit, UNCED was particularly notable as the conference that marked a tremendous surge in civil society participation in global arenas. An estimated 20,000 to 30,000 people from more than 2,400 nongovernmental organizations participated in the conference, held in Rio de Janeiro, Brazil. UNCED was also the first significant mobilization by transnational corporations in a UN conference (Bruno and Karliner 2002; Haas 2002).

UNCED differed from the much earlier Stockholm conference in a number of ways, the most notable being the scale and scope of popular participation. The numbers of civil society groups participating dwarfed all of the previous world conferences.[10] Another key—and not unrelated—difference was that the framework of discussion was more inclusive and less narrowly technical than the Stockholm conference (Seyfang 2003). This reflects the process through which conferences, including the civil society mobilization they facilitate, help governments reframe their understandings of problems through dialogue, information-gathering, and debate. Indeed, numerous observers have pointed out how civil society involvement in global negotiations has helped expand official agendas, forcing governments to address complex interdependencies among issues.[11] Also, as noted, an important part of the UN conference process has become the regional preparatory meetings facilitated by the conference secretariats. In the case of Rio, this regional work was notable for its ability to help Latin American governments and civil societies develop regional perspectives on the environment that had not existed previously (Friedman, Clark, and Hochstetler 2005).

Observers at UNCED noted that the conference was marked by major splits between the governments of the global North and South. Southern governments pressed for greater attention to economic development needs, whereas northern governments, in general, sought to focus on negotiations to curb environmental damage. Questions about the need to limit consumption in the global North or about the incompatibilities between the growth-based global trade regime and limited global carrying capacity were not addressed. However, although governments were and remain quite divided on these issues, Peter Willetts observed that "by mid-1990 [NGOs] were far ahead of governments in bridging the North-South political divide, both by NGOs from North and South working together and by environmental and development NGOs working together" (1996b, 73).

The extraordinary energy created by UNCED and its assemblage of thousands of activists, no doubt encouraged by the end of the Cold War and new hopes for large-scale global change, helped fuel a number of different movements beyond the environmental movement. For instance, the Women's Environment and Development Organization (WEDO), an important network of transnational feminists, was formed at UNCED. The analyses advanced at UNCED and its opportunities for networking helped draw together groups beginning to articulate the critiques of economic globalization that have undergirded the contemporary global justice movement. At UNCED, activists began—on a larger scale than possible before this conference—to compare experiences and frame their discussions and organizing strategies in ways that would both reflect the new realities being shaped by economic globalization and resonate across multiple issue-areas and the north-south divide (for example, Anand 1999; Broad and Hecksher 2003). For instance, Gita Sen, the feminist economist and organizer of Development Alternatives with Women for a New Era (DAWN), observed, "[DAWN's] message about development was really new, that you can't just talk about gender equality without considering equality of what. Do you want equal shares of a poisoned pie? It was a message that had a galvanizing effect on people. . . . No longer was it a situation where the North worries about gender equality and the South about development" (quoted in Thom 2000, 31).

The major official outcome of UNCED was Agenda 21, a blueprint for global environmental action adopted by the 178 governments attending the conference, which laid out frameworks for negotiations on two important environmental treaties, the Framework Convention on Climate Change and the Convention on Biodiversity. In addition, governments agreed to begin negotiations for new treaties on forest protection and combating desertification. These final documents and the subsequent treaty negotiations they generated provided ongoing opportunities for civil society groups to monitor government compliance with their commitments in Agenda 21 and to press governments to take stronger actions. Participants could learn about the process of treaty-making and be part of subsequent discussions with other activists about how to improve government compliance with international agreements (Friedman, Clark, and Hochstetler 2005; Krut 1997). For instance, Annelise Riles (2001) documents how organizations developed methods of tracking government performance following global women's conferences, illustrating how the conference process transformed organizational agendas and practices. New groups like Social Watch formed with the explicit purpose of helping collect and disseminate information on governments' compliance with international targets for improving social policy. This made it easier for more local and national groups to link their activities with global policy arenas.

The treaty processes themselves have generated ongoing series of conferences that regularly review governments' progress toward achieving their treaty commitments and establish stronger and more stringent commitments to environmental protection. Most treaties, for instance, incorporate review conferences every five years, and these Conferences of Parties (COPs) draw regular participation from activists. The conferences on global climate change have probably drawn the most attention from civil society groups, which have mobilized in increasing numbers to encourage governments to limit greenhouse gas emissions and to assist low-income countries with emissions reduction and adaptation to climate change (see, for example, Reimann 2002). The treaty bodies and COPs have thus provided some important avenues of global institutional access for environmental groups, and reflect key developments in the institutional architecture that defines the global environmental regime. But, in addition to encouraging the development and strengthening of international environmental treaties, UNCED led to the creation of the Commission on Sustainable Development, which provides another regular venue for activists to engage with the UN System.[12]

Shifting away from a top-down institutional perspective, we might ask next whether transnational organizing on the environment came in response to these changes in the institutional context or whether global environmental institutions were created in response to social movements' bottom-up pressure on elites. There is some debate about the origins of transnational environmental activism, and whether this has emerged in response to elite-initiated agendas and processes or whether social movements may be seen as a causal force (for example, Johnson and McCarthy 2005; Roberts 1996). Certainly the transborder nature of environmental problems would lead us to expect considerable environmental activism across national boundaries (Faber 2005). Indeed, a great deal of scholarship on environmental activism suggests that these movements are a key factor in explaining the emergence and development of transnational environmental institutions and related treaties (Conca 1995; Lipschutz 1996; Smith 1997, 1999). Quantitative studies add further support to the conclusions of more case-based research, documenting significant influences of transnational environmental activism on institutional and policy outcomes (Frank 1999; Roberts 1996; Jorgenson 2008).

At the same time, global institutions help legitimize environmental activism. Governments' participation in global environmental treaties and institutions encourages environmental activism by citizens (Economy 2004; Frank, Hironaka, and Schofer 2000; Meyer et al. 1997; Reimann 2002; Vasi 2007). Erik Johnson and John McCarthy's study of the founding patterns of environmental groups, however, suggest that transnational organizing followed the development of strong national movement sectors, at least in the United States (2005). Our perspective would posit that the relationships here are multidirectional, and that strong national environmental movements in some countries (that is, core countries with greater political openness and influence in the global political economy) helped encourage the spread of transnational environmental organizing. These transnational activist groups and global conferences contributed to the development of a transnational environmental regime that, in turn, encouraged the proliferation of both national and transnational environmental organizations world-wide.[13]

Although we do not address the origins of the transnational environmental movement here, we can show how patterns of transnational environmental activism relate to global institutional processes, and how organizational patterns have changed alongside broader global trends. Examining the literature on transnational environmental activism, we see a number of important tensions in this movement that we expect will be reflected in the data we have on transnational social movement organizations. The most important fault line is the global North-South conflict, which is a central one in environmental discourse, given the tensions between the material limits to the Earth's carrying capacity that an environmental critique highlights and the material needs of the world's poorest people whose very survival is at stake (Pellow 2000; Roberts and Parks 2006). Given the aim in global conferences of better integrating the perspectives and interests of people from the majority of UN member countries of the global South, we must consider how transnational organizations working on this particularly challenging issue compare with those working on issues where north-south divisions may be less polarized.

Global Conferences and Transnational Organizing

What we've shown is that, by creating spaces where activists come together around a shared agenda and set of targets or goals, UN global conferences provided focal points that reinforce particular sets of organizing principles and practices for groups that are emergent around the times the conferences are held. Organizational population dynamics are expected to generate more general logics and pressures that mean that even where activists in a group have not participated directly in a global conference, they will see the effects of conference-derived norms and practices reflected in the larger organizational field (see, for example, Kenis and Knoke 2002; Minkoff 1993; Minkoff and McCarthy 2005;

Singh, Tucker and Meinhard 1991). The widespread dissemination of accounts of the conferences by participants, networking among social movement organizations both before and after, availability of official and private funding, and the institutionalization of practices and discourses established through the conference process all serve to structure the larger culture and operational structures in which transnational social movement organizations and other actors operate (Finnemore 1993, 1996; Meyer et al. 1997; Riles 2001; Pianta 2005).

For instance, the dialogues at conferences and the need to build consensus and foster coalition work to effect them is likely to have long-term impacts on organization strategies long after the conference ends. Private foundations and public agencies funding civil society group work gather in conference settings as well to evaluate their work and develop funding priorities and guidelines (Riles 2001). Groups formed around global conferences may therefore be more likely to emphasize networking strategies and be well placed to develop multiple connections to other actors in the global environment than those formed at other periods (Gulati and Gargiulo 1999). Moreover, to the extent that access to resources and resourceful networks is shaped by the discourses and practices emerging from conferences, we would expect the larger organizational field to adapt in similar ways.

We now examine the data we have on transnational organizing to identify relationships between social movements and global conferences. Drawing from the accounts cited, we would expect that organizations' ability to mobilize in the global South, their decisions to organize regionally, and their embeddedness in the world polity will all be affected by global conference dynamics. Figure 4.1 presents evidence to help us assess these relationships. For each of the four leading issue areas—peace, human rights, women's rights, and the environment—we compare the differences between groups formed in the years surrounding conferences with those formed in other years. We compare the percentages of these organizations with headquarters or members in the global South, the extent to which they are organized within regions, and their connections to intergovernmental and nongovernmental organizations. We anticipate that the conferences would have the greatest impacts on the organizations specifically focused on the conference issue, even as the conference processes as a whole affect the overall population, as we saw, for instance, in table 4.2. Also, given the particular intensity of women's and environmental conferences, we expect the conference effects to be most pronounced in these two issue areas.

The comparisons of different founding cohorts demonstrate substantial effects of global conferences on the overall field of transnational

Figure 4.1   Conference Effects on Organizational Cohorts by Issue Area

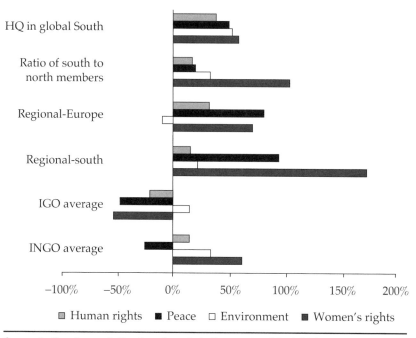

Source: Authors' compilation based on their Transnational Social Movement Organizations Dataset.
Note: This figure illustrates the percentage difference on features of transnational organizing between organizations founded in conference and non-conference years for four movement sectors.

social movement organizations. Comparing groups formed during each conference interval with those formed in other years, we find that all organizations formed in conference intervals, regardless of their issue-focus, were more likely to be based in the global South. They also have a higher ratio of southern to northern countries with members. Organizations formed in conference intervals were also more likely to adopt regional organizing structures. Other than for peace groups, whose conferences took place before the 1990s, conferences positively affected the number of ties that transnational movement organizations had with other INGOs.[14] Moreover, the effects of conference processes on ties to other INGOs and extensiveness of southern participation were most pronounced for environmental and women's groups. This suggests that the special efforts UN officials and civil society groups made to mobilize the public around these particular conferences brought more dramatic changes in these subpopulations' overall growth, and in their trends toward greater southern involvement, their more dense INGO networks, and for women groups, more regionalization. Interestingly, organizations founded during conference cycles were less likely to maintain ties to large numbers of intergovernmental organizations, a puzzle we take up in chapter 5.

These general patterns also held when we controlled for the timing of a group's formation and contrasted organizations working on the issues specific to the conference era with all other groups. So, for instance, women's groups were significantly more likely than other groups formed during the years of the global women's conferences to have southern headquarters, more southern members, regional structures, fewer ties to intergovernmental bodies, and more ties to other international nongovernmental organizations (see table 4.4). The evidence on transnational movement organizations thus demonstrates that the practices promoted through conference processes have ripple effects that spill across issue-specific organizational fields to affect the larger population.

Integrating Southern Participants. The conferences were probably most significant for helping integrate southern activists into transnational social movement organizations. As mentioned, conference logics created incentives and provided resources for organizations to expand the representation of southern activists in their memberships, and created spaces where activists from north and south could meet, exchange ideas, and develop strategies for working together. Conference eras tended to be associated with the creation of more south-based organizations for this reason.[15] Even groups based in the global North tended to expand the numbers of southern countries represented in their memberships. Regardless of issue-area, more south-based organizations were formed during conference intervals than in nonconference intervals. This effect was most pronounced for women's rights and environmental groups, at least a third of all such groups being based in the global South.

For environmental and women's rights organizations, the ratio of southern to northern countries with members in transnational organizations is significantly higher for groups formed during conference intervals than at other times. The conference effect on southern representation in transnational movement organizations is most pronounced for women's rights groups: those formed during conference intervals reported having, on average, nearly four times as many global South countries with members as they did global North countries with members. This represents slightly more than double the average ratio of

Table 4.4 Comparing Organizational Features of Specific TSMO Sectors to All Other Sectors for Organizations Founded in Conference and Non-Conference Years[a]

	Percentage Founded	Headquarters in Global South	Ratio of South to North Countries	Regional Structure	Average Number of IGO Ties	Average Number of INGO Ties
Human rights						
Non-conference years						
Human rights						
(N=2423)[b]	86.4%	20.3%	2.05	23.9%	2.73	3.80
Other sectors						
(N=6325)	87.7%	21.3% n.s.(−)[c]	2.46 ***(−)	24.6% n.s.(−)	1.78 ***(+)	3.33 **(+)
Conference years						
Human rights						
(N=380)	13.6%	27.9%	2.52	31.8%	2.23	4.32
Other sectors						
(N=964)	12.3%	28.2% n.s.(−)	2.81 n.s.(−)	36.3% ∫(−)	1.39 ***(+)	3.69 n.s.(+)
Peace						
Non-conference years						
Peace						
(N=1493)	79.2%	16.1%	2.34	14.6%	2.67	3.89
Other sectors						
(N=5584)	68.0%	19.6% **(−)	2.36 n.s.(−)	25.7% ***(−)	2.00 ***(+)	3.20 ***(+)

Conference years						
Peace (N=393)	20.8%	24.2%	2.82	28.0%	1.39	2.83
Other sectors (N=2622)	32.0%	29.8% *(−)	2.43 †(+)	32.0% n.s.(−)	1.68 *(−)	4.05 ***(−)
Environment						
Non-conference years						
Environment (N=1006)	72.5%	21.0%	2.17	27.1%	2.20	4.13
Other sectors (N=7790)	86.2%	20.4% n.s.(+)	2.35 n.s.(−)	23.7% *(+)	2.00 *(+)	3.26 ***(+)
Conference years						
Environment (N=283)	27.5%	32.2%	2.89	29.4%	2.50	5.46
Other sectors (N=1013)	13.8%	29.5% n.s.(+)	2.65 n.s.(+)	36.4% **(−)	1.62 ***(+)	4.05 ***(+)
Women						
Non-conference years						
Women's rights (N=513)	62.0%	25.5%	1.77	18.7%	2.72	3.26
Other sectors (N=5967)	64.4%	17.1% ***(+)	2.36 *(−)	22.9% *(−)	2.15 ***(+)	3.33 n.s.(−)

(Table continues on p. 126.)

Table 4.4 (Continued)

	Percentage Founded	Headquarters in Global South	Ratio of South to North Countries	Regional Structure	Average Number of IGO Ties	Average Number of INGO Ties
Conference years						
Women's rights (N=314)	38.0%	40.4%	3.60	40.8%	1.24	5.23
Other sectors (N=3298)	35.6%	28.4% ***(+)	2.45 ***(+)	30.6% ***(+)	1.66 **(−)	3.72 ***(+)

Source: Authors' calculations based on their Transnational Social Movement Organizations Dataset.

[a] The table shows a) the percentage of transnational social movement organizations in a specific sector and in all other sectors founded during sector-specific conference years and during non-conference years; b) the overall percentage, ratio, or average for transnational social movement organizations founded in sector-specific conference years and non-conference years; c) the results of statistical tests comparing organizations in a specific sector with organizations in other sectors founded during sector-specific conference years and during non-conference years.

[b] All figures in the table were calculated from the total number of organizations active over all years (organization/year spells) in conference and non-conference founding periods. In other words, an individual organization is included in the count for each year that it is active.

[c] For the nominal variables, "Headquarters in Global South" and "Regional Structure," Chi-square tests were used to assess differences between organizations. Independent sample *t*-test were used for comparisons of organizations on the scale variables "Ratio of South to North Countries," "Average IGO Ties," and "Average INGO Ties." + and − signs indicate that the percentage/ratio/mean for organizations in a specific sector was significantly higher or lower than the percentage/ratio/mean for organizations in other sectors in sector-specific conference and non-conference years. The *p*-values associated with the comparisons are: *$p \leq .05$; **$p \leq .01$; ***$p \leq .001$; ✝$p \leq .10$.

global South to global North countries for women's rights groups formed outside of conference intervals.

Encouraging Regional Organizing.   The data in table 4.4 show that regional organizing structures are more common among groups formed during conference intervals. Global conferences were important in helping encourage the expansion of regional forms of transnational organizing we discussed in chapter 3. It is understandable that organizations preparing to attend a global conference, or those simply monitoring the debates, will attempt to coordinate their work with like-minded groups situated in their geographic area. The need to economize, combined with the incentive of the external resources provided by private and official funders to assist regional preparatory conferences, has had a lasting impact on patterns of transnational social movement organizing. Also encouraging this move toward regionalization was the greater institutionalization of regional IGOs in response to changes in the system of globalized capitalism and the end of the Cold War (see chapter 3). Friedman and her colleagues noted that before the UN Conference on Environment and Development, there had been no clear articulation of a Latin American regional environmental perspective. This changed with the Rio conference, because environmentalists in Latin America met their counterparts and began to engage in dialogues about common aims and perspectives with respect to global conferences. People from the same region are more likely to share a common set of interests, but these interests cannot be effectively articulated in global contexts without prior discussions, coordination, and strategizing. Regional PrepComs helped mobilize actors within a given region and expand regional participation in the conference processes (Friedman, Clark, and Hochstetler 2005).

Connections to Other Actors.   Global conferences also helped shape the ways organizations connect with other actors in their environment. In particular, conferences helped facilitate the expansion of networks between transnational movement organizations and other INGOs. Across three of the issues, increases were fairly large and robust in the numbers of ties that transnational movement organizations reported having to other international nongovernmental organizations. This finding is consistent with case studies of global conferences, which reveal extensive NGO networking in these settings (for example, Krut 1997; Riles 2001; Friedman, Clark, and Hochstetler 2005). Analysts cite a number of reasons these events would foster networking. The most important is perhaps that movement activists participating in conferences learn new skills relevant to engaging in global politics. Specifically, they (and others active in the larger organizational field at the time of conferences) become more familiar with the UN conference processes, such as the need to involve southern participants, to make friends with or get friends appointed to national delegations at conferences, and to be involved early in the preparatory process when many key decisions are made. Activists learned the importance of having access to information and of building civil society consensus across major political divides and expanding coalitions to gain political influence. They developed new methods of transnational organizing to facilitate this, such as Women's Caucuses and creative applications of communications technology (Friedman, Clark, and Hochstetler 2005; Prügl and Meyer 1999; West 1999). Illustrating the innovations in organizing tactics, women's groups preparing for the Fourth World Conference on Women organized a "peace train" that traveled from western Europe through the former Soviet Republics and Russia on its way to Beijing. During the trip, activists exchanged ideas and experiences and worked to improve understandings of how racial and class differences operated in the group and in the larger movement (Snyder 2006).

Analysts of transnational feminist organizing point out that, over the course of routine meetings surrounding UN conference processes, feminist organizations and activists developed new ways of thinking and acting together. The diverse perspectives and priorities of activists led to significant conflicts, and feminists remained divided over many issues. Nevertheless, observers of these conferences noted significant changes in feminist frames and discourses. For feminists and other activists familiar with the conference scene, networking came to be seen as a political act that rivaled direct lobbying in its political import (Benchmark Environmental Consulting 1996; Krut 1997). Also, conferences enabled the creation of communication networks that spanned geographic and political as well as racial and class divides. Routine opportunities to meet face to face enabled longer-term conversations to take place, and fostered the creation of trust across diverse groups of activists (Snyder 2006; Riles 2001; Moghadam 2008).

This networking emphasis among transnational feminists might help explain that it is among transnational women's organizations we find the greatest difference in the growth of ties with other INGOs between groups founded during conference and nonconference periods. Representing a difference of 40 percent, the average number of INGOs with which women's groups founded during conference periods had ties with 5.23 versus an average of 3.26 for women's groups formed in other years. The effect was also evident for environmental groups (5.46 versus 4.13, a difference of 31 percent) and human rights organizations (4.30 versus 3.80, a difference of 13 percent).

Interestingly, and contrary to our initial expectations, for all issues except the environment, the numbers of ties to intergovernmental bodies was consistently smaller, on average, for groups formed during conference periods.[16] Our finding that transnational environmental organizations formed especially during the 1972 Stockholm conference had more ties to IGOs (rather than fewer, as was the case for all other issues) suggests that the particular institutional context for environmental activism provides more openings or incentives for those groups to maintain ties to a larger number of intergovernmental bodies. In contrast, for other issues, it seems that activists have either abandoned efforts to engage with global institutions (in favor of extra-institutional strategies) or they find it more efficient to maintain ties to fewer IGOs, perhaps using their networks with other INGOs to obtain the same information and avenues of influence that in the past had required direct relationships with intergovernmental agencies.

Another explanation for this finding is that the greater knowledge about intergovernmental agencies available to groups forming and active during global conferences may highlight for them the limitations of the intergovernmental arena as a site for addressing many of the world's most pressing problems. Indeed, many activists attending conferences complained at the time about the limited progress of official negotiations, compared with the vast amounts of resources these conferences require. Also, a retrospective look at the achievements of UN global conferences shows a pattern of disappointing results, including very limited gains in most issue areas and the gradual abandonment and reversal of earlier agreements. Many social movement groups are likely to seek alternative means of influence, given the high costs of maintaining ties to intergovernmental agencies and the perceptions of the futility of intergovernmental political negotiations. We return to this theme in chapter 5.

Conclusion

These analyses show important relationships between the UN global conferences and the evolution of the population of transnational social movement organizations. The most significant cluster of global conferences were held in response to changes in the post–Cold War geopolitical environment. The processes they institutionalized helped support the development and expansion of transnational social change organizations and networks (Campbell 2005; Haney 2005). The conferences also helped shift intergovernmental negotiations in directions that stressed international cooperation around laws and norms, thereby enhancing the potential influence of actors, such as social movements, that rely on persuasive rather than coercive forms of influence.

UN conferences have shaped the regulatory, normative, cognitive,

and network contexts in which activists seeking to shape global policies are increasingly embedded. Rules of access to formal institutions
have contributed to the professionalization and specialization of wom-
en's organizations, what Alvarez refers to as "NGO-ization." Efforts to
influence conference negotiations, monitor governments' compliance
with conference agreements, and respond to official funding opportunities all generate common pressures on groups and encourage groups
to adopt similar organizational forms. At the same time, conferences
helped expand the density of networks among feminist activists, which
contributed to the spread and consolidation of movements' discourses
and analyses, altering activists' notions of what is possible (Alvarez
1998, 294–95). Evolving ideas about conference practices and activists'
experience with political discourses helped activists articulate more
clearly defined norms that constrained the range of acceptable actions
and discourses for states.

In short, the organizing logics encouraged and reproduced at the
global conferences had larger repercussions for the wider population of
transnational social movement organizations. These spaces enhanced
the organizing capacities of transnational movements and introduced
activists to new ways of understanding and framing global problems,
thereby fueling new possibilities for transforming the world-system.

Friedman and her colleagues observed that, through the course of
the 1990s, civil society groups' participation in UN conferences became
well established and legitimized through official conference practices
and declarations (Friedman, Clark, and Hochstetler 2005, 155). Moreover, it became more routinized through the establishment of entities
such as the Commission on Sustainable Development and through
other treaty bodies that authorize civil society actors to monitor state
compliance with treaty provisions (Merry 2005). These processes help
replace and reproduce UN conferences as transnational focal points
and support structures that facilitate ongoing TSMO engagement with
global institutions and interstate politics.[17]

The global conferences and their institutional offshoots, moreover,
helped trigger changes in the wider organizational field. We see that
the patterns we have linked to global conferences persist across cohorts
of organizations founded around conference years, even among groups
not directly engaged with the conferences themselves. The data we
present here thus reveal that global institutions have shaped the larger
organizational fields in which transnational social movements operate,
even as movements seek to transform international institutions, agendas, and practices. The relatively limited effects of conferences on
changing actual government practices, moreover, have affected debates
within movements and shaped activist strategies over time. Many

movements have achieved important policy advances as a result of their work within global conferences, but the conferences have channeled transnational organizing in ways that may undermine movements' more transformative aims. Understanding the larger implications of social movement–institutional interactions for global social change requires attention to relational dynamics operating within global institutions, a subject that we investigate further in chapter 5.

═ Chapter 5 ═

Institutional Logics
and Paradoxes

*Contrary to popular wisdom, the [global financial institutions] were neither be-
nevolent do-gooders nor mechanistic tools in the hands of global capital opposed
to social justice and equity. Rather, they constituted a complex space in which
power and justice and security and humanitarianism functioned in contradictory and complementary ways. Indeed, these phenomena could not exist without
each other.*
—Balakrishnan Rajagopal (2003, 108)

*The limitations in equality, liberty, and solidarity [of social movements] are not
their responsibility but the consequence of the difficulties imposed upon them by
the defenders of the status quo.*
—Immanuel Wallerstein (1990, 39)

WHEREAS world-systems analysts speak of contradictions between the world economy and the set of principles, or geoculture, that has developed to justify and legitimate the modern world-system, analysts of global institutions have identified the
specific ways these contradictions are manifest in global institutions
such as the United Nations. For instance, Bruce Cronin speaks of the
"two faces of the United Nations," which must arbitrate between its
roles as an organization of member governments and as a guarantor of
a global common good (2002, 55–58). This "paradox of international
relations" pits intergovernmentalism against transnationalism as key
orienting practices in the UN, heightening tension within the organization at a time of rising demands. Moreover, Cronin sees a long-term
trend of increasing transnationalism, a development that increases the
ability of nonstate actors to influence global policies (2002, 60).

Further demonstrating the salience of basic contradictions in con-
temporary global politics, Peter Willetts (2006) highlights the ways the
UN's recent statement on its relations with civil society, known as the
Cardoso Report, reflects incompatibilities in the three distinct logics—

functionalist, corporatist, and pluralist—the report uses to justify civil society participation in the UN. Jaeger discusses further the ways that participation of civil society groups in the United Nations has contributed both to their depoliticization and to the development of a critical "subsystem of world politics" (2007, 271).

These discussions of institutional contradictions and their implications for transnational mobilization mirror the dynamics that Terry Boswell and Christopher Chase-Dunn describe in their discussion of the historical "spiral of capitalism and socialism" (2000, 11–13). In this view, interactions between groups challenging some aspect of the dominant order and the institutions put in place to support the interests of core powers generate a dialectic that shifts the orientation of state practices from capitalist to socialist tendencies over time. Moreover, the spiral image connotes transformations of structures and actors in ways that also change the forms of struggle over time. In this chapter, we explore this spiral dynamic in relation to changing patterns of transnational organizing during a period of hegemonic decline and crisis as well as expanding organizational and normative social movement capacities.

The late twentieth and early twenty-first centuries have been a period of declining U.S. hegemony. This does not mean that the period has been marked by unambiguous declines in U.S. leadership or in the momentum of capitalist tendencies, but rather that the strategies for capitalist expansion initiated in this period have made the system more crisis-prone while at the same time enhancing the underlying conditions supporting antisystemic mobilization (Arrighi and Silver 1999; Boswell and Chase-Dunn 2000). Thus, although economic globalization has expanded global trade and economic growth, it has also tested the physical limits of the planet for increased commodification, leading to the creation of markets in things like water, genetic resources, and clean air (for example, carbon trading) that have traditionally remained outside market relations. As more poor and formerly middle-class people are denied such basic necessities of life as clean water and air, the system's legitimacy and sustainability are increasingly threatened. As financialization replaces industrialization, the large pool of unemployed workers will continue to expand, threatening social stability. These tensions help fuel antisystemic movements by exacerbating popular grievances at a time when movements are better poised to advance claims based on universalized notions of rights.

In this book, we have portrayed global institutions as much products of interactions between authorities and challengers as the arenas in which these contests take place (Khagram 2004; McMichael 2006;

Munck 2002; Rajagopal 2003; Smith 2008). Dominant powers in the world system justify their claims to authority and their disproportionate access to resources through liberal ideologies of individualism, equality, and universalism. Norms of universalism, inclusion, and equity are thus professed within a system whose reliance on perpetual accumulation "requires active institutional discrimination against particular status-groups or identities" (Wallerstein 2004, 39). As long as most people accept—or at least do not question—the status quo, the contradictions between ideology and practice are largely irrelevant, and hegemony is maintained. But the ideals on which the legitimacy of existing institutions rest invite challenges by groups pointing out the incompatibilities between rhetoric and reality (Markoff 1996, 2011; Silver and Arrighi 2005). This makes institutions dynamic, and therefore our analyses of them must account for how interactions within them transform both institutions and actors over time.

Built on these inherent contradictions, institutions of our modern world-system constitute opportunities for counter-hegemonic projects even as they reinforce the hegemony of dominant discourses and practices. Designed to promote stability and to reproduce the interests of powerful actors, institutions tend to channel social movements in ways that depoliticize their demands and negate their transformative potential. For instance, John McCarthy and his colleagues have demonstrated how states constrain social movements through restrictive registration and tax laws as well as policing public demonstrations and other collective actions (McCarthy, Britt, and Wolfson 1991; McCarthy and McPhail 2006). Pamela Oliver further demonstrates the role of U.S. criminal justice institutions in preempting and repressing racial justice activism (2008).

Exploring how global institutions aided the transition from colonialism toward more culturally legitimate but no less exploitative forms of intervention in the name of development, Balakrishnan Rajagopal refers to international organizations as "shock absorbers against mass resistance" (2003, 48). The human rights and development discourses and policies of international organizations served to deradicalize "the contentious relationship between development interventions and many non-European societies" (2003, 48). Ferguson observes that international NGOs[1] should be viewed as part of a "new, transnational apparatus of governmentality," rather than as entities situated "below" the state (2006, 103). He notes that, especially since the end of the Cold War, NGOs have served as conduits for official development aid, helping donor states get around uncooperative national governments in recipient states. They also engage in more direct forms of social control by, for instance, hiring private security or military contractors to protect national parks or humanitarian operations staff from local populations. At a time when we see a rise in the global South of what Ferguson calls the "nongovernmental state," some groups typically seen as nongovernmental are becoming increasingly enmeshed in the work of governance (see also Hammack and Heydemann 2009).

At the same time, however, we have argued throughout this book that international organizations can expand opportunities for movements to challenge authorities and the hegemonic discourses they use to maintain their power. Ironically, movements frequently appeal to the very norms that legitimate global institutions when they mobilize support for their claims using what Keck and Sikkink have referred to as the boomerang strategy (1998). Governments' hypocrisy—reflected in the gaps between their legitimating ideologies, international treaty commitments, and actions—define opportunities for movements to mobilize (see, for example, Ball 2000; Hafner-Burton and Tsutsui 2005).

The previous chapter explored the ways UN global conferences shaped patterns of transnational social movement organizing. We described how global conferences are linked to rising southern participation, increased regionalization, and more dense connections between transnational social movement organizations (TSMOs) and other nongovernmental organizations. One somewhat surprising finding was that the movement organizations formed during periods of global conference organizing were significantly less likely than those formed at other times to maintain formal ties to intergovernmental organizations. All movement organizations formed in conference intervals, regardless of their age, were significantly less likely than those formed in other years to report a tie to at least one intergovernmental organization, and they reported, on average, fewer overall ties to them.[2]

Why were transnational movements less connected to global political institutions when governments and nongovernmental actors were actively engaged in increasingly institutionalized efforts to address global problems? Given the greater opportunities at conferences to engage more directly with global institutional actors, we would expect social movement activists to be more rather than less connected to intergovernmental bodies. Global conferences draw attention to the specific multilateral agencies charged with addressing important global problems such as environmental degradation, human rights, and development. Conference secretariats work deliberately to strengthen ties to civil society groups. Conferences can generate new institutional structures and monitoring bodies such as the Commission on Sustainable Development or the High Commissioner for Human Rights, and activists can get in on the ground floor to help shape these new institutions. Conference declarations and monitoring bodies can also be important sources of access and leverage for social movements seeking to change state behavior. So the relative lack of connection between conference-era TSMOs and intergovernmental agencies (IGOs) is somewhat puzzling. We draw from institutional theories to examine the logics that may be affecting these decisions by transnational activists, and we consider the larger implications of these choices for global social change.

Global Institutional Logics

Max Weber argued that the logic of rationalization and bureaucratization could lead to the creation of institutional "iron cages" that imprisoned their human creators (1994). Paul DiMaggio and Walter Powell extend Weber's metaphor to show how the state and the professions, which they call the "great rationalizers of the second half of the twentieth century" (1991, 64), help define the institutional logics of contemporary organizational fields, leading inexorably to organizational homogeneity, or isomorphism. For organizational theorists, cognitive mechanisms such as norms and cultural practices as well as relational mechanisms such as certification and brokerage all contribute to the tendency of organizations working in a similar industry or policy area to adopt similar structures, norms, and practices, regardless of whether these conform to the organization's central goals or function. The ways civil society actors are embedded in institutions affects their organizational forms, capacities for change, and connections to other actors in the environment (Campbell 2004, 2005; Powell and DiMaggio 1991). Actors are often aware of how institutions define their strategic choices, and may adapt their operating structures and activities in response to these constraints (Martens 2005). As a result, civil society actors may engage states as "sometimes rivals, sometimes servants, sometimes watchdogs, sometimes parasites, but in every case operating on the same level and in the same global space" (Ferguson 2006, 103).

To be seen as legitimate players in a given institutional context, actors must conform to particular organizational models and practices, discourses, and standards of behavior. Varying rules of engagement, or methods of "certification" (McAdam et al. 2001), are used by institutional gatekeepers to regulate who can participate in official policy realms. Actors' acceptance or standing in particular arenas depends on their conforming to established norms, regardless of whether these are consistent with their organizational logics and goals. For social movements, this typically requires some level of accommodation with dominant power structures, thereby constraining their ability to fully articulate and advocate for changes that are consistent with movement goals (McAdam and Scott 2005). Perhaps one of the most important and divisive sorts of conflicts within social movements is whether and how to respond to the incompatibilities between dominant institutions (including mass public opinion) and movement values and goals. For instance, as they have sought to gain access to political leaders and official negotiating forums, some feminist activists have justified decisions to engage in political strategies that are deemed effective in patriarchal institutions but that contradict key feminist values (Alvarez 1999). Marisa von Bülow (2010, 112) discusses how public opinion in the United States led a leading anti–free trade campaigner to mobilize around frames that had resonance in the United States (that is, border safety and the drug war) but that undermined transnational solidarity. This pattern is mirrored in many northern labor struggles (Fletcher and Gapasín 2008). Kersten Martens discusses how the process of obtaining formal consultative status in the UN leads groups to downplay controversial agendas in return for access to UN negotiation settings and the legitimacy that comes with this formal status (2005, chap. 5). Francis Shor shows how the strategic and political contradictions of U.S. anti-sweat campaigns have "scarred expressions of global solidarity while undermining the necessary struggle by those in an imperial culture against the privileges and mystifications that define that culture" (2010, 50). Gay Seidman (2009) and Ethel Brooks (2007) show how dominant logics of global capitalism have limited the transformative potential of transnational activism for workers' rights—including the rights of women and children workers and their families. Finally, Patricia Widener's analysis of transnational environmental campaigns found that many "ignor[e] or even contribut[e] to the global treadmill of production" (2011, 8–9).

Von Bülow observed that there are many "pathways to transnationalism," but institutional pressures lead transnational organizations and their larger networks to adopt organizational structures and practices that reflect those of other organizations in the environment (Zald and Garner 1987). That we can even speak of an entity called a transnational social movement organization reflects observable structural similarities in the patterns of transnational associational activity. National and international rules that regulate civil society organizations ensure that particular structures of accountability and governance are in place, and unless an organization conforms to those structures, it will have limited ability to generate resources and influence in the larger political environment (Anheier and Themudo 2002; McCarthy, Britt, and Wolfson 1991; McCarthy 1996; McCarthy and Zald 1990).

The more centralized a polity is, the more pressure on local movements to adapt to predominant organizational models and strategies (Garner and Zald 1988). Thus we see a tendency for citizens' organizations to become more formal and professionalized, even when the group's ideologies and values mitigate against this (Alvarez 1998; McCarthy and Zald 1987; Mendoza 2002; Riles 2001; Staggenborg 1988; Jenkins and Ekert 1986). Also, we saw in our data on transnational social movement organizations and elsewhere a predisposition for convergence around a more limited set of issues and policy agendas in centralized and consolidated polities. Thus, as we reported in chapter 2, in the early years of our dataset, fewer than half (44 percent) of organizations worked in the most populous issue areas of human rights, women's rights, environment, and development, whereas in the 2000s more than two-thirds (68 percent) did so. Along with issue convergence, another outcome of more centralized polities is discursive isomorphism, or the tendency for diverse actors to adopt similar discourses and ways of thinking about shared problems. Thus, Susan Olzak and Kiyoteru Tsutsui found that ethnic minorities have become increasingly likely to articulate their claims in human rights as opposed to nationalist-separatist terms (1998), a pattern that is also reflected in our dataset. Similarly, as we discuss shortly in regard to the environmental arena, we find a convergence of environmental debates around the language of sustainable development in the wake of the 1992 UN Conference on Environment and Development.

In addition to defining appropriate organizational forms, institutions also shape the cognitive arena in which organizations operate. They help delineate what the larger society thinks about and how they think about it. They define the "dominant symbolic repertoire," or a society's taken-for-granted ways of thinking, writing, talking, and acting (Woehrle, Coy, and Maney 2008, 29). This influence over people's understandings and their imaginations is the essence of what Antonio Gramsci referred to as hegemony (1971). Contemporary global institutions are built on an ideology that privileges globalized markets, which means that much of the public and policy discourse revolves around and prioritizes values of profit-making and economic growth. The notion that economic growth will trickle down and advance other social goals has become normalized—or widely and unquestioningly accepted—among much of the population. The interests of economic elites have thus come to be seen as universal, as benefitting all of society. Other social goods and values, such as health, a clean environment, and equity in the distribution of resources are assumed to be natural outgrowths of efficient markets, thereby marginalizing movements organizing to prioritize these concerns over market logics. At the same time, the dangers and vulnerabilities inherent to the global organization of trade and financial markets are downplayed or dismissed (see Sklair 2001). Thus the collapse of the U.S. housing market in 2008 and the subsequent global financial crisis came as a surprise to many, and much mainstream media discourse fails to portray the crisis's origins in the basic operations of the globalized economy.

Cecelia Lynch describes how the dominance of market ideology within the global institutional context contributed to the "discursive demobilization" of peace and justice movements in the 1980s and 1990s (1998). In particular, it led movements to focus on single issues, such as child labor, or on particular weapons systems, rather than on the larger systemic problems of globalized capitalism and the militarization and arms trade it encourages. These strategic choices made it more likely that groups could gain access to policy processes and policymakers, even as it reduced the likelihood that they would achieve larger movement aims of advancing peace and demilitarization. Discursive demobilization results in part from what Myra Marx Ferree refers to as "soft repression," or "the nonviolent uses of power that are specifically directed against movement collective identities and movement ideas that support 'cognitive liberation' or 'oppositional consciousness'" (2005, 141). Soft repression occurs in the symbolic or cognitive realm of "naming, speaking, labeling, defining, and knowing," but it can also spill over into more overt forms of violence and repression. Both discursive demobilization and soft repression are forms of "boundary policing" done through micro-level ridicule (Ferree 2005, 143).

Forms of political control that reinforce hegemony also result from the division of political agendas and policy arenas into distinct issues, such as environment, women's rights, human rights, and so on. The compartmentalization of global institutional agendas obstructs efforts to address the interconnections across issues and to identify common, systemic causes:

> UN rights conferences and conventions, including the convention on the Rights of the Child promoted by humanitarian NGOs and the series of international women's conferences promoted by women's groups, can both contribute to and distract attention from the way in which globalization threatens basic labor rights internationally. Where challenges to indentured servitude, slave labor . . . and child labor . . . do exist, they illuminate particular injustices while forgoing the opportunity to challenge the "right" of firms to base investment decisions on the relative cost and malleability of labor markets. (Lynch 1998, 151–52)

As is clear from this discussion, controlling discourse is a crucial feature of power and hegemony. Neil Cooper argues that discourses aimed at reinforcing dominant power relations are part of the "architecture of forgetting" (2010, 10). As they promote certain values and ideals, discourses can make invisible or otherwise distort interpretations of important historical relations and injustices, most notably colonialism (see also Farmer 2004; Eyben and Napier-Moore 2009).

Discursive and other forms of demobilization within institutions are often quite subtle, and movements, without intending to, can reinforce the interests and power of dominant forces (Kamat 2002). Development scholars such as Arturo Escobar (2004a), Paul Farmer (2004), and Balakrishnan Rajagopal (2003) highlight the ways dominant international discourses on development and human rights make invisible the economic violence inherent in the global capitalist system. As a consequence of the institutional context, many human rights groups (particularly those in the global North) have emphasized civil and political rights to the neglect of developmental rights. Many activists concerned with improving global equity are willing to mobilize large-scale campaigns for more aid but fail to consider how donor governments' policies systematically deny people of the global South access to economic opportunities at home and in international markets.

In addition to constraining the range of critical discourses in which the public engages, institutions also help define the organizational structures and agendas of social groups, including those groups that promote social transformation. Institutional demands and certification processes can thus lead social movement organizations toward more formal and professionalized, isomorphic structures. Such structures might, moreover, contradict common movement values of decentralized authority and participatory decision making (Polletta 2002). Dominant political institutions can also divert the attention of civil society groups from more transformative agendas toward activities that reinforce the status quo. Through international aid and development programs, many development NGOs have helped support conservative agendas either directly or by helping lend popular legitimacy to international financial institutions (see also Ferguson 2006; Macdonald 1997; Fisher 1997). For instance, Paul Nelson's analysis of the World Bank's engagement with civil society groups showed that the bank systematically limited civil society's participation to helping carry out World Bank projects, denying any role in defining larger program agendas (1995). Michael Goldman points to a similar dynamic in the bank, referring to it as the "neoliberalization of civil society" (2005, chap. 6).

The World Bank's central role in global development policy leads many groups to work with it rather than accept what they think may be worse social and environmental outcomes if they refuse to do so (Goldman 2005; see also O'Brien et al. 2000; Nelson 1995). Evelina Dagnino calls the intersection of dominant institutions and NGOs a "perverse convergence," where political leaders want and need civil society groups to help them carry out public functions and to legitimize dominant institutions, but they refuse to relinquish any decision-making power (2008, 57). Some groups have been willing to accept these unequal terms of cooperation in return for access, legitimacy, and resources, but others refuse to engage with institutions and are often penalized with political marginalization and limited access to resources (see Macdonald 1997).

But even when they do engage with institutions, movement actors do not necessarily accept the constraints authorities impose. Rather, many actively seek to shift public discourses and institutional contexts. Increasingly, as they gather more evidence of the failures of neoliberal policies to achieve "development," they gain leverage in international arenas. One common strategy transnational movements have used to counteract the "dominant symbolic repertoire" and contest authorities' claims is to develop strategies through which they can challenge, or "harness," hegemony (Woehrle, Coy, and Maney 2008). The boomerang strategy introduced earlier is such an effort. Keck and Sikkink (1998) first introduced the notion of the boomerang effect to illustrate the ways transnational advocacy groups engage the international political system to enhance their leverage with respect to states. Drawing largely from cases of human rights activism within repressive national contexts, these authors argued that transnational alliances could expand movements' political opportunities where national polities were closed. Activists with transnational ties draw international attention to a national conflict, bringing a government's international reputation, interstate alliances, as well as pressure from international institutions into play in its decisions about its treatment of internal dissidents and other citizens. The strategy essentially exploits contradictions between international norms and national practices with the aim of bringing the latter into conformity with the former. Strategically, this logic is not much different from that used by movements operating within some national contexts, such as civil rights activists in the United States drawing the national government into state and local conflicts over civil rights (McAdam 1999; Kolb 2007).

In addition to aiding the work of human rights activists, the boomerang strategy proved useful for transnational feminist networks seeking leverage within national political contexts that were dominated by men and patriarchic norms (Keck and Sikkink 1998, chap. 5; Meyer 1999; Miller 1999). It was also effective for environmental advocates seeking to bring global environmental norms into national legal systems (see Economy 2004; Hochstetler 2002; Keck and Sikkink 1998), a process referred to as "domesticating" international law (Tarrow 2005). Since Keck and Sikkink's initial statement of the boomerang theory appeared, other scholars have identified conditions where such a strategy is most likely to be used, adapted by activists, and to succeed (Hertel 2006; Hochstetler 2002; Stewart 2004).[3]

Even though international norms and institutions can expand movement potential, ironies remain in how institutional logics shape the possibilities for movements to achieve their broader aims. For instance, Tammy Lewis (2002) shows how the need for strong civil society partners led transnational conservation groups to opt to work in countries where environmental threats were relatively less urgent. Clifford Bob (2005) demonstrates how transnational campaigns have tended to privilege communities with leaders who could speak to and whose stories appealed to international media. And Neil Cooper (forthcoming) shows how the institutionalized discourses around pariah weapons and the rhetoric of "human security" prevented the emergence of more broadly critical movement framings of global militarism and the international arms trade. INCITE! Women of Color Against Violence has argued that "the revolution will not be funded," and offers a strident critique of the "nonprofit industrial complex" (2007). The group encourages more movements to critically assess how their reliance on external funding can deradicalize their work.[4]

The key point is that the institutionalization of norms and values is a complex process, involving cooperation as well as competition between authorities and challengers over cultural norms, values, and priorities (for example, Campbell 2001). The proliferation of transnational institutions has created both new challenges and new opportunities for movements. An understanding of institutional logics can help us assess the effectiveness of various movement strategies for social change. In the following section, we consider how global institutional contexts are related to patterns of transnational organizing. We consider whether international institutions appear more as constraints on movements, channeling and co-opting movement efforts toward more system-supporting forms, or whether there is evidence that they provide opportunities for movements to transform the world-system.

Isomorphism, Institutional Embeddedness, and Transnational Social Movement Organizations

To investigate the impact of institutional logics on patterns of transnational movement activity, we first consider the extent to which transnational movement organizations are embedded within institutional contexts and how much their organizational structures conform to dominant models. We measure institutional embeddedness as the numbers and nature of ties that transnational movement organizations report to intergovernmental organizations. Conformity to dominant organizational templates, known also as isomorphism, is measured as the degree to which an organization develops specialized structures designed to maximize their access and influence in the world polity. Our investigation of the ways the global polity affects the population of transnational social movement organizations focuses our attention on whether and how these tendencies have changed over time. Our concern with the possibilities for transnational movements to affect global change leads us to ask whether more extensive links to the intergovernmental arena and greater isomorphism with dominant organizing models weakens movements' commitment to expanding their ties with less powerful actors in the world polity—including people in the global South, as well as other NGOs. More ties to marginalized actors are expected to enhance groups' antisystemic or counter-hegemonic tendencies, and therefore should be less prevalent for organizations more firmly connected to formal intergovernmental institutions and processes. Ironically, ties to these same actors can also indicate an organization's greater legitimacy or acceptance within the world polity because the democratic norms governing global institutions mean that a group's standing depends on representativeness of a broad population, including groups known to be underrepresented in formal political arenas. This is part of the inherent tension and contradiction of the modern world-system we have discussed.

Isomorphism refers to the tendency of organizations to adopt similar structures and practices in response to coercive processes and in mimicry of dominant models through professionalization. Our dataset provides us with three measures of the extensiveness of a group's conformity with dominant organizing models: organizational structure, membership, and mobilizing agenda. We use the term *specialization* to refer to these features, because they reflect organizing strategies aimed at maximizing a group's potential influence within the dominant political system. Regarding organizational structure, we distinguish transnational organizations according to how centralized they are. Within centralized transnational organizations such as Amnesty International, movement agendas and activities tend to be defined and managed by an international secretariat; chapters and sections are accountable to international rules and standards, which may overshadow local interests and preferences (see, for example, Siméant 2005; on parallels in national-level organizations, see Oliver and Furman 1989). More decentralized structures, by contrast, allow affiliates or partners a wide range of choices about organizational practices and strategies.

Our second measure of specialization relates to the structure of organizational membership. We conceptualize movement organizations with professional members only (for example, lawyers or doctors) as more specialized or adapted to dominant institutional logics than those with no such restrictions on membership. Finally, we consider organizations that adopt a single-issue agenda as more specialized than those that adopt a multi-issue agenda, because issue specialization is a response to the larger institutional environment, which divides complex global problems into issue-specific negotiating frameworks. Issue specialization also enhances the organization's ability to compete for limited resources in the larger multi-organizational environment. These three features—centralized structure, professional membership, and single-issue agenda—reflect organizations' rational adaptation to national and international institutional contexts as they seek to generate resources and influence in the political environment.

To measure institutional embeddedness, we consider whether a movement organization has any tie to an intergovernmental body, has ties to many intergovernmental bodies, or has consultative status with a multilateral agency. We acknowledge that our measures capture neither the extensiveness or substance of the ties, nor the full range of possible connections between social movement organizations and bilateral and multilateral agencies, but they do tell us something about whether and how extensively a group associates its work with that of IGOs.

For the analysis of the correlates of embeddedness, we coded movement organizations 1 if they exhibited at least two of these features and 0 if they exhibited one or none. Figure 5.1 displays the trend in organizational specialization and institutional embeddedness over time.

Over all years, the percentage of institutionally embedded organizations is greater than the percentage that is specialized. Institutionally embedded groups went from a high of just over 60 percent of the population in 1953, declined through the 1990s, and rose again to around 45 percent in 2003. Much of the fluctuation can be explained by the rapid growth in the population at the time, and that new groups may take time to develop ties to other organizations, especially IGOs. The percentage of groups exhibiting specialization starts much lower, with just over 30 percent of movement organizations scoring high on our measure in 1953, and declining to under 20 percent by 2003.[5]

Is there a relationship between institutional embeddedness and organizational specialization? Organizational theory would lead us to expect it. Following our discussion, organizations most densely linked to international institutions are expected to also conform more closely to specialized organizational models. This is because organizations most linked to the realm of formal politics are expected to adopt organizational features that maximize their ability to attract resources and

Figure 5.1   Institutional Embeddedness and Specialization over Time

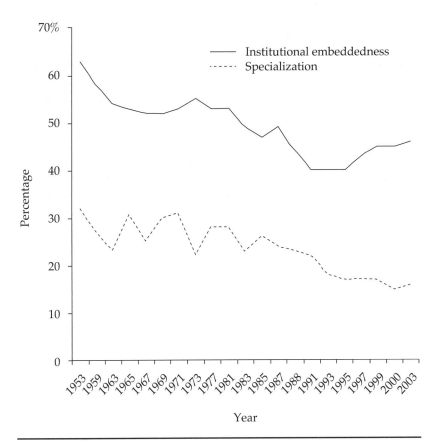

Year

Source: Authors' compilation based on their Transnational Social Movement Organizations Dataset.
Note: The figure displays the percentage of transnational social movement organizations that had two or more of the following indicators of specialization: a centralized structure, professional membership, and a single-issue agenda, and the percentage of transnational social movement organizations that had two or more of the following indicators of institutional embeddedness: consultative status with an multilateral agency, any tie to an intergovernmental agency, or ties to a high number of intergovernmental agencies.

support. However, contrary to what the literature suggests, we found that more institutionally embedded organizations did not exhibit higher levels of specialization than those with fewer institutional ties. In addition, organizations that were more highly embedded in global institutions also tended to have higher levels of southern participation. Specialization, in contrast, tended to be associated with somewhat lower levels of southern participation, but this difference was only present for groups based in the global South.

How might we account for these patterns? Isomorphic pressures channel all organizations toward similar forms and similar relations within the institutional realm. The adoption of widely accepted organizational forms is expected to bring legitimacy to the organization and to reduce costs of operating in the larger multi-organizational environment. It is also expected to generate the most payoffs in terms of a group's access to resources and policy arenas controlled by elites. There is reason to believe that groups in the global North will be more likely to adopt specialized structures, given that their constituencies will be more likely to view global institutions as essentially benevolent and functional, whereas in the global South, perceptions of global institutions are likely more critical.

However, groups in the global South—and especially in the periphery—may be more likely to adopt globally legitimated models to try to enhance their standing in global arenas. Although they may see the limited influence of their countries on the global stage, they may still aspire, as James Ferguson observes, to "assert membership and equality through likeness and to claim . . . 'semblant solidarity'" (2006, 21–22). Consistent with this interpretation, data analyzed by Roy Kwon and his colleagues on participants at World Social Forum gatherings demonstrates a tendency for activists from the core and from the periphery to be most supportive of global institutional arrangements, and the most critical voices come from semiperiphery countries (2008).

To compare south- and north-based organizations, we categorized organizations by founding period to control for age and for changes in geopolitics and institutional opportunities. We chose a simple dichotomous categorization, using 1990 as a cut-off year, grouping organizations founded during or before 1990 into one category, and the remaining organizations into a second category. This year coincides with the hastening breakdown of the bipolar world order, as well as the beginning of the UN conference cycle, both of which have had tremendous implications for transnational mobilization.

In general, the younger cohort of organizations shows less specialization than the older cohort. But regardless of founding cohort, north-based groups are more highly specialized generally, and are more likely than south-based groups to have professional members, although the percentage of organizations having only professionals as members declines somewhat for the younger north-based cohort (from 28.5 percent to 23.9 percent). Among the older cohort, north-based groups are more likely to have a centralized structure, but the percentage declines for the younger cohort to just below that of southern groups (13.4 percent of north-based groups versus 14.1 percent of south-based groups). Finally, with regard to single-issue advocacy, northern groups are more likely than southern ones to have single-issue frames, regardless of cohort. Among younger organizations, for example, 53.7 percent of north-based groups versus 38.4 percent of south-based groups embraced a single-issue agenda. Because a larger percentage of southern transnational social movement organizations were formed in more recent years, variation in organizing models should be seen as reflecting not purely geographic preferences but also changes in organizational environments over time.

Institutional embeddedness in general has declined across age cohorts, but more so for north-based organizations. Although just under 50 percent of these founded through 1990 scored high on our measure, only 25 percent of those based in the global North and founded after 1990 did so. This compares with 33 percent of south-based organizations in the post-1990 cohort. The overall percentage of organizations with IGO connections is smaller for the younger cohort than for the older one, but interestingly younger south-based organizations are slightly more connected to IGOs than their north-based counterparts. The south-based groups founded after 1990 are more likely to have ties to at least one IGO, and also more likely to have ties to numerous IGOs than north-based groups in the same founding cohort.

The most striking difference between cohorts of both north- and south-based organizations is in the percentage of organizations having consultative status with any IGO, such status being far less common among newer organizations. This is at least partly a function of the more limited time that newer groups have had to establish their reputations and relationships with IGOs. For north-based groups, the difference between old and young cohorts is more than 25 percentage points. This rather dramatic difference is the puzzle we first identified in chapter 4 and with which we began this chapter. As noted, this counterintuitive finding might reflect transnational social movements' shift away from the institutional arena, probably from a sense that such ties do not help groups achieve their goals or that they compromise organizations' core values or agenda. It might also mean that organizations are developing different kinds of networks to help them manage the demands on their time and other resources that engagement with IGOs requires. Establishing ties with other NGOs that have formal ties to IGOs rather than maintaining their own independent links allows groups to gain access to relevant information and communication channels without having to devote their own resources toward maintaining contact with IGOs and fulfilling the other requirements associated with consultative relations.[6] Beth Caniglia's work, for instance, showed that transnational environmental groups with consultative status tended to be more central, that is, maintain higher numbers of ties to other groups, within organizational networks (2000). Case study research shows that both logics may be operating simultaneously (see, for example, Martens 2005; von Bülow 2010).

What impact does isomorphism and institutional embeddedness have on representation from the global South? Organizations that conformed more closely to dominant organizational models tended to have less representation from the global South, and this was mainly so for south-based organizations. Disaggregating our isomorphism measure, we see that this is largely because of differential effects of professional memberships and organizational centralization in each region. Although having a single-issue focus reduced participation from the global South for all groups, among north-based groups, those with professional members were far more likely than groups with no such restrictions on membership to have higher representation from the global South (64.7 percent versus 43.2 percent). But south-based organizations did not show such differences, suggesting that professional networks create useful ties for mobilizing across the north-south divide but are less important for mobilizing within the south. The impact of having a centralized structure also differs for north- and south-based organizations. Having a centralized structure does not increase southern representation, and is in fact a detriment to southern representation among the northern organizations. The inverse was true for south-based groups: 84 percent of south-based groups with a centralized structure had a higher than 1:1 ratio of southern to northern participation, versus 74 percent of more decentralized organizations.

Whereas high specialization (isomorphism) has a negative or neutral effect on southern representation in transnational social movement organizations, institutional embeddedness has a strongly positive effect for both north- and south-based groups. Among north-based organizations, 58.7 percent of institutionally embedded groups had a higher than 1:1 ratio of south to north participation, versus 43.9 percent of organizations with fewer institutional links. South-based groups that were more densely linked to intergovernmental organizations were 16 percentage points more likely than less embedded groups to have high southern representation. The disaggregated measures show that, regardless of headquarters location, having any tie to an IGO enhances southern representation, but having ties to a high number of IGOs matters far more for north-based than for south-based groups. Among northern groups, those with high IGO ties are 25 percentage points more likely to have a high southern membership than groups with fewer IGO ties are. Consultative status made an important difference for both south- and north-based groups: among the latter, those with consultative status were 13 percentage points more likely to have high southern representation, and among south-based groups, 17 percentage points more likely. This pattern supports the conclusion Caniglia (2000) makes that groups with consultative status are important brokers between transnational social movement organizations and IGOs.

In sum, institutional embeddedness does indeed seem to benefit movement goals such as higher representation from the global South. Specialization has mixed effects: northern organizations with professional members are more effective at generating southern participation than other types of north-based organizations are, but having professional members reduces the expansiveness of southern representation within south-based organizations. Having a single-issue agenda restricts the possibility that an organization will attract more participation from the south, regardless of headquarters location.

On another measure of movement activity, ties to other international nongovernmental organizations (INGOs), we find that specialization has mixed effects. It is somewhat detrimental to establishing ties to a large number of international nongovernmental organizations, though this effect is not large and is more pronounced for south-based groups. The impact of professional membership on the networking abilities of transnational social movement organizations is also not very large, and varies according to the geographical location of headquarters. North-based groups with professional members have a slightly higher average number of ties to other international nongovernmental organizations than north-based groups with other types of members do. The effect is the opposite within the population of south-based transnational social movement organizations. Finally, for both north and south-based organizations, having a single-issue agenda constricts the number of other INGOs that an organization has ties with by an average of two.

As with southern representation, institutional embeddedness has a much larger impact on networking than organizational characteristics do, especially for north-based groups. Organizations with more links to intergovernmental organizations have ties to an average of three more INGOs than less embedded groups, regardless of headquarters location. Having consultative status increases the number of INGOs with which a movement organization has ties by an average of two, regardless of headquarters location. Thus, having ties to IGOs enhances the motivation and ability of TSMOs to cultivate relationships with other NGOs. Attendance at intergovernmental conferences and communications with intergovernmental officials provide increased opportunities for organizations to maintain dense networks with other civil society actors.

The patterns we uncover here reinforce the idea that institutions have contradictory and paradoxical effects on the movements seeking to challenge dominant power relations. Overall, we saw a general tendency for groups conforming most closely to dominant organizational models (specialization) to be comparatively less effective at engaging with more marginalized groups such as members in the global South or other NGOs. At the same time—and supporting Keck and Sikkink's contention that the boomerang strategic logic motivates many transnational challengers—groups with more dense connections to global institutions (embeddedness) were better able to forge connections to less powerful actors in the world polity. To illustrate these paradoxical institutional dynamics further, in the next section we examine discursive shifts within the transnational human rights and environmental movements.

Human Rights and the Rise of a Global System Critique

For Rajagopal, international institutions and human rights norms represent distinct but complementary "cosmopolitan projects" (2003, 9). Both projects have the potential to be hegemonic (that is, reinforcing the interests of dominant political and economic elites), or counter-hegemonic and emancipatory. In the postcolonial context, social movements have had to find culturally legitimate forms of resistance to the dominant legal and development institutions that avoid exclusionary nationalist discourses, and human rights has provided a primary avenue for such struggles. However, Rajagopal also points out important contradictions in the international human rights regime, which has used human rights language to justify large-scale structural inequality, military interventions, and other actions that contradict basic human rights: "By ignoring the history of resistance to imperialism, by endorsing wars while opposing their consequences, and by failing to link itself with social movements of resistance to hegemony, the main protagonists of the Western human rights discourse are undermining the future of human rights itself" (2006, 775). In effect, the contemporary world polity allows for the coexistence of hegemonic and counter-hegemonic uses of human rights, and it is unclear which human rights agenda will emerge victorious (Rajagopal 2006, 770; Santos 2007b).

The end of the Cold War opened space on the international agenda both for capitalist economic expansion and for greater discussion and international cooperation to advance human rights. These two tendencies created a new hegemonic role for rights-based discourse, especially as global norms of liberal democracy and "good governance" were consolidated around the aims of spreading global markets and incorporating "emerging economies" into global markets (Rajagopal 2006, 770; Ferguson 2006). Institutions like the World Bank and the IMF abandoned their earlier hostility toward human rights discourse as they articulated and embraced a market-friendly conception of human rights. This helped advance what Rajagopal refers to as a "totalising discourse" (2006, 770) that justified a variety of coercive economic and military interventions in the name of human rights (see also Pugh, Cooper, and Turner 2008).

But though new challenges to human rights emerged with the post–Cold War expansion of both political and economic international institutions, the rise of neoliberalism generated a counter-mobilization by the growing numbers of people being excluded from the benefits of economic globalization: "With the emergence of counter-hegemonic globalization, the global South began to question [conventional conceptions of human rights] by showing, in striking ways, that the global North and its imperial domination over the South—now intensified by neoliberal global capitalism—was indeed the root source of the most massive violations of human rights" (Santos 2007b, 5).

This led to greater levels of contention in the human rights field during the 1990s, with the rise of a more consolidated "insurgent cosmopolitanism" in the global justice movement (Santos 2007b). In other words, the contradictions between the legitimating rhetoric of human rights and the realities of neoliberal economic development have fueled the recent emergence and convergence of diverse social groups around claims for global economic justice.

This discussion suggests divergent trends in the transnational human rights movement that simultaneously reinforce and challenge dominant institutions and unequal power relations. On the one hand, human rights advocates are encouraged to conform to institutionalized practices and to abandon more radical or transformative agendas. Institutionalized human rights politics have shifted attention largely toward monitoring and enforcing political and civil rights while devoting less attention to the more expansive economic and social rights captured in notions of the right to development. Because many in the legal profession are attracted to international human rights activism, moreover, there is likely more attention to the formal and practical dimensions of human rights law than to larger questions about the limits and contradictions of the international legal system. Within legal frameworks, calls for more ambiguous or nontraditional rights, such as the right to development, are seen as impractical or even as a threat to established precedents in human rights law.

Rajagopal summarizes the important ways that institutionalized human rights limit the possibilities for people of the global South especially to realize universal human rights (2006, 172–73). First, institutional logics privilege Western legal thinking and ways of knowing, foreclosing opportunities to envision alternative models for articulating and protecting human rights. Second, the state plays an important role as a protector of human rights, but existing international law does not account for variations in states' historical relations and their related capacities for meeting both positive and negative human rights requirements.[7] Moreover, international law is limited in its ability to hold states accountable for rights violations that their economic policies and other actions cause outside their own borders (Gibney 2008). This is related to the overall failure of international legal and institutional discourses to confront the violence inherent in development as carried out through international policies and practices (Escobar 2004b). As Rajagopal observed, human rights discourse "remains caught up in the discursive formations of colonialism that makes it blind to many types of violence" (2006, 186).[8]

Evidence of a discursive shift around human rights in the population of transnational social movement organizations is seen in an increasing percentage of human rights groups incorporating a critical assessment of the global economy in their mobilizing agendas after 1990. We refer to these groups as having a critical frame. Sixty-five percent of these groups were founded in the global South, compared with 35 percent founded in the global North. Of the human rights organizations founded after 1990, nearly 10 percent advanced a critical frame, compared with around 4 percent formed in 1990 or earlier.[9] Although this is not a tremendous increase, the growth in the size of the population does suggest an important shift in the overall amount of critical human rights discourse. This discursive shift, moreover, coincides with the 1993 World Conference on Human Rights in Vienna, which affirmed the right to development, and the rise of the transnational global justice movement.

Not surprisingly, groups adopting a critical rights frame reported more ties to other international nongovernmental organizations, averaging ties to around nine INGOs compared to an average of five for other human rights groups. Figure 5.2 reveals further differences between the two sets of groups.

**Figure 5.2   Characteristics of Transnational Social Movement
Organizations by Human Rights Frame**

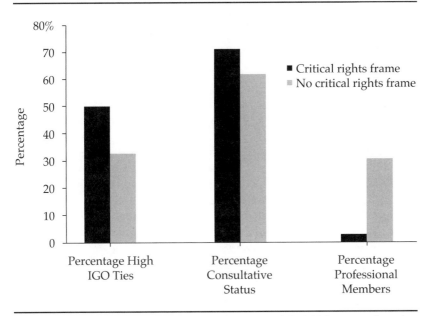

Source: Authors' compilation based on their Transnational Social Movement Organizations Dataset.

Highlighting the paradox of institutional dynamics, groups adopting a critical rights frame tended to have ties to more intergovernmental organizations than other rights organizations did. As figure 5.2 shows, 51 percent of critical rights groups had ties to a high number of IGOs, versus 33 percent of other rights groups. Whereas groups with conventional human rights frames are also likely to be working with intergovernmental agencies to enact the boomerang effect as a remedy to government hypocrisy, the consolidation of the international human rights legal architecture seems to be channeling these groups into a small number of institutional hubs (Tsutsui, Wiest, and Smith forthcoming). However, because there are fewer institutionalized channels through which critical human rights advocates can advance their claims that the global economy contributes to rights violations, these groups may be forming more ties to intergovernmental agencies simply to expand the number of targets and amplify their claims about states' hypocrisy. Interestingly, and again highlighting institutional paradoxes, a slightly higher percentage of groups embracing a critical rights frame had a consultative relationship with IGOs (71 percent versus 62 percent).

These patterns demonstrate how newer TSMOs have responded to the persistence of massive inequality and related human rights violations despite more than a half century of growth in the international human rights legal regime. Coming at a time of a rapidly growing global movement for economic justice, they suggest that human rights movements will increasingly advance a more critical perspective on human rights, given that it is the newer groups as well as those formed in the far more populous global South that tend to advance a critical rights frame. This reflects the learning and socialization that takes place within social movements. Activists join movements to address a social problem, and often they begin working within existing institutions to promote change. With time, however, they confront the limitations that institutionalized norms and practices place on achieving the sort of changes they hoped to realize. Some activists come to embrace more radical critiques of the social order. Sam Marullo and his colleagues, for instance, documented this dynamic among U.S. peace movement organizations. Following the failed nuclear freeze legislation in the U.S. Congress, U.S. peace groups were more likely to mobilize around frames that were critical of the larger structures of U.S. militarism and unilateralism and less singularly focused on opposition to nuclear weapons (Marullo, Pagnucco, and Smith 1996).

Similarly, our data on transnational social movement organizations as well as the contemporary activities of the global justice movement show that many more groups advocating critical, systemic framings of global problems have emerged since the 1990s. Many of these groups point to the lessons learned from years of activism around World Bank and global economic policies as they articulate claims for a more just world economic and political order (Broad and Hecksher 2003). The massive protests against the G8 and World Trade Organization in the late 1990s and economic crises in Asia, Latin America, and in the core countries of the world-system attest to the fact that the contemporary global order is more susceptible to antisystemic social movements than in earlier times.

From Environmental Protection to Sustainable Development

Global institutions can be seen as disciplining environmental organizations in two key ways. First, they have structured environmental discourse in a way that demobilizes critics of economic globalization who stress the impossibility of perpetual economic growth within the natural limits of the planet.[10] Second, global environmental institutions established after the UN Conference on Environment and Development reinforce the political access and influence of transnational corporations and other elites with an interest in preserving the existing global capitalist order. They have done so around a discourse that Michael Goldman refers to as "green neoliberalism" (2005, 93) bringing the vast resources and convening power of the World Bank and related institutions to bear in the struggle to define the environmental agenda.

As the United Nations prepared for its first environmental conference in 1972, many scientists and a rising collection of environmental activists were arguing that protecting the environment required a dramatic shift away from an emphasis on globalized markets and economic growth. Instead, they saw a need for greater understandings and recognition of environmental limits. But Bernstein demonstrates how the language of sustainable development advanced within the UN in the 1980s and '90s reinforced market ideology and growth-oriented policies, despite the earlier arguments by environmentalists that such policies threatened the long-term viability of the planet: "Liberal environmentalism accepts the liberalization of trade and finance as consistent with, and even necessary for, international environmental protection. It also promotes market and other economic mechanisms . . . as the preferred method of environmental management. The concept of sustainable development, while it legitimated this shift in norms, now masks this compromise that characterizes international environmental governance" (2001, 7).

The mid-1980s saw a shift in global environmental discourse toward what became known as sustainable development. The move was in response both to the rise of environmental movements and to the demands of countries of the global South that their development goals not be subordinated to environmental protection measures.[11] Social movements were increasingly highlighting the incompatibilities between the endless economic growth demanded by the neoliberal development agenda and the physical limits of the planet. They drew from a growing body of evidence demonstrating the zero-sum competition between the development program of the World Bank and its allies and the protection of the environment (Broad and Hecksher 2003; Rich 1994; Khagram 2004).

The language of sustainable development, however, conveniently provided space for those concerned with maintaining international flows of trade and investment—such as transnational corporations—to make their voices heard in global environmental debates. UNCED Secretary-General Maurice Strong played an important role, moreover, in reaching out to the business community and encouraging their active involvement in the UN system (Paine 2000). Although many leaders recognized the need for collective action to preserve environmental resources, they were also wary of the intentions of northern countries, which were positioned to take economic advantage of new environmental regulations. They demanded, in exchange for policies limiting environmental degradation within their countries, that northern governments support environmentally friendly technology transfer and other assistance to reduce the economic costs to poor countries (Porter, Brown, and Chasek 2000; Morphet 1996; Williams 1993).

Thus the introduction of the term *sustainable development* both responded to important conflicts over environmental matters and provided space for those whose interests were decidedly not in favor of environmental protection to affect how this new language would be interpreted. The use of the sustainable development discourse in the UN framework can be seen as reflecting what we discussed earlier as discursive demobilization of challengers. Proponents of neoliberal or market globalization advocate for a world free of government regulations where all resources—including basic ones such as water, clean air, and arable land—are allocated through markets. Environmental opponents of neoliberalism have argued that markets fail to account for environmental costs, which include such things as the long-term economic costs of depleting nonrenewable resources, and the larger health and ecosystem costs of air and water pollution (Daly 1996; Woodward and Simms 2006). The costs of such "environmental externalities" are typically borne disproportionately by communities rather than corporations, and most commonly by subnational communities that tend to be poor and politically marginalized (Bullard 1994; Pellow 2000).

Economic globalization itself exacerbates the problems of environmental as well as social externalities by increasing the distance between the places where goods are produced and consumed (Schnaiberg and Gould 1994). As richer countries began to place more regulations on production processes to reduce environmental costs, high-polluting companies moved their production to poorer countries that lacked environmental regulations, the capacity to enforce them, or both. Financial institutions like the World Bank and IMF encouraged such moves by forcing southern governments to liberalize their trade and investment policies (Shandra et al. 2008). Limited governmental regulation of the environment and protection of workers was seen as the best way to attract the foreign investment needed to expand the country's economic output (Daly 1996; Khagram 2004; Peet 2003; Rich 1994).

A major source of profits for transnational companies has been their ability to squeeze maximum profits from the production process, which means reducing their own costs for both labor and environmental protection. Roberts and Parks have outlined some of the ways the globalization of production systematically devalues the environments of the global South but allows consumers in the global North to expand their consumption well beyond what is ecologically sustainable (Roberts and Parks 2006, 2007). The failure to acknowledge and account for what activists have called the north-south "ecological debt" has been an essential tool for global economic expansion because it delinks the problem of environmental degradation from globalized capitalism and its colonial past. Thus, more than other transnational movements, environmental movements have encouraged countermobilizations by transnational corporate actors defending their interests in global trade and financial liberalization (Bruno and Karliner 2002; Karliner 1997; McCright and Dunlap 2003; Bernstein 2001).

Our data on transnational social movement organizations illustrates how the debates of the UNCED era affected transnational environmental mobilization. Specifically, the UNCED conference helped produce an important shift in how environmental groups framed their concerns. Although the majority of environmental movement organizations still organize around a concern with a broad environmental protection frame, the UNCED conference interval saw growing numbers of groups including sustainable development on their main agendas. Transnational environmental movement organizations founded during the time of the Rio conference were more likely to organize around sustainable development than groups formed in other periods. Before 1990, just 8 percent of transnational environmental movement organizations were mobilized around the sustainable development frame, versus 37 percent after the Rio conference. We also saw a consolidation of the environmental agenda around a smaller set of environmental frames in the aftermath of UNCED.[12] Table 5.1 summarizes our data on differences between the transnational social movement organizations adopting sustainable development or environmental protection frames. We examine differences in geographic representation and ties with international nongovernmental organizations and intergovernmental agencies by headquarters location.

South-based environmental organizations were much more likely than their northern counterparts to mobilize around sustainable development than around environmental protection alone (43 percent versus 27 percent). The location of the UN Environment Program headquarters in Nairobi, Kenya, may have facilitated the spread of the sustainable development frame among south-based groups, as did UNCED Secretary-General Maurice Strong's commitment to strength-

Table 5.1   **Characteristics of Transnational Environmental Movement Organizations**

	All	North-Based	South-Based
Number transnational environmental movement organizations	259	193	66
Sustainable development	31%	27%	43%
Number southern countries in membership	23.4	25.3	19.9
Ratio of south to north member countries	3:1	2:1	4:1
IGO ties	3.2	3.5	2.8
INGO ties	6.4	6.8	5.5
Environmental protection	65%	67%	57%
Number southern countries in membership	21.5	21.3	22.2
Ratio of south to north member countries	2:1	2:1	5:1
IGO ties	1.8	1.9	1.6
INGO ties	4.0	3.8	4.8

Source: Authors' compilation based on their Transnational Social Movement Organizations Dataset.

ening the UN's ties to southern NGOs. However, the UNCED conference produced a notable shift in this north-south divide, and northern groups formed in the years surrounding UNCED became much more likely to embrace the sustainable development agenda. Still, southern groups remained somewhat less focused on environmental protection frames (57 percent versus 67 percent).

Many environmental activists have been highly critical of the sustainable development discourse because in practice it has allowed the subordination of environmental protection to economic development and left the definition of sustainability ambiguous enough to allow the growth-oriented market logic to remain unchallenged. But the ability of the UN and other global institutions—most notably the World Bank—to mobilize resources and cultivate the support of civil society for an environmental agenda that would not be rejected by major governments and corporations contributed to the success of the sustainable development discourse (see, for example, Goldman 2005; Sklair 2001). Also, the political context within which southern activists work certainly contributed to the attractiveness of the sustainable development frame. To embrace more restrictive environmental protection goals might draw charges that an environmental group was subject to foreign influences, promoting the imperial agendas of the West, and hindering southern prospects for economic development. In the larger context of the global political economy, environmentalism has been portrayed by some southern governments and advocates as a northern ploy to preempt national development efforts.

However, Peter Newell argues that transnational environmental groups differ significantly in regard to their views of the role of markets in addressing environmental problems. Northern groups tend to be more optimistic about market-based mechanisms for addressing environmental problems. In the south, however, solutions to environmental problems are seen as "inseparable from larger issues of poverty, trade and globalisation" (2006, 109). Southern groups are therefore more likely to link their environmentalism with global and environmental justice networks than their northern counterparts, reflecting a more radical articulation of sustainable development (see also Rohrschneider and Dalton 2002).[13]

We also see that it is organizations embracing the sustainable development discourse that tend to be most firmly embedded within global networks of IGOs and INGOs. Transnational environmental movement organizations adopting a sustainable development frame had ties to an average of 3.2 IGOs and 6.4 INGOs, compared with averages of 1.8 IGOs and 4.0 INGOs for the those mobilized around environmental protection. Attracting global allies is easier for groups that embrace institutionally legitimated discourses. But as we have argued throughout this chapter, social movements' links with intergovernmental organizations can have both taming and radicalizing effects. Global institutions can shape the discourses and agendas of transnational movement networks and make these more consistent with elite interests. But in the case of sustainable development, it may well be that elites appropriated the language of movements without necessarily generating movements' full allegiance or support. The framing of sustainable development has enabled elite actors to neutralize the effects of their critics, in part by encouraging some activists to engage in work to help "green" the World Bank and by conveying a sense among the wider public that the environmental problems to which movements had drawn attention were being addressed (Goldman 2005).

The dominance of neoliberal discourse during the 1990s and the concerted mobilization of transnational corporate actors to oppose and co-opt movements that link environmental problems to the structures of the world economy helps explain why there has been less unity and focus in the transnational environmental movement around a more critical, antisystemic frame (see, for example Bruno and Karliner 2002; Smith 2008, chap. 4). Nevertheless, the global justice movement and the expanding and overlapping demands for global climate justice, food sovereignty, and for northern accountability for the ecological debt are coming together to advance antisystemic analyses that counter the sustainable development discourse. They are doing so as intergovernmental negotiations on climate change have stalled and as scientific evidence on global warming has generated more urgent calls for action. The spiral dynamic we have used to portray global conflicts illustrates how the articulation of new antisystemic discourses and analyses can enhance the normative and political leverage of social movements, particularly at times of global crises.

For instance, in April 2010, following failed interstate negotiations in Copenhagen a few months earlier, the Bolivian government convened the World People's Conference on Climate Change and the Rights of Mother Earth, which drew more than 30,000 citizens and government representatives. The resulting Cochabamba Declaration put forward an alternative to the voluntary, market-oriented approaches favored by the United States. It also called for efforts to establish the Universal Rights of Mother Earth, and to set up an International Climate Court to hold states accountable for the environmental impacts of their policies.[14] Another example shows popular responses to the increasingly urgent issue of access to food. Volatile energy prices are threatening poor people's access to food, and the problem has been exacerbated by neoliberal policies that have been displacing people from their land and otherwise denying people the ability to engage in subsistence food production. The food sovereignty movement has been led by a global network of peasant farmers, Via Campesina, which has worked in larger global justice alliances to seek to fundamentally alter discourses on environment and development and to bridge movements working for farmers' and consumers' rights with other movements. As McMichael observes, "food sovereignty serves to appropriate and reframe dominant discourse, as a mobilizing slogan, and as a political tactic to gain traction in the international political-economy en route to a global moral economy organized around 'cooperative advantage'—as a counterpoint to 'comparative advantage'" (2008, 51).

As global institutions have developed, they have shifted the bases of power and authority in the world-system, requiring actors to rely more on persuasion and normative-moral authority than upon brute force. Social movements have long contributed to the articulation and strengthening of international laws and institutions. In today's movements we see evidence that they also draw on global norms to amplify their challenges to the world-system. They do so by highlighting fundamental contradictions of the modern world-system that contribute to chronic global problems such as poverty, hunger, and environmental devastation.

Conclusion

Institutions constitute opportunities for counter-hegemonic projects, even as they reinforce the hegemony of dominant forces. Over the years, transnational movements have in some ways become less tied to the formal institutions of the world polity, and more skeptical of these institutions as mechanisms for progressive social change. Yet engagement with the institutional realm of world polity facilitates and supports transnational movements by helping expand mobilization in the global South, increasing networking with other international NGOs, and advancing and legitimizing global norms. This observation complicates the idea that institutionalization necessarily undermines the counter-hegemonic or antisystemic potential of social movements. Institutional processes and connections are not incompatible with the emergence of critical discursive repertoires and networks. Moreover, ties to the institutional realm of world polity do not appear to restrict in a consistent way organizations' structures and discursive content. In fact, over time the complex interactions between authorities and challengers within global institutions contribute to the ongoing transformation of the world-system.

Connections to the formal institutions of the world polity facilitate broadscale networking among international nongovernmental organizations as well as across the north-south divide, and they promote learning and diversity in the cultural content of social movement agendas. This can contribute to the potential of transnational movements to transform global social relations. As world-systems analysts have argued, the structures of the world-system are developing in response to both periodic crises of capitalism and to ongoing challenges from a diverse collection of social movements. At the same time, the very social groups that rise up to contest the dominant order are themselves being transformed by this ongoing spiral of contention.

It is important for scholars to recognize the complexity in the strategic thinking and acting of social movement actors and to resist the common tendency to reduce these complexities to binary classifications such as north versus south, or radical versus reformist goals and strategies. Operating within global institutional contexts may lead some groups away from more transformative strategies and critiques, but it is clear from our data that, over time, institutions have helped shape networks among subaltern groups that can advance counter-hegemonic and even antisystemic agendas and otherwise challenge the legitimacy of dominant ideologies and institutions. Their ability to do so, moreover, is enhanced in times of systemic crisis and hegemonic decline.

= Chapter 6 =

Antisystemic Movements and Global Transformation

THREE BASIC CLAIMS have oriented our analysis of transnational organizing over the closing decades of the twentieth and early years of the twenty-first centuries. Specifically, we have argued that today's social movements must be understood in world-historical terms. The contemporary context of U.S. decline as a dominant force in the world economy and polity affects the opportunities for challengers of all types to advance new claims and build strategic alliances with other global actors. To understand the possibilities for social movements to contribute to radical social change, we must consider this larger global context and the structures of alliance and conflict it embeds. Second, the world-systemic arrangements that helped the United States advance to the role of global hegemon also helped build the social infrastructures that support contemporary transnational social movements. The practice of democracy in the core countries of the world economy and the global diffusion of democracy, organization of global labor markets, expansion of communications and other technologies, and spread of globalizing ideologies both supported global capitalism and nurtured the growth of transnational associations and networks around more coherent identities and claims. These networks are more capable than ever before of mounting collective actions to challenge states and other global actors as well as the interstate system itself. Third, the strengthening of international law and institutions has been shifting the bases of power and authority from claims of territorial sovereignty, backed by coercion, to normative claims based on persuasion. This has empowered new actors in the global political arena, including social movements and less powerful states.

These observations suggest that the political foundations of the contemporary world-system themselves are shifting during this time frame, from an interstate system to what James Rosenau has called a "multicentric global system" involving states, international institutions, and nonstate actors of various kinds (2002). Hans Jaeger speaks of this as the emergence of a critical "subsystem of world politics," which results from the institutionalized interactions between civil society groups and the United Nations (2007, 271). Similarly, Boaventura de Sousa Santos sees the "insurgent cosmopolitanism" of today's movements as a vital response to the challenges of our day (2007b, 9). The expansion of transnational organizing capacity among popular groups has generated a foundation for critical analyses and discourses that are contributing to efforts by many to envision alternatives to capitalism as the organizing logic for our world. These analyses are also questioning nationalism as the primary basis for collective identity. Moreover, the proliferation and expanded scope of transnational organizations and networks has extended their ability to generate new transnational identities and collective action capable of advancing these alternatives.

In light of this, we might ask ourselves, "what would a twenty-first century revolution look like?" Is there reason to think it would resemble those revolutions of the past, which were largely focused on taking over state power and which relied on coercion as a means of furthering their aims? Can a revolution take place within a single country, without changes in the larger world-system (compare Boswell and Chase-Dunn 2000)? Has the proliferation and expansion of international law and institutions, including the spread of ideas of human rights, had an effect on how major change in the world is likely to happen? The trends documented in this book may be uncovering a global revolution in the making. As power is becoming more diffuse and multifaceted, and as social movements have developed an organizational and ideational basis—a subsystem of world politics—to challenge the interstate system's monopoly over global politics, we may need to revise our conventional thinking about revolutionary change. In the past, the interstate system could largely define global agendas and command the attention of movements seeking to shape global affairs. But, over time, movements have built capacities and analyses that have enabled them to expand the spaces and scope for popular engagement in debates about how the world should be organized. In other words, they have expanded the possible "pathways to transnationalism" (von Bülow 2010, 5) available to people in local and national settings, and in the process they have been nurturing a multicentric global system. This has generated more movement-centered, as opposed to state-centered, focal points for transnational activism, opening new possibilities for global transformation.

The shifts in organizational emphases and discourses documented here parallel observations made by other scholars and observers of contemporary transnational activism in spaces like the World Social Forum (WSF) process. There, we find attentiveness to and even continued engagement with interstate politics and debates taking place in the United Nations or in the World Trade Organization, but new levels of

Figure 6.1   Autonomous Transnational Civil Society Meetings

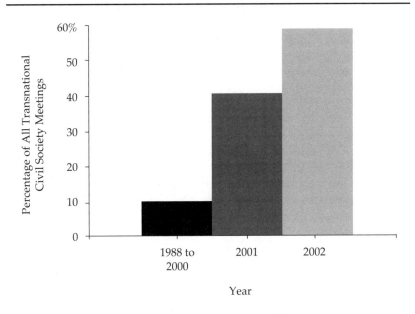

Source: Authors' adaptation of Pianta and Silva (2003, 389).

passion and energy are being directed toward more autonomous movement spaces. In these spaces, people develop networks and strategies and engage in actions that seek to influence interstate debates without being constrained by the rules and procedures of interstate politics (see, for example, Adamovsky 2005; Bond 2008).

This greater movement autonomy is reflected in the proliferation over the past decade of autonomous transnational meetings of civil society groups. Reflecting on long-term changes in civil society engagement with global politics, Chadwick Alger observes that "widespread, complicated new forms of global governance are being invented" (2002, 115). Mario Pianta and Federico Silva further document this trend, showing that civil society actors are increasingly looking outside state-centered arenas to engage in transnational politics (2003). Figure 6.1 illustrates the rapid shift in locus of transnational organizing. Whereas just 10 percent of all transnational civil society gatherings were organized outside interstate arenas during the 1990s, by the early 2000s more than half were held outside these state-centered arenas.

These autonomous spaces are not necessarily the exclusive domain of civil society, in that governments, intergovernmental officials, and other global actors seem increasingly engaged with them. For instance, Latin American heads of state have staged events alongside and sent their delegates to meetings of the World Social Forum, even as activists debated whether or not government leaders should be able to participate. UN agency officials also participate in the WSFs, typically in their personal capacities.[1] The 2010 People's World Conference on Climate Change and the Rights of Mother Earth, held in Cochabamba, Bolivia, at the initiation of President Evo Morales, is another example that shows how even states are seeking alternatives to the existing interstate order. The important shift that we see is that instead of movements and other civil society groups seeking entry into interstate arenas to advance their social change agendas, state leaders and representatives of global institutions are seeking alliances with autonomous civil society gatherings to build support for their policy initiatives.

In this closing chapter we draw from our empirical findings and discussions in earlier chapters to outline a model of global change that better accounts for the ways civil society actors interact with the larger world polity to advance social change. Figure 6.2 summarizes our findings and theorizing about the various pathways through which social movement organizations engage with global institutions. We consider the larger implications of these patterns for our understandings of the politics of global change.

Key drivers of our model are institutional processes of isomorphism and the underlying contradictions between the norms that help legitimate institutional authority and the operation of the world economy. These contradictions are inescapable outcomes of the logic of global capitalism, which prioritizes the endless accumulation of wealth despite the physical and social limits to accumulation (Wallerstein 1991, 105). The liberal ideology emphasizing individual rights and democracy, coupled with the marginalization of popular groups and limited public scrutiny in interstate arenas, have masked the system's many contradictions.[2] But these contradictions and tensions have contributed to growing popular resistance, exacerbated crises, and eventually will overwhelm the ability of authorities to maintain popular quiescence (Arrighi and Silver 2001; Chase-Dunn 1998; Wallerstein 1976, 2004a).

The contradictions between national government practices and a growing body of global-level norms facilitated the rapid expansion of transnational social movement organizations in the late twentieth century. Although supported by opportunities to engage the boomerang strategy to win leverage with respect to states, the population of transnational movement organizations also grew as the technologies of transnational organizing became more widely accessible to people of various classes around the world. These technologies include both

Figure 6.2 Systemic Contradictions, Movement Contestation, and Global Transformation

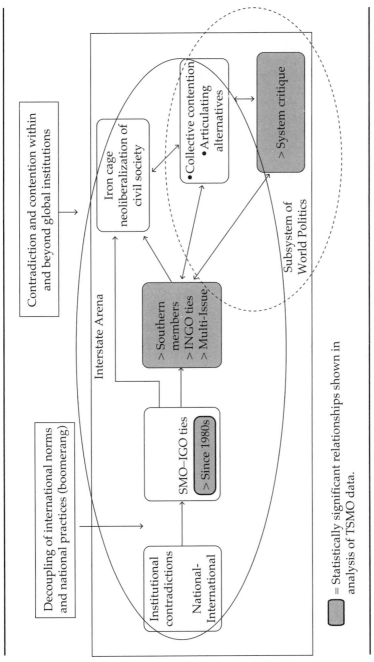

Source: Authors' figure.

physical machinery such as telephones, fax machines, and the Internet as well as skills and knowledge relevant to organizing across national and cultural differences. Thus, the proliferation of higher education and the expansion of international communications and travel—both required by elites hoping to promote the aim of economic globalization—broke down the walls protecting states' privileged role in global politics and thereby facilitated the rise of social movement challengers. Significantly, the proliferation of transnational groups and activism also expanded the class diversity of those engaged in and attentive to global politics because it created new avenues for local and national groups to participate.

Our data show that as regional transnational social movement sectors have grown, so has the proportion of these organizations that establish ties to regional IGOs. In doing so, social movements affect the trajectory of regionalism, often using a boomerang strategy in efforts to bring state practices into line with regional as well as global normative regimes. As we showed in chapter 3, these regional efforts can contribute to the counter-hegemonic tendencies in regional IGOs and also highlight some of the system's basic contradictions. Links to the world-level polity help strengthen counter-hegemonic and antisystemic challenges, as in the ongoing subhemispheric efforts in Latin America, because they provide counter-hegemonic forces with important sources of legitimacy, allies, and leverage that can be a counterweight to U.S. intervention in the region.

As we saw in previous chapters, the population of transnational social movements was further strengthened and developed through ongoing engagement between movements, governments, and intergovernmental actors. The United Nations helped establish the norm of civil society involvement in formal intergovernmental arenas, thereby legitimating civil society participation in new intergovernmental bodies, including regional institutions. This development was in part a recognition of the actual and potential influence of nonstate actors in the work of multilateral governance. Civil society engagement with the UN has allowed the system to address, for a time, inherent contradictions between universalizing norms of equity and participation and the hierarchical and discriminatory practices of both the interstate system and of globalized capitalism. Official engagement with civil society actors has also helped contain antisystemic movement potential by focusing activists' attention on interstate agendas and approaches to addressing global problems, thereby marginalizing alternatives (the iron cage).

At the same time, however, UN global conferences helped new transnational networks of social movements and other global actors flourish and expand. Our analysis showed that the conferences contributed to important changes in the population of transnational social movement organizations, such as increasing participation from the countries of the global South, denser ties between social movement organizations and other NGOs, and a greater tendency to organize regionally. They were also associated with more complex, critical, multi-issue framings of global problems than with the narrow, single-issue frames that conform to conventional interstate negotiating frameworks.

Participation in regional interstate politics, global conferences, and other transnational advocacy campaigns encourages actors to develop and expand transnational repertoires of contention. Collective action generates relationships among groups and individuals that can inspire further collective action as well as tactical innovation. As people come together across national borders and engage with global institutions and related political processes, they gain insights into the operation of power and develop strategies for improving their effectiveness. As at the national level, transnational collective action may be highly contentious—such as the protests at global financial institutional meetings—or it may advance cultural change through media or educational work, or it may seek to engage directly with international officials and institutions to affect policy change. For instance, activists in the World Social Forum process continue to be engaged with the global climate change negotiations, and they use the spaces of the WSF to develop and coordinate strategies for challenging international negotiations. Transnational activists also work outside institutions to generate alternatives to dominant institutions and culture, creating autonomous spaces of movement activity outside elite control.

Officially sponsored international conferences and regionalism were thus not the only processes contributing to these changes in the transnational social movement organizational population. Studies of transnational campaigns demonstrate how movements themselves furthered global transformation and helped animate a growing subsystem of world politics. As they engaged in transnational conversations about global problems, activists came to embrace more complex issue-frames that reflected the diverse experiences of activists from the global North and South. Thus we see a radicalization of analyses as a result of work to challenge environmentally destructive development projects (Rothman and Oliver 1999), child labor (Brooks 2007), threats to indigenous peoples (Brysk 2000; Passy 1999; Hall and Fenelon 2009), and gender discrimination (Alvarez 1998; Snyder 2006; Hertel 2006; Moghadam 2008). The global prominence of the UN conferences as well as the organizing opportunities they provided helped emerging transnational groups meet each other and focused their attention and energies on shared global projects. This helped strengthen the population of organizations and aided in the elaboration of new, transnational "repertoires of contention" (compare Tilly 1978). Although the conferences gave organizers a chance to learn more about the opportunities for action in the larger UN system, it also sensitized them to the limitations of these forums for advancing social change.

As we move along the pathways specified in our model, we recall our earlier analyses that showed how global institutions have supported transnational social movement mobilization by providing symbolic resources and organizational templates for challenging domination, fostering participation in transnational movements from the global South, encouraging the development of stronger networks among civil society actors, and shaping the emergence of more expansive multi-issue framings of global issues. We saw that organizations with these characteristics were both more embedded in intergovernmental organizational networks and more likely to embrace critical framings of the global economic order. However, institutional theory reminds us of the tendencies of modern bureaucratic structures to become iron cages that divert movements from their emancipatory agendas. We must therefore take seriously the observations that social movements' engagement with the state and with intergovernmental institutions has not always contributed to advancing movements' more transformative goals, and in fact may be preempting such agendas.

In assessing movement outcomes, William Gamson distinguishes between gaining access to political authorities and winning new advantages or concessions from them (1990). He argues that authorities often respond to challenges with co-optation—that is, efforts to neutralize movements by mobilizing them into elite projects, providing symbolic access to decision processes, or otherwise deradicalizing the claims of movements (see, for example, Meyer and Tarrow 1998). Looking at transnational mobilizing efforts, we referred in chapter 5 to research showing how transnational campaigns tend to privilege groups with more formal and well-resourced organizing capacities and those that are most appealing to Western audiences and funders. These tend not to be those groups most marginalized by the existing world economy, such as those from the global South, people of color, low-income people, small-scale farmers, and women, among others (Lewis 2002; Bob 2005; INCITE! Women of Color Against Violence 2007; Martinez 2000; Guerrero 2010). In addition to privileging particular kinds of groups, the interstate arena can also constrain the range of discourse and policy options, causing a depoliticization of group claims (Jaeger 2007).

Further illustrating the operation of hegemony in interstate politics, we discussed how work like that of Sada Aksartova and others shows that transnational organizing is often shaped by official aid and grant flows, in what can be called a "Western grant economy" (2009, 161). Aksartova shows how socializing rituals of sponsored training sessions and workshops generated privileged discourses within the organizational fields where activist groups worked. This NGO-speak privileged those activists and groups most fluent in English and most familiar with Western culture over indigenous organizing networks (see also Goldman 2005; Riles 2001). Analyzing three prominent and large transnational movement organizations, Johanna Siméant showed how pressure from funding agencies led groups to develop their transnational structures and fueled competition between movement groups (2005; see also Edwards 2008; Bebbington et al. 2008; Bob 2005).

Such forms of co-optation are responses by elites to short- and medium- term challenges, but according to Wallerstein it "is a process that, in the long run, attacks both the economic and the political underpinnings of the system" (1991, 110; see also Silver 2003). Thus, by involving civil society groups in World Bank projects, authorities provide activist groups with the access to local networks as well as direct evidence of the system's lack of transparency and of the incompatibilities between social and community benefits and the global development project (see, for example, Rich 1994; SAPRIN 2002). For instance, Médecins Sans Frontières (Doctors without Borders) may receive official funding for its medical services in refugee camps, but this work can inform its global campaign against pharmaceutical companies' global patents on essential medicines.

When institutions seek to incorporate peripheries or to co-opt opponents, as is seen in the attempts of the UN and other global institutions to engage civil society critics as "partners" or supporters, the results don't always produce the anticipated outcomes. As Ann Swidler found, the extensive resources devoted to engaging civil society actors in multilateral efforts to fight HIV/AIDS has yielded relatively little effect, due to the incompatibilities between authorities' and civil society group aims (2009). Similarly, work on civil society groups' engagement with the World Bank and other global institutions shows that many groups are motivated more by their sense that it might prevent more disastrous outcomes than would otherwise result than by a conviction that such a strategy will solve the problems they seek to address (Goldman 2005, 188–90; Nelson 1995). The key problem is that authorities define the terms of the negotiations, and movements have remained rather powerless to challenge dominant assumptions (Kamat 2002).[3]

In addition to efforts to co-opt movements, authorities have also sought to undercut the appeal of social movements' claims by questioning their representativeness and accountability to grassroots constituents in whose interests they claim to act. In part, this strategy aims to reassert states' monopoly in global politics, but it has also been used to assert corporate interests in global arenas. Beginning in the 1990s, at the same time social movements were becoming more engaged with and successful at influencing global conferences and institutional processes, governments, corporate actors, and intergovernmental officials increasingly called on civil society groups to defend charges that they were not representative or accountable (Charnovitz 1997; Wapner 2002). Paul Wapner offers a systematic critique of these charges, indicating that they both misconstrue the claims being made by advocacy groups—most of which do not claim to represent specific constituencies but do call on governments to enhance their own representativeness and accountability and to democratize global governance. This has diverted civil society energies to the work of demonstrating and enhancing their own accountability and representativeness, rather than placing the burden clearly on states to establish formal mechanisms for participation and representation in interstate arenas. Governments and corporate actors continue to wield accusations against civil society groups, because movements are less able to counter false or misleading claims in mainstream political and media arenas. Jaeger identifies the paradox inherent in the UN system's welcoming of civil society groups and simultaneous disciplining of groups that dare to be critical:

> Paradoxically . . . from the perspective of the system, it was the very function of NGOs to challenge the system. Challenges in the name of "world opinion" allowed the political system of world society to observe itself, helping it to identify its "blind spots" and potential remedies. Criticisms of the insufficient independence of NGOs from official structures thus exposed the international public sphere as both a self-referential context of communication and a subsystem of the political system of world society. (Jaeger 2007, 271)

This discussion demonstrates that the boomerang strategy enabled by global institutions provides access but limited advantages for movements, and that it can undermine the radical potential of transnational social movements. Institutional processes help maintain the privilege and power of elite groups by defining and constraining the "discursive opportunities" of movements (Ferree 2003), by diverting the attention and energies of activists towards interstate projects and away from social change, and by fostering competition and division among movements.

Research by scholars like Michael Goldman (2005) and James Ferguson (1990, 2006) go a few steps farther to uncover the larger implications of the relationships between global institutions and transnational civil society organizations,[4] even considering them part of the larger project of neoliberal governance. Goldman's analysis of the World Bank's role in elaborating discourses on development, including how it uses its convening power to host workshops and training sessions to reinforce neoliberal ideologies and interpretations, shows how the Bank channels development efforts in ways that reinforce its institutional power (see also Nelson 1995). He discusses this as the "neoliberalization of civil society," whereby transnational organizations help organize and channel grassroots efforts in ways that directly support what McMichael calls the globalization project, by, for instance, promoting micro-credit projects and by collaborating in Bank-sponsored water privatization schemes (Goldman 2005, 270–71; see also Davis 2006). Thus Ferguson indicates the role transnational civil society groups play as part of a "new, transnational apparatus of governmentality," which projects globalized norms and practices well beyond the reach of national governments in Africa and other parts of the global South (2006, 102).

Nevertheless, although it is clear that institutions can undermine the transformative potential of transnational movements, we caution against overstating the power of institutions to imprint or project their own interests and perspectives on groups that are organized to resist the projects of global elites (Heydemann and Hammack 2009). Institutional theorists routinely stress the pervasiveness of what they call decoupling between institutional functions and forms, logics and practices, purposes or rationales, and outcomes (DiMaggio and Powell 1991). Thus it is problematic to infer that when a civil society group engages or even partners with, for instance, the UN Global Compact or the World Bank, it is necessarily co-opted by the neoliberal globalization project. To the extent that organizational partners have mismatched organizational goals, there will always be tensions and slippage in the projection of elite agendas. Thus, Heydemann and Hammack cite the need to "move beyond frameworks that situate local actors and their international counterparts in neatly packaged zero-sum relationships." They further argue that "processes of reception . . . are not unambiguous expressions of subordination, resistance, assimilation, or hierarchy. They do not produce consistent coalitions of support and opposition, of altruism and opportunism. Nor do they permit us to draw generalizable conclusions about those aspects of projection that are more likely to 'stick' than others" (2009, 18).

Looking more closely at the discourses about engagement with the state and intergovernmental organizations, the absence of a "cultural match" between the institutional logics and norms of governments and intergovernmental organizations and those of social movements can be expected to complicate elite efforts to effectively project their organizational aims and goals on civil society challengers (Swidler 2009, 211).

Similarly, Mary Fainshod Katzenstein points out how the strategy of bringing critics into institutions has altered movement dynamics since the 1960s. Whereas in the United States no blacks and few, if any, women held political office before the 1960s, those earlier movements brought marginalized voices at least to the table. This has changed the nature of politics and contention so that "it is hard to know what radicalism means in the context of the contemporary age" (Katzenstein 1998, 212). Whereas earlier movements had only the streets as their arena of action, movements today have multiple options for advancing critical discourses and perspectives within the institutions themselves. But they also are more wary of the limitations of states and interstate institutions in addressing basic issues of inequality and social-political exclusion.

Given these contradictions, at this point in the twenty-first century, we see the strongest momentum for global change within the subsystem of world politics, which encompasses the World Social Forum process and other alternative spaces that movements have helped generate to expand the focus of movement energies outside formal intergovernmental processes. This subsystem is linked to the experiences of earlier movements during the Cold War period as well as the neoliberal period of the 1980s and 1990s, and it continues to both engage with and operate parallel to the interstate arena (see Jaeger 2007). Collective action in the subsystem of world politics reinforces some of the patterns seen in our analysis of transnational organizing within interstate contexts. Thus we can expect groups that participate in transnational collective action in this sphere to have more southern members, more dense ties to INGOs, and more multi-issue frames—all features that should enhance the antisystemic tendencies of social movements. As more marginalized actors are engaged in global political spaces, other activists are more likely to adapt their views of global problems in more critical ways (see, for example, Ford 2003). Furthermore, although some groups will remain engaged with the interstate arena, they will do so with increased attentiveness to the more movement-centered subsystem of world politics.

As movement-centered spaces and networks become stronger and better able to project a competing set of norms and logics, the growing subsystem of world politics will help activists articulate a more coherent set of goals and principles and become more accountable to each other. Movement-generated norms rather than state-centric ones will become more potent references and guides for action. Moreover, more radical elements of movements can exert greater influence within the subsystem of world politics than they can in arenas dominated by states. This dynamic is apparent in Jeffrey Juris's work on anarchist networks in the global justice movement and the World Social Forums. He shows how anarchist networks' interventions in the World Social Forum pushed its organizers to adopt practices that were more consistent with movement values of equality, opposition to hierarchy, and participation—particularly by the most marginalized groups. These values were advanced against practices like the sponsoring of a VIP room for government officials and media. Activists challenged this privileging of elites, claiming "we are all VIPs!" (Juris 2008b, 233). Patrick Bond (2008) discusses other efforts by more radical networks to shift activist attention in the WSF from more "reformist" approaches such as the Global Campaign Against Poverty to efforts to cancel Third World debt and win reparations for slavery. Heather Gautney (2010) offers a more critical assessment of the forum's ability to integrate anarchist and other radical voices, but her work makes clear that the forum is indeed a space where such strategic debates and conflicts can be confronted and potentially addressed in a meaningful way.

Movements and organizations are routinely engaged in conflicts over the failures of much movement practice to realize their alternative visions of how the world should be organized. Many movements for justice and liberation have been plagued by the problem of racism and sexism within movement ranks (McAdam 1988; Polletta 2002; Robnett 1997; Rupp 1997; Macdonald 2005; INCITE! Women of Color Against Violence 2007). Scholars of the WSF process have documented persistent sexism in this process, despite the fact that feminist organizing principles and values have animated it from its origins (Doerr 2007; Eschle and Maiguashca 2010). These scholars also demonstrate, however, that activists struggle with this reality and that many are aware of how the system reproduces hierarchies of sexism, racism, and classism within their ranks. For instance, Lyndi Hewitt and Marina Karides (2011) document actions of feminists to transform discriminatory practices in the social forums. These tensions are the result of the fact that, as movements advance a fundamentally different global order, they must operate within the existing world-system, which is antithetical to these aims.

Contemporary movements seem to have embraced projects that address this dilemma more effectively than in the past. Juris, for instance, shows how new norms and practices aimed at overcoming systemic exclusions are being integrated into the U.S. Social Forum process (2008a). By transforming the social forum's open space to what Juris calls an "intentional space," activists in the United States have made explicit the need for the movement to seek leadership from those groups most marginalized by the capitalist world-economy (see also Karides et al. 2010). Although in practice this has proved challenging to implement, it is clear that the process is contributing to the socialization of activists into a new culture that might define a transformed world-system.[5] "But, of course, it is not as easy to know what shall be the culture, a culture, of the future. We design our utopias in terms of what we know now. . . . We act in the end, and at best, as prisoners of our present reality who permit ourselves to daydream" (Wallerstein 1991, 180).

Transnational advocacy groups are diverse entities that bring together people with varying notions about what sort of change is desirable and feasible. Often activists—even within the same organization—can agree on basic goals but differ widely in their assessment of how best to further them. Conflicts over strategies and tactics permeate social movements and often hinder their effectiveness. The dynamic in our model suggests that the context of intramovement conflict may be shifting in ways that could enhance movement unity and effectiveness. Transnational campaigns to rebuke organizations that act in ways that contradict prevailing movement norms illustrate the importance of intramovement relationships in contemporary global justice movements. For instance, in 2002 when Oxfam launched its Market Access Campaign to promote wider access for goods and services from global South countries to northern markets, it faced a flurry of criticism from leading voices in the movement.[6] Numerous groups have engaged in critiques of Oxfam and other NGOs' support for the Global Campaign Against Poverty, which has become increasingly tame as it has gained more attention from government and intergovernmental officials (Quarmby 2005; Bond 2008). Most recently, Oxfam is facing open criticism from social movements critical of a book it commissioned, *Biotechnology and Agricultural Development: Transgenic Cotton, Rural Institutions and Resource-Poor Farmers* (Trip 2009), which promotes biotechnology as a solution to hunger. An April 2010 letter launched by the Oakland Institute and signed, as of May 10, 2010, by nearly one hundred organizations offers a detailed analysis and critique of Oxfam's position, most notably highlighting Oxfam's failure to recognize that the use of biotech seeds has made small farmers beholden to the transnational corporations producing the seeds, leading to the loss of small farms and an epidemic of rural suicides in some countries. The letter concludes that "the publication betrays the vibrant global movement that is demanding a more ecologically sustainable and socially just agriculture, free from corporate control."[7] This large and well-funded organization demonstrated its interest in maintaining its reputation and standing among other organizations by entering into dialogue with its critics and by publishing a response to the open letter that qualified significantly its support for biotechnology, saying that Oxfam "does not support GMOs as the solution to hunger, poverty, and development."[8] Certainly the experience of receiving such criticism can be expected to shape its decisions about future campaigns and practices.

Another example of how relationships among social movement actors can deflect attempts by dominant institutions to co-opt challengers is the emergence of groups like the Funders Network on Transforming the Global Economy. This organization emerged in the wake of the 1999 protests against the World Trade Organization and in response to a growing body of evidence of the failures of philanthropic efforts to achieve goals such as promoting development, enhancing civil society, and gender equality (Edwards 2008; Heydemann and Hammack 2009). The network brings together foundations that recognize "the global and systemic nature of the challenges confronting us . . . to empower funders to more effectively support the transformation of the global economy into one that fosters a just, responsible and sustainable world." It provides symposia, reports, and other resources to help its members develop strategies and identify practices that support more transformative movements for global change. This group has been important to the World Social Forum process, particularly in the United States, and it sees itself as "accompanying" the process. Its representatives attend regional and international meetings of WSF activists and consult with organizers about fundraising while working to educate and socialize its own funder-members in the WSF process and methods. The emergence and development of this organization reflects the ways actors in the world polity adapt in response to threats that their work may become a tool for reproducing the hegemony of the order they seek to transform.

The World Social Forums have thus become important spaces where diverse organizations and activists can come together to articulate and build consensus around movement norms, socialize new groups and activists, and hold groups accountable to movement norms. The WSF process is important evidence of how relationships among movement actors contribute to the evolution and adaptation of transnational organizing models and discourses. Each forum has generated public debate among activists about the persistence of inequalities and hypocrisies in the forum's operation. Throughout its ten-year history, analysts have observed persistent tensions between the forum's desire to be an open space for the free exchange of ideas and experiences and the wish of some to make it a platform for uniting diverse movements around common actions. There are also debates about the place of governments and parties in the forums and tensions between organizing efforts at global and more localized levels. These "creative tensions" have been key to the forum's growth and dynamism (Smith, Karides, et al. 2007). Over time, new formats for engaging movements in shared action have been tested with the aim of both preserving open space and fostering united action (Juris 2008b; Santos 2006a). There is constant attention to the lessons of past actions and a concerted effort to foster reflexivity among participants and organizers in the social forum process. Many activists in the social forum process appear content with its ambiguities, and resolving these questions is less important than their sense that the process itself is generating new ideas, models, and lessons that can contribute to the long-term effort to make "another world possible."

One final observation from our model is that as social movement actors engage with the global political order, they expand the numbers of potential paths through which individuals and other civil society actors can become engaged in transnational activism, thereby democratizing the global polity and expanding the space for antisystemic movement. Thus we have an arrow connecting the national sphere with the subsystem of world politics. Keck and Sikkink's boomerang pattern may have characterized much of the early transnational activism, but we argue that contemporary transnational contention is driven more by the systemic contradictions that are increasingly apparent as the twenty-first century unfolds.[9] Thus, Keck and Sikkink observed that much of the boomerang strategy involved what they called "information politics" (1998, 2).[10] Today's activism also involves more contentious collective action against global institutions as well as the articulation of alternatives to the global economic and political order (Bennett 2005; Sikkink 2005). It also contains far more local level action and efforts to connect local struggles with analyses of global structures (see, for example, Juris 2008b; von Bülow 2010). The World Social Forum process in particular has helped advance strategies for strengthening links between global politics and local action, most notably through the proliferation of local, national, and regional social forums and through its social movement assemblies, which aim to generate local action in response to global campaigns and days of action. A further example of autonomous spaces for movement convergence is the World March for Women, which also aids the work of expanding local mobilization and consolidating analyses and identities of transnational activists (Dufour and Giraud 2007). These new forms of transnational contention may make it easier for more local and less privileged activists (including those from the global South and those with lower incomes) to be engaged in global protest, thereby expanding the potential base of counter-hegemonic movement.

The expanded field of transnational social movement organizations, coupled with the accumulated experiences of a growing pool of transnational activists and organizations, has thus democratized the world polity and enhanced the capacities of social movements. Whereas earlier challenges to international policy required great investments of resources to sustain transnational links among activists and to make protests heard in the sites of international governance, electronic communications, enhanced organizing capacity, and more decentralized strategies of global activism facilitate local action for global change agendas. An antisystemic analysis, moreover, is not required before an individual activist's or organization's embrace of a larger system critique. For instance, many participants in the World Social Forum are uncertain about their views on neoliberalism, and thus may not come to the forum agreeing with one of its key organizing principles. However, through participation in the forums, activists are exposed to different ideas and perspectives that will tend to support a critical stance toward neoliberal globalization. Thus, participation in transnational networks of civil society groups can both result from and produce more critical understandings of the global political and economic order. Networks, transnational activism, and critical perspectives on the global political economy, in other words, are mutually reinforcing. What is more, they are facilitated by the presence of global institutions, and it is through movements' critical engagement with these institutions that we find the potential for global transformation.

Conclusion: Civil Society and the Construction of a New World-System?

The modern world-system is not simply a structure for organizing economic life, but rather the material relations that undergird the system and shape the structures of knowledge production, discourses, and systems of meaning or culture. Thus the identities, models of organization, symbols, and practices we take for granted need to be contested because they are both products of the particular world-system that produced them and essential to its continued operation. The organizations and movements we have explored in this book are struggling to bring about fundamental changes to this world-system, but they are operating within "social prisons" (Wallerstein 2004a, 22). If states, gender, racial, and ethnic categories, and organizational forms are all artifacts of the current world-system, and if this world-system is in crisis because of its fundamental limits and contradictions, what sort of identities, institutions, and practices might replace those with which we are familiar? Moreover, how can human society discover such forms even as the current world-system persists, albeit within crisis mode? The changes we have documented and discussed in this book suggest that transnational activists are asking these questions and developing new approaches to addressing them. The ways they do so have been shaped by earlier struggles, and so contemporary movements are part of an ongoing spiral of capitalism and socialism-democracy.

If movements are working to create new forms of identity and social belonging, then our accepted categories must be scrutinized. As Ferguson observes, the nature of contemporary globalization and the problems it generates requires new ways of thinking about and constituting global actors:

> [If] transnational relations of power are no longer routed so centrally through the state, and if forms of governmentality increasingly exist that bypass states altogether, then political resistance needs to be reconceptualized in a parallel fashion. . . . Can we learn to conceive, theoretically and politically, of a "grassroots" that would not be local, communal and authentic, but worldly, well connected, and opportunistic? Are we ready for social movements that fight not "from below" but "across," using their "foreign policy" to fight struggles not against "the state" but against that hydra headed transnational apparatus of banks, international agencies and market institutions through which contemporary capitalist domination functions? (Ferguson 2006, 106–7)

Although some social scientists debate questions about whether globalization is eclipsing the state, about the conceptual boundaries distinguishing political actors, and about the nature of local-global relationships, it is clear that many social movement actors are following their instincts to seek out new forms of social political engagement that remedy the failures of states and IGOs.

Our analysis of the history of transnational social movement organizing and its engagement with formal intergovernmental institutions helps inform our understandings of these contemporary struggles, identifying factors that have shaped activists' experiences, their transnational relationships, and their ways of thinking and acting in the world. Because these movements have built on a long history of transnational struggles for social emancipation and to protect the earth, they have theories about and know the workings of the global polity. Observing their operations and evolution can shed light on the ways our complex global polity has evolved and can inform thinking about ways of addressing major global problems.

Activists in the contemporary global justice movement, as well as in some earlier movements, frequently speak of the need for "new forms of politics" (Smith, Kutz-Flamenbaum, and Hausmann 2008; Sen 2007), and observers of the World Social Forum process have noted the rise of new types of "flexible identities" that allow for "multiple belongings" (della Porta et al. 2006). A spirit of exploration, experimentation and "political imagination" permeates these spaces, as activists seek to enhance their effectiveness with innovative collective identities and strategies for social change (Smith, Karides, et al. 2007; Khasnabish 2008; Smith and Doerr 2011). Our account has shown, for instance, that it was not a big leap for social movement actors to move from the "counter-politics" (West 1999) of the UN global conferences to expand and develop their own autonomous organizing spaces, including, most significantly, the World Social Forum process.

The seeds for reimagining and reconstructing the world were planted long ago, even before the negotiations and debates about how to recreate the world in the aftermath of the atrocities of World War II. Through centuries of contestation and collaboration, and by challenging entrenched political, economic, social, and cultural hierarchies, political elites and civil society actors have together constructed the scaffolding for a new world-system based on the durable ideals from the French Revolution of liberty, equality, and fraternity or solidarity (Wallerstein 1990). This has occurred both within and outside the formal institutions of states and intergovernmental organizations, reflecting a mutually constitutive, rather than mutually exclusive, relationship between insider and outsider politics, between states and social movements, between global, national, and local.

In this particular historical moment, we see the manifestation of these sorts of interactions in the form of hybrid challenges to domination and hegemony in the world-system. Political leaders outside the core and social movements are drawing on world cultural scripts to rework the map of social, economic, and political power on the American hemisphere; activists within the U.S. and World Social Forums are discussing radical strategies for targeting UN conferences such as those on development and migration and on climate change. In doing so, they have increasingly integrated the perspectives and voices of indigenous peoples—thereby drawing upon knowledge and cultural materials from outside the dominant world-system (for example, Becker and Koda 2011; Hall and Fenelon 2009). They therefore pose several basic challenges to the logic of the current system, and expand openings for more critical contestation of the system.

The emerging subsystem of world politics may contribute to the realization of a more democratic and equitable world. But the contemporary historical moment does not guarantee that such an outcome will emerge. In fact, many would argue that the odds are in favor of a world in which the continued scramble for a shrinking pool of resources will generate increased violence, exploitation, and chaos. This is, of course, a real possibility, although it is one that most would hope to avoid. To the extent social movements can build upon past lessons and articulate new visions of how the world should be organized, those seeking a world based on ideals of liberty, equality, and solidarity may win out in the end.

$=$ Notes $=$

Introduction

1. These elite actors help form what Jackie Smith (2008) calls the "neoliberal globalization network." The network is a loose alliance of actors united mainly in their shared interest in advancing globalized markets (see, for example, Sklair 2001).
2. We use the terms *global North* to refer to the richer, core states of the world system and *global South* to refer to countries of the semiperiphery and periphery. We are following common conventions in academic and UN circles.
3. Routine meetings of the World Social Forum (WSF) took place annually between 2001 and 2007 and subsequently convene biannually. They regularly attract many tens of thousands of activists from scores of countries, and the most recent WSFs in Brazil have attracted up to 150,000 attendees. In addition, hundreds of social forums have been held at local, national, and regional levels around the world, as have dozens of thematic forums addressing issues such as migration, education, and health (Smith and Karides et al. 2007; Smith et al. 2011; della Porta et al. 2006).
4. Indeed, the emergence and strengthening of international institutions and law in the post–World War II era has dramatically increased the numbers of interstate interactions overall, especially those based on norms of cooperation and reflecting a shared commitment to international law. The proportion of violent interstate interactions is comparatively very small.
5. Writing in *The Guardian*, economist Jayati Ghosh noted, "Before the great recession of 2008 it was an international institution on life support: ignored by most developing countries; derided for its failure to predict most crises and then for its counterproductive responses; even called to book by its own auditors for poor management of its own funds" ("To Make the IMF Relevant Will Take More Than a New Leader," April 20, 2001).
6. At the same time, however, groups such as al Qaeda and others seeking to counter U.S. hegemony to advance particular group identities and interests will also become more attractive, especially in the absence of groups mobilizing around inclusive, transversal identities and goals.
7. The institutional foundation for the defense of human rights norms has grown significantly over the past decade or more. The International Criminal Court represents the most significant attempt to hold individual violators of rights accountable, and it has jurisdiction in cases of domestic as

well as international abuses of human rights. The UN's recognition of states' Responsibility to Protect allows international intervention against states accused of rights violations. Although implementation is uneven and often used to serve the interests of major powers, the articulation of these norms provides leverage for those seeking to constrain states' use of coercion.

8. We refer to these as conference processes because their significance is not limited to the relatively short period of time in which the actual world conferences meet, but rather it extends over many years to include conference preparatory meetings during which the terms of negotiation are initially defined and follow-up conferences where parties review and renegotiate their commitments.

Chapter 1

1. The study by Mark Weisbrot and his colleagues demonstrates that the tremendous growth of noncore countries like China and India were largely the result of their refusal to follow neoliberal policy prescriptions advocated by the World Bank and IMF. In contrast, Argentina is a poster child for World Bank structural adjustment lending, and, like other countries following neoliberal scripts, was more devastated by economic volatility and crisis than countries that did not open their economies as extensively as prescribed.

2. A growing body of postcolonial literature has been critical of the Northern-centric perspectives in much of the Western literature on world politics (see, for example, Connell 2007; Santos 2007a; Farmer 2004).

3. Earlier hegemonic crises therefore saw increased centralization and consolidation of state power. In the current period, marked by high concentration of state power and high polarization among states, it appears that interstate regional configurations will become the locus for counter-hegemonic challenges.

4. These movements were part of a worldwide clustering of protest at this time, and Wallerstein and other world-systems analysts have referred to the period as the world revolution of 1968.

5. IGOs are formal organizations formed by agreements among states. Their members can include nonstate actors, but states typically retain decisive influence in these organizations.

6. The UN Human Rights Council was created by the UN General Assembly in 2006 to replace the weaker Human Rights Commission, which was seen as being overly political and allowing countries with poor human rights records to hold seats.

7. Counter-hegemonic movements are those oriented toward challenging the leadership of the dominant state actor in the world-system, which since the mid-twentieth century has been the United States. These movements are a subset of the larger collection of antisystemic movements, which have the potential to threaten the basic operation of the world-sys-

tem even if activists themselves have not framed their struggles in anti-systemic terms (see Arrighi, Hopkins, and Wallerstein 1989).

8. In a similar way, Annelise Riles sees UN processes and international philanthropic practices as serving to "subvert critique of the aesthetics of politics by rendering it impossible to imagine a political life without 'aesthetics.' Conversely, in the world conferences and the designs described in this book, we find design already 'politicized' and even generating political commitment from within" (2001, 182).

9. The data we present in this volume allow us to examine the presence or absence of ties between organizations and ties between people and groups within countries to TSMOs. Thus we can assess the relative density of ties a country or organization has, but these aggregate data do not say much about the content or direction of these ties. They should therefore be seen as a basis for further investigation of network dynamics in transnational movements.

Chapter 2

1. The Union of International Associations is a nongovernmental entity charged by the UN General Assembly in one of its early resolutions with the task of keeping a census of all international associations, both intergovernmental and nongovernmental.

2. INGOs is the common term used among practitioners and in much of the political science literature and within the UN system to refer to voluntary, nonprofit citizen associations. It includes groups as diverse as the International Olympic Committee, Amnesty International, and the International Elvis Presley Fan Club.

3. Our time series includes alternate years from 1950 to 2003 with the exception of 1961, 1975, and 1979 due to the absence of any or of an English-language edition of the yearbook in those years. Data for 1987 through 1989 was collected from the 1986–1987 and 1987–1988 editions of the yearbook, which had been collected before our decision to code odd-numbered years for the entire time series.

4. Additionally, it was difficult to trace the labor unions over time because unions so often merged and changed names. Thus, the labor union data is less reliable than the data on other types of transnational social movement organizations, whose name changes and mergers were fewer and much easier to trace.

5. Organizations are asked to list both INGOs with which they have links or contacts and those with which they have formal consultative status (where that is an option). They are also asked for names of those with which they have links. Of course, it is impossible to discern from this evidence the extensiveness or the content of these links.

6. The main criterion for inclusion in the yearbook is that an organization must have members in at least three countries.

7. Yearbook editors do make an effort, however, to identify prominent infor-

mal networks that lack a conventional organizational presence. For instance, they have listed the Trilateral Commission since before it was a well-known entity, and they have included groups like People's Global Action, which explicitly rejects a formal organizational structure.

8. This reliance on NGOs coincided with neoliberal ideology, which sought to reduce the role of the state while expanding private actors' role in society.

9. We use the term *Washington Consensus* here to refer to the set of neoliberal policy prescriptions designed to expand the globalization of markets by encouraging international trade and financial investment, minimizing governmental involvement in the economy, and privatization of public services (Broad and Cavanagh 1999).

10. Proponents of trade and financial liberalization have continued to advance international trade agreements regionally and bilaterally even as multilateral negotiations in the WTO stalled. But even this shift signaled an end to a period marked by a sense that global rules governing trade and investment would inevitably advance.

11. The patterns we see of transnational labor organizations mirror data on world patterns of labor unrest, which peaked in the early post–World War II period and declined through the 1960s, 1970s, 1980s, and 1990s (Silver 2003, 126–27).

12. World-systems analysts anticipate different patterns of mobilization in the semiperiphery from those in the periphery. Specifically, more radical analyses and challenges are expected to come from the semiperiphery, where activists have relatively more power in global commodity chains and better access to resources, and where states are more subject to pressures to conform to human rights and other world polity norms (Silver 2003; Chase-Dunn et al. 2010; Markoff 2003). In the periphery, the relative lack of resources and worker power undermine the prospects for radical organizing. The scope of this particular study, however, limits our comparisons to the main divide between the global North and South.

13. The tendency of transnational movement organizations to base their headquarters in the global North is related in part to the fact that most international agencies are based in that part of the world, and the communications and transportation infrastructures in that region generally are better able to serve the needs of transnational groups. Thus, the decisions about organizational location are sometimes pragmatic responses to existing global inequalities rather than conscious or unconscious attempts to reproduce privileges of activists in richer states (compare Sassen 1991).

14. Increasingly, however, changes in donor organizations and in the capacities of organizations in the global South have reduced, but not eliminated, such dependence.

15. The implication of this for movements is ambiguous, and does not necessarily suggest much greater movement capacity for collective action. Many individuals are not actively engaged in political action, but rather participate by information-sharing and financial support. Also, individu-

als may lack the local social networks to support engaged participation in transnational movements.

17. Data on organizations' ties to other groups is based on reports in their yearbook entries of IGO links, NGO links, or as reports of consultative status with relevant intergovernmental agencies.

18. For both south- and north-based movement organizations, disbanded organizations had, on average, fewer IGO ties than surviving organizations did.

19. Latin American feminists and peasant organizations were meeting during the 1980s in gatherings called *encuentros,* or encounters aimed at sharing analyses and reports on local conditions and developing understandings of the global sources of local challenges. These movements and the organizing forms they developed contributed to the World Social Forum process (Hewitt and Karides 2011; Alvarez 1998; Martinez-Torres and Rosset 2010).

Chapter 3

1. As we discuss in more detail, case study research suggests that significant transnational social movement activity was taking place in Latin America and South America at this time, but was largely informal and therefore not accounted for in the *Yearbook of International Organizations* and thus the dataset we have assembled.

2. In Oliver Stone's 2010 film, *South of the Border,* for instance, Bolivian president Evo Morales credits liberation theology with providing the foundation for the recent rise of leftist governments in South America. In 2008, the liberation theology activist and Catholic "Bishop of the Poor," Fernando Lugo, won the presidency of Paraguay, toppling the long-incumbent right-wing Colorado Party.

3. The role of a UN agency in shaping counter-hegemonic discourse illustrates a theme we emphasize throughout this book, which is also an essential idea in world-systems analysis—that is, the structures and idea-systems created by hegemonic powers to further their interests contain the seeds of their own demise. Encouraging regional cooperation through the United Nations helped create stability within the system and supported U.S. hegemony. But these regional organizations helped support the articulation and coordination of critical discourses that have supported antisystemic movements. Interestingly, world-systems theory has built on the intellectual traditions of dependency theorists working within the UN's Economic Commision on Latin America.

4. The Andean Community of Nations (AC) was established by the Cartagena Agreement in 1969. The country composition of the AC has changed over the years and currently includes Peru, Bolivia, Columbia, and Ecuador as member-states. Chile, Argentina, Brazil, Paraguay, and Uruguay are associate members.

5. Debra Minkoff (1995, 2002) shows how organizations involved in provid-

ing services to marginalized sectors of society evolved over time into political advocacy groups, making it clear that the boundaries between
movement organizations and other civil society groups are often quite po-
rous and evolving.

6. These bodies are not yet entirely functional, but the point is that the AU
has ratified legal measures that lay the foundation for representative and
constitutive bodies.

7. As Mary Kaldor points out, such appeals to international norms can both
enhance civil society groups' leverage in contests against national and
other authorities while also strengthening international norms by demonstrating their applicability and legitimacy. She refers to this dynamic as a
"double boomerang" (2003, 96).

Chapter 4

1. The New International Economic Order arose from analyses by dependency theorists coming from the global South (see chapter 2), which at-
tributed the relative underdevelopment of the global South to colonial
practices and the resulting dependent relationships that persisted between
the global North and South. If the south were to advance economically,
more equitable relationships were necessary to allow southern countries
to overcome this structural disadvantage. The NIEO agenda was largely
marginalized by the United States and other northern powers and eventually supplanted by the neoliberal agenda and the Washington Consensus
(Bello 1999; Smith 2008, chap. 4).

2. Of course, international agendas are not independent of the debates and
political tensions within the nation-states that are the membership of the
United Nations. Thus, we would expect conflicts articulated in national
polities to be expressed in global forums. Similarly, transnational movements rely upon strong national movements to build diverse membership
bases. Scholars have found that transnational organizational networks are
most likely where strong national movements or civil societies are present,
and where governments face some international pressure to recognize
citizens' basic rights (Ball 2000; Hafner-Burton and Tsutsui 2005; Lewis
2002; Smith and Wiest 2005).

3. Indeed, as Jackie Smith (2008) observes, a key strategy for contemporary
social movements is to highlight the contradictions within global institutions, pointing for instance to the ways global trade agreements violate
states' human rights or environmental commitments (see also Rajagopal
2006).

4. Modal years were determined by an examination of the frequency distribution of organizational foundings within each sector by headquarters
location. We selected the three years in which a higher number of organizations were founded compared with other years. As an example, we
identified the modal years for north-based peace organizations as 1964,
1981, and 1993 when, respectively, eleven, ten, and ten north-based organizations were founded.

5. This was despite repression on the part of the Chinese government that prevented many activists from attending the Beijing conference and NGO forum.

6. Robert O'Brien and his colleagues observed that "the painful debates between First and Third World feminists have had a fruitful outcome: they triggered the articulation of a new gendered political economy by socialist feminists and feminists in the South, a fundamental critique of economic development which now animates the position of many women's movements in relation to multilateral economic institutions" (2000, 35). Much of this debate and subsequent learning has taken place within the context of the multiple UN global conferences, which structured ongoing meetings of transnational groups of feminists.

7. Ironically, although women's movements had been using UN Conferences to enact what Margaret Keck and Kathryn Sikkink (1998) call a boomerang effect that brings international leverage to bear in making national practices and policies more open to women's voices, conservative Christian movements viewed this as a fundamentally undemocratic strategy. As Buss and Herman note, "the UN conference, far from being a democratizing space, is seen by the [Christian right UN campaign] as profoundly *un*democratic, allowing activists, such as feminists, to pursue a social policy agenda through the backdoor of international law and policy that was unsuccessful when introduced through the front door of domestic policy" (2003, 45 [emphasis in original]).

8. Just eight states have failed to ratify CEDAW, including Iran, Nauru, Palau, Qatar, Somalia, Sudan, Tonga, and the United States. We note, however, that official recognition of women's rights has not meant that the stipulations of CEDAW have been followed in practice in even a minority of states. Women's activists continue to press national governments to bring their practices into greater alignment with CEDAW (see Merry 2005).

9. There are few records of this meeting, which took place in Nairobi in 1982. The final declaration is available online (see http://www.unep.org/Docu ments.Multilingual/Default.asp?DocumentID=70&ArticleID=737&l=en; accessed October 26, 2011).

10. This expansion of civil society participation is attributable to a number of factors, including the proliferation of transnational organizations during the 1980s and early 1990s, facilitated in part by new technologies that reduced the costs and other obstacles to transnational association. Also important was the end of the Cold War, which made the time of the UNCED conference one of great hope and enthusiasm that the world could begin to come together to address the environment and other problems not directly related to military security.

11. For instance, David Atwood discusses this dynamic in the United Nations Special Sessions on Disarmament (1997) and Tony Porter (2005) identifies it within the global financial arena.

12. The Commission on Sustainable Development (CSD) was established in 1993 to coordinate UN activities on the environment and to monitor local,

national, and international implementation of UNCED's Agenda 21. It is also expected to make policy recommendations to the General Assembly, and to promote dialogue and cooperation among governments and other major actors in the global political arena (Caniglia forthcoming; Conca 1995; Kaasa 2007). The CSD has fifty-three member states, selected through a formula that ensures proportional regional representation, and meets annually in New York for about two weeks. Some civil society activists have been critical of the CSD, arguing that it privileges corporate "stakeholders" and reinforces dominant discourses on development. We examine these critiques further in chapter 5.

13. Similarly, John Markoff (2003) argues that semiperipheral countries helped incubate successful movements for women's suffrage, which affected the transnational diffusion of this movement to core countries. In the environmental sector, the important role international development agencies play in structuring the environmental policies of the global periphery affect the relative influence that environmental movements in core, or donor, countries can have on global environmental discourses.

14. Peace TSMOs formed after 1989 reported significantly more ties to INGOs than older groups.

15. A further consequence of global conferences in this regard is the growth in the population of nongovernmental organizations within countries of the global South. For instance, southern environmental groups seem to have flourished sometime following, and perhaps in relation to, the Stockholm Conference on the Human Environment. In 1982, the Environmental Liaison Center in Nairobi documented 2,230 environmental NGOs in developing countries, 60 percent of which were formed after 1972. In contrast, an estimated 13,000 environmental NGOs were located in the north, 30 percent of which were formed after 1972 (Morphet 1996, 128). Marc Williams (1993) cites growth in environmental activism in the global South in the 1970s and 1980s as helping explain the shifting position of Third World governments in regard to the environment.

16. Environmental groups formed during years surrounding the Stockholm Conference reported an average of nearly four IGO ties (3.97), compared with an average of 1.78 IGO ties for nonenvironmental TSMOs. The difference was much smaller for the later UNCED conference, at which environmental groups formed during the years surrounding the conference reported an average of 1.90 IGO ties, compared with 1.17 ties for nonenvironmental groups formed in the same years.

17. Civil society actors are frequently given formal opportunities to report to the UN on states' practices as they relate to treaty obligations, and are invited to respond to official reports submitted by governments to report on their progress in achieving treaty commitments.

Chapter 5

1. As noted in chapter 2, NGOs include a large category of nonstate actors, and most are not contained in our category of transnational social move-

ment organization. Many NGOs are engaged in humanitarian and development assistance, operating closely with governments and international financial institutions. Their organizational mandates emphasize service provision and conventional market development over advocacy for political or social change (see figure 2.1).

2. An exception is the environmental sector, where groups formed in years surrounding the 1972 UN Conference on the Human Environment in Stockholm tended to sustain more ties to IGOs. For both older (more than ten years) and younger (ten years or younger) women's TSMOs, we found significant, negative relationships between being formed during conference intervals and the numbers of ties to IGOs (the correlations were −.127 for younger and −.237 for older organizations).

3. Kathryn Sikkink (2005) later expanded a model for accounting for other strategies transnational advocacy groups adopt, depending upon the relative openness of both national and international institutions. Whereas the boomerang is most effective where national political structures are closed and international institutions relatively open, in more open domestic contexts, activists may adopt an *insider-outsider coalition* strategy to try to influence international and national policy. Where domestic institutions are more open and international institutions more closed—such as in the global financial institutions—a strategy of *defensive transnationalization* is more likely. The latter reflects how the contemporary global justice movement has operated to try to strengthen domestic control over national economies and resist international pressures for trade and financial liberalization and deregulation.

4. The term *nonprofit industrial complex* has been used increasingly among activists in the global justice movement and the related World Social Forums, where INCITE! has been active.

5. Each distinct measure of specialization mirrored this downward trend, with the declines in the percentage of groups with single-issue agendas showing the sharpest decline from a high of over 70 percent in 1953 to just over 40 percent in 2000. The trends for our measures of institutional embeddedness also decline in the early part of our time series, but begin to trend upward following the end of the Cold War and the UN global conferences of the 1990s.

6. This strategy may be more common since the UN system for accrediting organizations has not expanded much beyond the one hundred applications it reviews each year, despite the fact that it receives three hundred to four hundred new applications each year (Martens 2005, 130–33).

7. Negative human rights protections refers to a state's respect for the right to due process and physical integrity of citizens; positive rights refers to the provision of basic needs and the right to development.

8. Although this makes it difficult for groups advancing notions of human rights that go beyond civil and political rights, it also undermines the legitimacy of global institutions by highlighting the contradictions between Western ideologies and practices.

9. We note that our measure is based on organization's description of their

aims in the *Yearbook of International Organizations*, and is therefore likely to underestimate the extent to which organizations embrace more radical formulations of their goals. Although organizations may in practice embrace more critical agendas, they may not record such emphases in external publications like the yearbook, especially if they are working with intergovernmental agencies or seeking foundation grants. Our measure does, however, help us estimate the timing of the emergence of more critical discourses as well as the features of groups most willing to be public in their association with such frames.

10. Fewer than 1 percent of transnational environmental organizations in our dataset include an explicit structural critique of the global economy on their agenda, although we note that this is likely an underestimate of the number of organizations with critical analyses of the global economy, given that many groups are likely to provide a more moderate description of their organizational aims for the audience of the yearbook, which might include their funders and authorities.

11. This attention to the relationship between environment and development was not new at this time, but had yet to be explicitly taken up as an agenda for governmental action in the UN context. Sally Morphet documents the extensive efforts of environmental groups to press governments to make this connection. She notes that as early as 1962, following the influence of the International Union for the Conservation of Nature (IUCN), UNESCO and the UN General Assembly passed resolutions on the relationship between conservation and development (1996, 122). In 1971, a UN-sponsored conference of experts held in Founex stressed the links between environment and development, arguing that "environmental problems had their origin in both poverty and industrialization" (1996, 122–23). In 1980, UNEP launched the World Conservation Strategy, which called for attention to the connections between sustainability in developing countries and overconsumption in the North (Morphet 1996, 129).

12. This was a key goal of UNCED Secretary-General Maurice Strong, who saw the conference as "the beginning of a global partnership and a new phase of development and environment cooperation" (quoted in Morphet 1996, 134).

13. This was particularly evident in the international climate negotiations in Bali in 2007 and in Copenhagen in 2009, when southern governments aligned with social movements to challenge the failures of northern governments to assume responsibility for past environmental practices and to accept more stringent regulations to curb global warming. In 2010, the government of Bolivia worked with climate justice activists to host a conference outside the official negotiating framework that aimed to build momentum for progress on a climate agreement.

14. As we write, a resolution calling on for international recognition of the Universal Rights of Mother Earth is being advanced in the United Nations General Assembly by the Bolivian government and numerous cosponsors.

Chapter 6

1. The World Social Forum forbids governments and political parties to register as organizational participants, but allows individuals from these entities to participate outside their official capacities.
2. One need only take note of the official response to the 2010 release of internal State Department documents by Wikileaks to see how important state secrecy is to the operation of the system.
3. Experience shows, however, that as more groups have the opportunity to work within institutional contexts, many individual activists and organizations come to shift their views about the prospects for achieving change in this manner. Much of the critical literature on the World Bank comes from individuals and groups that had been engaged in its operations (Kamat 2002; Goldman 2005; Broad and Cavanaugh 1994; Rich 1994; compare Marullo, Pagnucco, and Smith 1996; Daly 1996).
4. The term *transnational civil society groups* is often used to refer to large, well-funded organizations that provide humanitarian relief and development aid to the global South. Many such groups are recipients of large amounts of official government assistance and multilateral aid flows and include groups such as Christian Aid, Save the Children, Oxfam, and other well-known groups. Of the advocacy-oriented groups we discuss in this book, many either refuse government aid or are not candidates for these flows of resources because they do not engage in service work.
5. From Smith's field notes on meetings of the U.S. Social Forum's National Planning Committee, March 2009–October 2010 (see also Smith and Doerr 2011).
6. Most notable is the open debate between the leading global justice organizer Wadlen Bello of Focus on the Global South and Oxfam (see http://www.focusweb.org/publications/2002/oxfam-debate-controversy-to-common-strategy.html; accessed August 22, 2011).
7. See http://www.pambazuka.org/en/category/letters/63898 (accessed August 4, 2011).
8. See http://www.oxfam.org/campaigns/agriculture/oxfam-position-transgenic-crops (accessed August 17, 2011).
9. The visibility of these contradictions is in part structural, but it also stems from social movements' own work to frame understandings of problems in world-systemic terms.
10. Information politics involves activists documenting national violations of global norms and bringing international attention to these violations.

= References =

Acharya, Amitav. 2002. "Regionalism and the Emerging World Order: Sovereignty, Autonomy, Identity." In *New Regionalisms in the Global Political Economy*, edited by Shaun Breslin, Chrisopher W. Hughes, Nicola Phillips, and Ben Rosamond. New York: Routledge.

———. 2003. "Democratization and the Prospects for Participatory Regionalism in Southeast Asia." *Third World Quarterly* 24(2): 375–90.

Adamovsky, Ezequiel. 2005. "Beyond the World Social Forum: The Need for New Institutions." Opendemocracy.net. Available at: http://www.open democracy.net/globalization-world/article_2314.jsp (accessed October 27, 2011).

Ahmad, Zakaria Haji, and Baladas Ghoshal. 1999. "The Political Future of ASEAN After the Asian Crisis." *International Affairs* 75(4): 759–78.

Aksartova, Sada. 2009. "Promoting Civil Society or Diffusing NGOs? U.S. Donors in the Former Soviet Union." In *Globalization, Philanthropy, and Civil Society*, edited by David C. Hammack and Steven Heydemann. Bloomington: Indiana University Press.

Alger, Chadwick. 2002. "The Emerging Roles of NGOs in the UN System: From Article 71 to a Millennium People's Assembly." *Global Governance* 8(1): 93–117.

Alvarez, Sonia. 1998. "Latin American Feminisms 'Go Global': Trends of the 1990s and Challenges of the New Millennium." In *Cultures of Politics, Politics of Culture: Re-visioning Latin American Social Movements*, edited by Sonia Alvarez, Evelina Dagnino, and Artuor Escobar. Boulder, Colo.: Westview Press.

———. 1999. "The Latin American Feminist NGO 'Boom'." *International Feminist Journal of Politics* 1(2): 181–209.

Alvarez, Sonia, Evelina Dagnino, and Artuor Escobar, eds. 1998. *Cultures of Politics, Politics of Culture: Re-Visioning Latin American Social Movements*. Boulder, Colo.: Westview Press.

Amin, Samir. 1994. *Re-Reading the Postwar Period: An Intellectual History*. Danvers, Mass.: Monthly Review Press.

———. 2006. *Beyond U.S. Hegemony? Assessing the Prospects for a Multipolar World*. Translated by Patrick Camiller. New York: Zed Books.

Amin, Samir, Giovanni Arrighi, Andre Gunder Frank, and Immanuel Wallerstein, eds. 1990. *Transforming the Revolution: Social Movements and the World-System*. New York: Monthly Review Press.

Anand, Anita. 1999. "Global Meeting Place: United Nations' World Conferences and Civil Society." In *Whose World Is It Anyway? Civil Society, the United*

Nations and the Multilateral Future, edited by John W. Foster and Anita Anand. Ottawa: United Nations Association in Canada.

Anderson-Sherman, Arnold, and Doug McAdam. 1982. "American Black Insurgency and the World Economy: A Political Process Model." In *Ascent and Decline in the World System*, edited by Edward Friedman. Beverly Hills, Calif.: Sage Publications.

Anheier, Helmut, and Nuno Themudo. 2002. "Organisational Forms of Global Civil Society: Implications of Going Global." In *Global Civil Society Yearbook, 2002*, edited by Marlies Glasius, Mary Kaldor, and Helmut Anheier. Oxford: Oxford University Press.

An-Na'im, Abdullahi. 2002. "Religion and Global Civil Society: Inherent Incompatibility or Synergy and Interdependence?" In *Global Civil Society Yearbook, 2002*, edited by Marlies Glasius, Mary Kaldor, and Helmut Anheier. Oxford: Oxford University Press.

Arrighi, Giovanni. 1999a. "Globalization and Historical Macrosociology." In *Sociology for the Twenty-First Century*, edited by Janet L. Abu-Lughod. Chicago: University of Chicago Press.

———. 1999b. "The Global Market." *Journal of World-Systems Research* 5(2): 217–51.

———. 2010. *The Long Twentieth Century: Money, Power and the Origins of Our Times*, new and updated ed. New York: Verso.

Arrighi, Giovanni, Terence K. Hopkins, and Immanuel Wallerstein. 1989. *Antisystemic Movements*. New York: Verso.

Arrighi, Giovanni, and Beverly J. Silver. 1999. *Chaos and Governance in the Modern World System*. Minneapolis: University of Minnesota Press.

———. 2001. "Capitalism and World (Dis)Order." *Review of International Studies* 27(5): 257–79.

Atwood, David. 1997. "Mobilizing Around the United Nations Special Session on Disarmament." In *Transnational Social Movements and Global Politics: Solidarity Beyond the State*, edited by Jackie Smith, Charles Chatfield, and Ron Pagnucco. Syracuse, N.Y.: Syracuse University Press.

Ayres, Jeffrey M. 1998. *Defying Conventional Wisdom: Political Movements and Popular Contention Against North American Free Trade*. Toronto: University of Toronto Press.

Babb, Sarah. 2003. "The IMF in Sociological Perspective: A Tale of Organizational Slippage." *Studies in Comparative International Development* 38(2): 3–27.

———. 2005. "The Social Consequences of Structural Adjustment: Recent Evidence and Current Debates." *Annual Review of Sociology* 31: 199–222.

Babones, Salvatore J., and Jonathan H. Turner. 2003. "Global Inequality." In *Handbook of Social Problems: A Comparative and International Perspective*, edited by George Ritzer. Thousand Oaks, Calif.: Sage Publications.

Ball, Patrick. 2000. "State Terror, Constitutional Traditions, and National Human Rights Movements: A Cross-National Quantitative Comparison." In *Globalizations and Social Movements: Culture, Power, and the Transnational Public Sphere*, edited by John A. Guidry, Michael D. Kennedy, and Mayer N. Zald. Ann Arbor: University of Michigan Press.

Bandy, Joe, and Jackie Smith, eds. 2005. *Coalitions Across Borders: Transnational Protest and the Neoliberal Order*. Lanham, Md.: Rowman & Littlefield.

Barabási, Albert-László. 2002. *Linked*. New York: Plume.

Barber, Benjamin. 1995. *Jihad vs. McWorld*. New York: Random House.

Beausang, Francesca. 2003. "Is There a Development Case for United Nations–Business Partnerships?" London: Development Studies Institute, London School of Economics.

Bebbington, Anthony J., Samuel Hickey, and Diana C. Mitlin, eds. 2008. *Can NGOs Make a Difference?: The Challenge of Development Alternatives*. New York: Zed Books.

Becker, Marc, and Ashley N. Koda. 2011. "Indigenous Peoples and Social Forums." In *Handbook of the World Social Forums*, edited by Jackie Smith, Scott Byrd, Ellen Reese, and Elizabeth Smythe.

Beckfield, Jason. 2003. "Inequality in the World Polity: The Structure of International Organization." *American Sociological Review* 68(3): 401–24.

———. 2007. "The Social Structure of the World Polity." Unpublished paper, Chicago.

Bello, Walden. 1999. *Dark Victory: The United States and Global Poverty*. London: Pluto Press.

Benchmark Environmental Consulting. 1996. "Democratic Global Civil Governance Report of the 1995 Benchmark Survey of NGOs." Oslo: Royal Ministry of Foreign Affairs.

Bennett, W. Lance. 2005. "Social Movements Beyond Borders: Understanding Two Eras of Transnational Activism." In *Transnational Protest and Global Activism*, edited by Donatella della Porta and Sidney Tarrow. Lanham, Md.: Rowman & Littlefield.

Bergesen, Albert J., and Omar A. Lizardo. 2005. "Terrorism and Hegemonic Decline." In *Hegemonic Declines Present and Past*, edited by Jonathan Friedman and Christopher Chase-Dunn. Boulder, Colo.: Paradigm Publishers.

Bernstein, Steven. 2001. *The Compromise of Liberal Environmentalism*. New York: Columbia University Press.

Bob, Clifford. 2005. *The Marketing of Rebellion: Insurgents, Media, and International Support*. Cambridge.: Cambridge University Press.

Boli, John, and George Thomas. 1997. "World Culture in the World Polity." *American Sociological Review* 62(2): 171–90.

———, eds. 1999. *Constructing World Culture: International Nongovernmental Organizations Since 1875*. Palo Alto, Calif.: Stanford University Press.

Bond, Patrick. 2008. "Reformist Reforms, Non-Reformist Reforms, and Global Justice: Activist, NGO, and Intellectual Challenges in the World Social Forum." In *The World and the U.S. Social Forums: A Better World Is Possible and Necessary*, edited by J. Blau and M. Karides. Leiden, The Netherlands: Brill.

Borras, Saturnino M., Jr., Marc Edelman, and Cristóbal Kay, eds. 2008. *Transnational Agrarian Movements: Confronting Globalization*. Malden, Mass.: Wiley-Blackwell.

Boswell, Terry, and Christopher Chase-Dunn. 2000. *The Spiral of Capitalism and Socialism*. Boulder, Colo.: Lynne Rienner.

Braun, Robert, and Ruud Koopmans. 2008. "The Diffusion of Ethnic Violence in Germany:The Role of Social Similarity." Berlin: Wissenschaftszentrum Berlin für Sozialforschung (WZB).

Bretton Woods Project. 2006. "Latin America Sends IMF packing." In *Bretton Woods Update/No. 49*: Bretton Woods Project. Available at: http://www.bretonwoodsproject.org/art-507679 (accessed April 21, 2011).

Broad, Robin, and John Cavanaugh. 1994. *Plundering Paradise: The Struggle for the Environment in the Philippines*. Berkeley: University of California Press.

———. 1999. "The Death of the Washington Consensus?" *World Policy Journal* 16(3): 79–88.

Broad, Robin, and Zahara Hecksher. 2003. "Before Seattle: The Historical Roots of the Current Movement Against Corporate-led Globalisation." *Third World Quarterly* 24(4): 713–28.

Brooks, Ethel. 2005. "Transnational Campaigns Against Child Labor: The Garment Industry in Bangladesh." In *Coalitions Across Borders: Transnational Protest and the Neoliberal Order*, edited by Joe Bandy and Jackie Smith. Lanham, Md.: Rowman & Littlefield.

———. 2007. *Unraveling the Garment Industry; Transnational Organizing and Women's Work*. Minneapolis: University of Minnesota Press.

Brown, L. David, and Jonathan A. Fox. 1998. "Accountability Within Transnational Coalitions." In *The Struggle for Accountability: The World Bank, NGOs, and Grassroots Movements*, edited by Jonathan A. Fox and L. David Brown. Cambridge, Mass.: MIT Press.

Bruno, Kenny, and Joshua Karliner. 2002. *Earthsummit.biz: The Corporate Takeover of Sustainable Development*. Oakland, Calif.: Food First Books.

Brysk, Allison. 2000. *From Tribal Village to Global Village: Indigenous Peoples Struggles in Latin America*. Palo Alto: Stanford University Press.

Bullard, Robert D. 1994. *Unequal Protection: Environmental Justice and Communities of Color*. New York: Random House.

Buss, Doris, and Didi Herman. 2003. *Globalizing Family Values: The Christian Right in International Politics.* Minneapolis: University of Minnesota Press.

Byrd, Scott, and Lorien Jasny. Forthcoming. "Transnational Movement Innovation and Collaboration: An Analysis of World Social Forum Networks." *Social Movement Studies.*

Calder, Kent E., and Francis Fukuyama. 2008. *East Asian Multilateralism: Prospects for Regional Stability*. Baltimore, Md.: Johns Hopkins University Press.

Campbell, John L. 2001. "Institutional Analysis and the Role of Ideas in Political Economy." In *The Rise of Neoliberalism and Institutional Analysis*, edited by John L. Campbell and Ove K. Pedersen. Princeton, N.J.: Princeton University Press.

———. 2004. *Institutional Change and Globalization*. Princeton, N.J.: Princeton University Press.

———. 2005. "Where Do We Stand? Common Mechanisms in Organizations and Social Movements Research." In *Social Movements and Organization Theory*, edited by Gerald F. Davis, Doug McAdam, W. Richard Scott, and Mayer N. Zald. New York: Cambridge University Press.

Caniglia, Beth Schaefer. 2000. "Do Elite Alliances Matter? Structural Power in the Environmental TSMO Network." Ph.D. diss. University of Notre Dame, South Bend, Ind.

———. Forthcoming. "Talk Shops: Non-State Actors and the Articulation of Environmental Discourse."

Castells, Manuel. 1998. *The Information Age: Economy, Society, and Culture*, vol. 3. Oxford: Basil Blackwell.

Cavanagh, John, and Jerry Mander. 2004. *Alternatives to Economic Globalization: A Better World Is Possible*, 2d ed. San Francisco: Berrett-Koehler Publishers.

Cavendish, James. 1994. "Christian Base Communities and the Building of Democracy: Brazil and Chile." *Sociology of Religion* 55(2): 179–95.

Chabal, Patrick. 2009. *Africa: The Politics of Suffering and Smiling*. New York: Zed Books.

Chandra, Alexandra. 2004. "Indonesia's Non-State Actors in ASEAN: A New Regionalism Agenda for Southeast Asia?" *Contemporary Southeast Asia* 26(1): 155–74.

Charnovitz, Steve. 1997. "Two Centuries of Participation: NGOs and International Governance." *Michigan Journal of International Law* 18(2): 183–286.

Chase-Dunn, Christopher. 1998. *Global Formation*, updated ed. Boulder, Colo.: Rowman & Littlefield.

Chatfield, Charles. 1997. "Intergovernmental and Nongovernmental Associations to 1945." In *Transnational Social Movements and World Politics: Solidarity Beyond the State*, edited by Jackie Smith, Charles Chatfield, and Ron Pagnucco. Syracuse, N.Y.: Syracuse University Press.

Chilton, Patricia. 1995. "Mechanics of Change: Social Movements, Transnational Coalitions, and the Transformation Process in Eastern Europe." In *Bringing Transnational Relations Back In*, edited by Thomas Risse-Kappen. New York: Cambridge University Press.

Chirot, Daniel, and Thomas D. Hall. 1982. "World System Theory." *Annual Review of Sociology* 8: 81–106.

Clark, Ann Marie. 2003. *Diplomacy of Conscience: Amnesty International and Changing Human Rights Norms*. Princeton, N.J.: Princeton University Press.

Clark, Ann Marie, Elisabeth Jay Friedman, and Kathryn Hochstetler. 1998. "The Sovereign Limits of Global Civil Society: A Comparison of NGO Participation in World Conferences on the Environment, Human Rights, and Women." *World Politics* 51(1998): 1–35.

Clemens, Elisabeth. 1996. *The People's Lobby*. Chicago: University of Chicago Press.

Conca, Ken. 1995. "Greening the United Nations: Environmental Organisations and the UN System." *Third World Quarterly* 16(3): 441–57.

Connell, Raewyn. 2007. "The Northern Theory of Globalization." *Sociological Theory* 25(4): 368–85.

Cooper, Neil. 2010. "Training Goldfish in a Desert: Ethical Trading Initiatives and Neoliberalism." In *Advances in Peace and Conflict Studies*, edited by Oliver Richmond. New York: Palgrave Macmillan.

———. Forthcoming. "From Crossbows to Landmines: Continuity, Discursive

Collateral Damage and the Regulation of Pariah Weapons." In *Globalization, Social Movements, and Peacebuilding*, edited by Jackie Smith and Ernesto Verdeja. Syracuse, N.Y.: Syracuse University Press.

Cortright, David, and Ron Pagnucco. 1997. "Limits to Transnationalism: The 1980s Freeze Campaign." In *Solidarity Beyond the State: The Dynamics of Transnational Social Movements*, edited by Jackie Smith, Charles Chatfield, and Ron Pagnucco. Syracuse, N.Y.: Syracuse University Press.

Cotton, James. 1999. "The 'Haze' over Southeast Asia: Challenging the ASEAN Mode of Regional Engagement." *Pacific Affairs* 72(3): 331–51.

Cronin, Bruce. 2002. "The Two Faces of the United Nations: The Tension Between Intergovernmentalism and Transnationalism." *Global Governance* 8(1): 53–71.

Cullen, Pauline. 2005. "Conflict and Cooperation Within the Platform of European Social NGOs." In *Coalitions Across Borders*, edited by Joe Bandy and Jackie Smith. Lanham, Md.: Rowman & Littlefield.

Dagnino, Evelina. 2008. "Challenges to Participation, Citizenship and Democracy: Perverse Confluence and Displacement of Meanings." In *Can NGOs Make a Difference: The Challenge of Development Alternatives*, edited by Anthony J. Bebbington, Samuel Hickey, and Diana C. Mitlin. New York: Zed Books.

Daly, Herman. 1996. *Beyond Growth: The Economics of Sustainable Development*. Boston: Beacon Press.

———. 1999. "Globalization versus Internationalization—Some Implications." *Ecological Economics* 31(1): 31–37.

Davis, Mike. 2001. *Late Victorian Holocausts: El Niño Famines and the Making of the Third World*. London: Verso.

———. 2006. *Planet of Slums*. New York: Verso.

Davis, Gerald, Doug McAdam, W. Richard Scott, and Mayer Zald, eds. 2005. *Social Movements and Organizational Theory*. New York: Cambridge University Press.

della Porta, Donatella. 2005a. "Making the Polis: Social Forums and Democracy in the Global Justice Movement." *Mobilization* 10(1): 73–94.

———. 2005b. "Multiple Belongings, Tolerant Identities, and the Construction of 'Another Politics': Between the European Social Forum and the Local Social Fora." In *Transnational Protest and Global Activism*, edited by Donatella della Porta and Sidney Tarrow. Lanham, Md.: Rowman & Littlefield.

della Porta, Donatella, Massimiliano Andretta, Lorenzo Mosca, and Herbert Reiter. 2006. *Globalization from Below: Transnational Activists and Protest Networks*. Minneapolis: University of Minnesota Press.

della Porta, Donatella and Hanspeter Kriesi. 1999. "Social Movements in a Globalizing World: An Introduction." In *Social Movements in a Globalizing World*, edited by Donatella della Porta, Hanspeter Kriesi, and Dieter Rucht. New York: St. Martin's Press.

della Porta, Donatella, Abby Peterson, and Herbert Reiter, eds. 2006. *The Policing of Transnational Protest*. London: Ashgate.

della Porta, Donatella, and Herbert Reiter. 2006. "The Policing of Global Protest: the G8 at Genoa and its Aftermath." in *The Policing of Transnational Pro-

test, edited by Donatella Della Porta, Abby Peterson, and Herbert Reiter. London: Ashgate.

Diani, Mario. 1995. *Green Networks: A Structural Analysis of the Italian Environmental Movement.* Edinburgh: Edinburgh University Press.

Diani, Mario, and Doug McAdam, eds. 2003. *Social Movements and Networks.* Oxford: Oxford University Press.

Dichter, Thomas W. 1999. "Globalization and its Effects on NGOs: Efflorescence or a Blurring of Roles and Relevance?" *Nonprofit and Voluntary Sector Quarterly* 28(1): 38–58.

DiMaggio, Paul J., and Walter W. Powell. 1991. "The Iron Cage Revisited: Institutional Isomorphism and Collective Rationality in Organization Fields." In *The New Institutionalism in Organizational Analysis*, edited by Walter W. Powell and Paul J. DiMaggio. Chicago: University of Chicago Press.

Doerr, Nicole. 2007. "Is 'Another' Public Sphere Actually Possible? The Case of 'Women Without' in the European Social Forum Process as a Critical Test for Deliberative Democracy." *Journal of International Women's Studies* 8(1): 71–88.

Dominguez, Jorge I. 1999. "US–Latin American Relations During the Cold War and its Aftermath." In *The United States and Latin America: The New Agenda*, edited by Victor Bulmer-Thomas and James Dunkerly. Cambridge, Mass.: Harvard University Press.

Dufour, Pascale, and Isabelle Giraud. 2007. "The Continuity of Transnational Solidarities in the World March for Women, 2000 and 2005: A Collective Identity-Building Approach." *Mobilization* 12(3): 307–22.

Duménil, Gerard, and Dominique Lévy. 2005. "The Neoliberal (Counter)Revolution." In *Neoliberalism*, edited by Alfredo Saad-Filho and Deborah Johnston. London: Pluto Press.

Easterly, William. 2002. *The Elusive Quest for Growth: Economists' Adventures and Misadventures in the Tropics.* Cambridge, Mass.: MIT Press.

Economy, Elizabeth C. 2004. *The River Runs Black: The Environmental Challenge to China's Future.* Ithaca, N.Y.: Cornell University Press.

Edelman, Marc. 1999. *Peasants Against Globalization: Rural Social Movements in Costa Rica.* Palo Alto, Calif.: Stanford University Press.

———. 2001. "Social Movements: Changing Paradigms and Forms of Politics." *Annual Review of Anthropology* 30(2001): 285–317.

———. 2005. "When Networks Don't Work: The Rise and Fall and Rise of Civil Society Initiatives in Central America." In *Social Movements: An Anthropological Reader*, edited by June C. Nash. Malden, Mass.: Blackwell.

Edwards, Bob, and Sam Marullo. 1995. "Organizational Mortality in a Declining Movement: The Demise of Peace Movement Organizations in the End of the Cold War Era." *American Sociological Review* 60(6): 805–25.

Edwards, Michael. 2008. *Just Another Emperor? The Rise of Philanthrocapitalism.* New York: Demos: A Network for Ideas and Action.

Ericson, Richard, and Aaron Doyle. 1999. "Globalization and the Policing of Protest: The Case of APEC 1997." *British Journal of Sociology* 50(4): 589–608.

Eschle, Catherine. 2005. "'Skeleton Women': Feminism and the Antiglobalization Movement." *Signs: Journal of Women in Culture and Society* 30(3): 1741–69.

Eschle, Catherine, and Bice Maiguashca. 2010. *Making Feminist Sense of the Global Justice Movement*. Lanham, Md.: Rowman & Littlefield.

Escobar, Arturo. 2003. "Other Worlds Are (Already) Possible: Self-Organisation, Complexity, and Post-Capitalist Cultures." In *Challenging Empires: The World Social Forum*, edited by Jai Sen, A. Anand, Arturo Escobar, and Peter Waterman. Montevideo, Uruguay: Third World Institute: Available at: www.choike.org (accessed August 22, 2011).

———. 2004a. "Development, Violence and the New Imperial Order." *Development* 47(1): 15–21.

———. 2004b. "Beyond the Third World: Imperial Globality, Global Coloniality and Anti-Globalisation Social Movements." *Third World Quarterly* 25(1): 207–30.

Evangelista, Matthew. 1995. "The Paradox of State Strength: Transnational Relations, Domestic Structures and Security Policy in Russia and the Soviet Union." *International Organization* 49(1): 1–38.

Evans, Peter B. 1997. "The Eclipse of the State? Reflections on Stateness in an Era of Globalization." *World Politics* 50(1): 62–87.

Eyben, Rosalind, and Rebecca Napier-Moore. 2009. "Choosing Words with Care? Shifting Meanings of Women's Empowerment in International Development." *Third World Quarterly* 30(2): 285–300.

Faber, Daniel. 2005. "Building a Transnational Environmental Justice Movement: Obstacles and Opportunities in the Age of Globalization." In *Coalitions Across Borders: Transnational Protest and the Neoliberal Order*, edited by Joe Bandy and Jackie Smith. Lanham, Md.: Rowman & Littlefield.

Fantasia, Rick, and Judith Stepan-Norris. 2004. "The Labor Movement in Motion." In *The Blackwell Companion to Social Movements*, edited by David A. Snow, Sarah A. Soule, and Hanspeter Kriesi. New York: Blackwell.

Farmer, Paul. 2004. "An Anthropology of Structural Violence." *Current Anthropology* 45(3): 305–25.

Farrell, Mary, Bjorn Hettne, and Luk van Langenhove. 2005. *Global Politics of Regionalism: Theory and Practice*. London: Pluto Press.

Ferguson, James. 1990. *The Anti-Politics Machine: 'Development,' Depoliticization, and Bureaucratic Power in Lesotho*. Cambridge: Cambridge University Press.

———. 2006. *Global Shadows: Africa in the Neoliberal World Order*. Durham, N.C.: Duke University Press.

Ferree, Myra Marx. 2003. "Resonance and Radicalism: Feminist Framing in the Abortion Debates of the United States and Germany." *American Journal of Sociology* 109(2): 304–44.

———. 2005. "Soft Repression: Ridicule, Stigma, and Silencing in Gender-Based Movements." In *Mobilization and Repression*, edited by Christian Davenport, Hank Johnston, and Carol Mueller. Minneapolis: University of Minnesota Press.

Ferree, Myra Marx, and Carol Mueller. 2004. "Feminism and the Women's Movement: A Global Perspective." In *The Blackwell Companion to Social Movements*, edited by David A. Snow, Sarah A. Soule, and Hanspeter Kriesi. New York: Blackwell.

Finnemore, Martha. 1993. "International Organizations as Teachers of Norms:

The United Nations Educational, Scientific and Cultural Organization and Science Policy." *International Organization* 47(4): 565–97.

———. 1996. *National Interests in International Society.* Ithaca, N.Y.: Cornell University Press.

Fisher, Julie. 1993. *The Road From Rio: Sustainable Development and the Nongovernmental Movement in the Third World.* Westport, Conn.: Praeger.

Fisher, William. 1997. "Doing Good? The Politics and Antipolitics of NGO Practices." *Annual Review of Anthropology* 26(1997): 439–64.

Fisher, William, and Thomas Ponniah, eds. 2003. *Another World is Possible: Popular Alternatives to Globalization at the World Social Forum.* New York: Zed Books.

Fisk, Robert. 2011. "Why No Outcry over These Torturing Tyrants?" *The Independent/UK.* May 14, 2011. Available at: http://www.independent.co.uk/opinion/commentators/fisk/robert-fisk-why-no-outcry-over-these-torturing-tyrants-2283907.html (accessed October 26, 2011).

Fletcher, Bill, Jr., and Fernando Gapasín. 2008. *Solidarity Divided: The Crisis in Organized Labor and a New Path Toward Social Justice.* Berkeley: University of California Press.

Ford, Lucy. 2003. "Challenging Global Environmental Governance: Social Movement Agency and Global Civil Society." *Global Environmental Politics* 3(2): 120–34.

Forsythe, David. 1991. *The Internationalization of Human Rights.* Lexington, Mass.: Lexington Books.

Foster, John. 1999. "Civil Society and Multilateral Theatres." In *Whose World Is It Anyway? Civil Society, the United Nations, and the Multilateral Future*, edited by John W. Foster and Anita Anand. Ottawa: United Nations Association of Canada.

———. 2005. "The Trinational Alliance Against NAFTA: Sinews of Solidarity." In *Coalitions Across Borders: Transnational Protest and the Neoliberal Order*, edited by Joe Bandy and Jackie Smith. Lanham, Md.: Rowman & Littlefield.

Foster, John W., and Anita Anand, eds. 1999. *Whose World Is It Anyway? Civil Society, the United Nations, and the Multilateral Future.* Ottawa: United Nations Association of Canada.

Frank, David John. 1999. "The Social Bases of Environmental Treaty Ratification." *Sociological Inquiry* 69(4): 523–50.

Frank, David John, Ann Hironaka, and Evan Schofer. 2000. "The Nation-State and the Natural Environment over the Twentieth Century." *American Sociological Review* 65(1): 96–116.

Frank, David John, Wesley Longhofer, and Evan Schofer. 2007. "World Society, NGOs and Environmental Policy Reform in Asia." *International Journal of Comparative Sociology* 48(4–5): 275–95.

Friedland, Roger, and Robert R. Alford. 1991. "Bringing Society Back In: Symbols, Practices, and Institutional Contradictions." In *The New Institutionalism in Organizational Analysis*, edited by Walter W. Powell and Paul J. DiMaggio. Chicago: University of Chicago Press.

Friedman, Elisabeth Jay, Ann Marie Clark, and Kathryn Hochstetler. 2005. *Sovereignty, Democracy, and Global Civil Society: State-Society Relations at the UN World Conferences.* New York: State University of New York Press.

Friedman, Jonathan, and Christopher Chase-Dunn, eds. 2005. *Hegemonic Declines Present and Past*. Boulder, Colo.: Paradigm Publishers.

Gallup. 2008. "Global Survey Hightlights Fear of Future and Lack of Faith in World Leaders." World Economic Forum.

Gamson, William. 1990. *Strategy of Social Protest*, 2d ed. Belmont, Calif.: Wadsworth.

Gamson, William, and David Meyer. 1996. "The Framing of Political Opportunity." In *Political Opportunities, Mobilizing Structures and Framing: Social Movement Dynamics in Cross-National Perspective*, edited by Doug McAdam, John McCarthy, and Mayer Zald. New York: Cambridge University Press.

Garner, Roberta Ash, and Mayer N. Zald. 1988. "The Political Economy of Social Movement Sectors." In *Social Movements in an Organizational Society*, edited by Mayer N. Zald and John D. McCarthy. New Brunswick, N.J.: Transaction.

Gautney, Heather. 2010. *Protest and Organization in the Alternative Globalization Era: NGOs, Social Movements, and Political Parties*. New York: Palgrave Macmillan.

George, Susan. 2005. *Another World Is Possible If...* New York: Verso.

Gerhards, Jurgen, and Dieter Rucht. 1992. "Mesomobilization Contexts: Organizing and Framing in Two Protest Campaigns in West Germany." *American Journal of Sociology* 98(3): 555–96.

Gibney, Mark. 2008. *International Human Rights Law: Returning to Universal Principles*. Lanham, Md.: Rowman & Littlefield.

Gillham, Patrick F., and Gary T. Marx. 2000. "Complexity and Irony in Policing and Protesting: The World Trade Organization in Seattle." *Social Justice* 27(2): 212–36.

Giugni, Marco, Ruud Koopmans, Florence Passy, and Paul Statham. 2005. "Institutional and Discursive Opportunities for Extreme-Right Mobilization in Five Countries." *Mobilization* 10(1): 145–62.

Goldman, Michael. 2005. *Imperial Nature: The World Bank and Struggles for Social Justice in the Age of Globalization*. New Haven, Conn.: Yale University Press.

Gramsci, Antonio. 1971. *Selections from the Prison Notebooks*. London: Lawrence and Wishart.

Gray, Rob, and Jan Bebbington. 2006. "NGOs, Civil Society and Accountability: Making the People Accountable to Capital." *Accounting, Auditing, and Accountability Journal* 19(3): 319–48.

Grugel, Jean B. 2004. "New Regionalism and Modes of Governance: Comparing US and EU Strategies in Latin America." *European Journal of International Relations* 10(4): 603–26.

———. 2006. "Regionalist Governance and Transnational Collective Action in Latin America." *Economy and Society* 35(2): 209–31.

Grzybowski, Candido. 2006. "The World Social Forum: Reinventing Global Politics." *Global Governance* 12(1): 7–13.

Guerrero, Michael Leon. 2010. "You Can't Spell Fundraising Without F-U-N: The Resource Mob, the Non-Profit Industrial Complex, and the USSF." In *The United States Social Forum: Perspectives of a Movement*, edited by Marina Karides, Walda Katz-Fishman, Rose M. Brewer, Jerome Scott, and Alice Lovelace. Chicago: Changemaker Publications.

Gulati, Ranjay, and Martin Gargiulo. 1999. "Where Do Interorganizational Networks Come From?" *American Journal of Sociology* 104(5): 1439–493.

Haas, Peter. 1992. "Epistemic Communities and International Policy Coordination." *International Organization* 46(1): 1–35.

———. 2002. "UN Conferences and Constructivist Governance of the Environment." *Global Governance* 8(1): 73–91.

Hafner-Burton, Emilie M., and Kiyotero Tsutsui. 2005. "Human Rights in a Globalizing World: The Paradox of Empty Promises." *American Journal of Sociology* 110(5): 1373–411.

Hahn, Niels S. C. 2008. "Neoliberal Imperialism and Pan-African Resistance." *Journal of World-Systems Research* 13(2): 142–78.

Hall, Thomas D., and F. James Fenelon. 2009. *Indigenous Peoples and Globalization*. Boulder, Colo.: Paradigm Publishers.

Hammack, David C., and Steven Heydemann, eds. 2009. *Globalization, Philanthropy, and Civil Society*. Bloomington: Indiana University Press.

Haney, Mary P. 2005. "Women's NGOs at UN Conferences: The 1992 Rio Conference on the Environment as a Watershed Event." *Journal of Women, Politics & Policy* 27(1): 181–87.

Harvey, David. 2005. *A Brief History of Neoliberalism*. New York: Oxford University Press.

———. 2009. "Organizing for the Anti-Capitalist Transition." *MR Zine: Monthly Review*. Available at: http://mrzine.monthlyreview.org/2009/harvey151209.html (accessed August 9, 2011).

Held, David, and Anthony G. McGrew. 2007. *Globalization/Anti-Globalization: Beyond the Great Divide*. Cambridge: Polity Press.

Herod, Andrew. 2001. *Labor Geographies: Workers and the Landscapes of Capitalism*. New York: The Guilford Press.

Hertel, Shareen. 2006. *Unexpected Power: Conflict and Change Among Transnational Activists*. Ithaca, N.Y.: Cornell University Press.

Hewitt, Lyndi, and Marina Karides. 2011. "More than a Shadow of a Difference? Feminists at the World Social Forums." In *Handbook of World Social Forum Activism*, edited by Jackie Smith, Scott Byrd, Ellen Reese, and Elizabeth Smythe. Boulder, Colo.: Paradigm Publishers.

Heydemann, Steven, and David C. Hammack. 2009. "Philanthropic Projections." In *Globalization, Philanthropy, and Civil Society*, edited by David C. Hammack and Steven Heydemann. Bloomington: Indiana University Press.

Hochstetler, Kathryn. 2002. "After the Boomerang: Environmental Movements and Politics in the La Plata River Basin." *Global Environmental Politics* 4(1): 35–57.

Howell, Jude, Armine Ishkanian, Ebenezer Obadare, Hakan Seckinelgin, and Marlies Glasius. 2008. "The Backlash Against Civil Society in the Wake of the Long War on Terror." *Development in Practice* 18(1): 82–93.

Hussey, Antonia. 1991. "Regional Development and Cooperation Through ASEAN." *Geographical Review* 18(1): 87–98.

Imig, Doug, and Sidney Tarrow. 2001. "Studying Contention in an Emerging Polity." In *Contentious Europeans: Protest and Politics in an Emerging Polity*, edited by Doug Imig and Sidney Tarrow. Lanham, Md.: Rowman & Littlefield.

INCITE! Women of Color Against Violence (INCITE). 2007. *The Revolution Will Not Be Funded: Beyond the Non-Profit Industrial Complex*. Cambridge, Mass.: South End Press.

Jacobson, David, and Galya Benarieh Ruffer. 2003. "Courts Across Borders: The Implications of Judicial Agency for Human Rights and Democracy." *Human Rights Quarterly* 25(1): 74–92.

Jaeger, Hans-Martin. 2007. "'Global Civil Society' and the Political Depoliticization of Global Governance." *International Political Sociology* 1(3): 257–77.

Jain, Devaki, and Shubha Chacko. 2009. "Walking Together: The Journey of the Non-Aligned Movement and the Women's Movement." *Development in Practice* 19(7): 895–905.

Jenkins, J. Craig, and Craig M. Ekert. 1986. "Channeling Black Insurgency." *American Sociological Review* 51(6): 812–29.

Jepperson, Ronald L., and John Meyer. 1991. "The Public Order and the Construction of Formal Organizations." In *The New Institutionalism in Organizational Analysis*, edited by Walter W. Powell and Paul J. DiMaggio. Chicago: University of Chicago Press.

Johnson, Erik, and John McCarthy. 2005. "The Sequencing of Transnational and National Social Movement Mobilization: The Organizational Mobilization of the Global and U.S. Environmental Movements." In *Transnational Protest and Global Activism*, edited by Donatella della Porta and Sidney Tarrow. Lanham, Md.: Rowman & Littlefield.

Jorgenson, Andrew K. 2008. "Structural Integration and the Trees: An Analysis of Deforestation in Less-Developed Countries, 1990–2005." *Sociological Quarterly* 49(3): 503–27.

Juris, Jeffrey. 2008a. "Spaces of Intentionality: Race, Class and Horizontality at the United States Social Forum." *Mobilization* 13(4): 353–72.

———. 2008b. *Networking Futures: The Movements Against Corporate Globalization*. Durham, N.C.: Duke University Press.

Kaasa, Stine Madland. 2007. "The UN Commission on Sustainable Development: Which Mechanisms Explain Its Accomplishments?" *Global Environmental Politics* 7(3): 107–29.

Kaldor, Mary. 2003. *Global Civil Society: An Answer to War*. Cambridge: Polity Press.

Kamat, Sangeeta. 2002. *Development Hegemony: NGOs and the State in India*. London: Oxford University Press.

Karides, Marina, Walda Katz-Fishman, Rose M. Brewer, Jerome Scott, and Alice Lovelace, eds. 2010. *The United States Social Forum: Perspectives of a Movement*. Chicago: Changemaker Publications.

Karliner, Joshua. 1997. *The Corporate Planet: Ecology and Politics in the Age of Globalization*. San Francisco: Sierra Club.

Katz, Hagai. 2007. "Global Civil Society Networks and Counter-Hegemony." In *Civil Society: Local and Regional Responses to Global Challenges*, edited by Mark Herkenrath. New Brunswick, N.J.: Transaction.

Katzenstein, Mary Fainshod. 1998. "Stepsisters: Feminist Movement Activism in Different Instituitonal Spaces." In *The Social Movement Society: Contentious Politics for a New Century*, edited by David S. Meyer and Sidney Tarrow. Lanham, Md.: Rowman & Littlefield.

Keck, Margaret, and Kathryn Sikkink. 1998. *Activists Beyond Borders*. Ithaca, N.Y.: Cornell University Press.

Kenis, Patrick, and David Knoke. 2002. "How Organizational Field Networks Shape Interorganizational Tie Formation Rates." *Academy of Management Review* 27(2): 275–93.

Kennedy, Paul. 1989. *The Rise and Fall of the Great Powers*. New York: Vintage Books.

Khagram, Sanjeev. 2004. *Dams and Development: Transnational Struggles for Water and Power*. Ithaca, N.Y.: Cornell University Press.

Khasnabish, Alex. 2008. *Zapatismo Beyond Borders: New Imaginations of Political Possibility*. Toronto: University of Toronto Press.

King, Anthony D., ed. 1997. *Culture, Globalization and the World-System*. Minneapolis: Unviersity of Minnesota Press.

Klare, Michael. 2001. *Resource Wars: The New Landscape of Global Conflict*. New York: Henry Holt.

Kolb, Felix. 2005. "The Impact of Transnational Protest on Social Movement Organizations: Mass Media and the Making of ATTAC Germany." In *Transnational Protest and Global Activism*, edited by Donatella della Porta and Sidney Tarrow. Lanham, Md.: Rowman & Littlefield.

———. 2007. *Protest and Opportunities: A Theory of Social Movements and Political Change*. Chicago: University of Chicago Press.

Korzeniewicz, Roberto Patricio, and Timothy Patrick Moran. 2009. *Unveiling Inequality: A World-Historical Perspective*. New York: Russell Sage Foundation.

Korzeniewicz, Roberto Patricio, and William C. Smith. 2001. "Protest and Collaboration: Transnational Civil Society Networks and the Politics of Summitry and Free Trade in the Americas." North-South Center Agenda Paper no. 51. Miami: North-South Center, University of Miami, Florida.

Krasner, Stephen D. 1985. *Structural Conflict: The Third World Against Global Liberalism*. Berkeley: University of California Press.

Kriesberg, Louis. 1997. "Social Movements and Global Transformation." In *Transnational Social Movements and World Politics: Solidarity Beyond the State*, edited by Jackie Smith, Charles Chatfield, and Ron Pagnucco. Syracuse, N.Y.: Syracuse University Press.

Kriesi, Hanspeter. 1996. "Organizational Development of New Social Movements in a Political Contexts." In *Political Opportunities, Mobilizing Structures and Framing: Social Movement Dynamics in Cross-National Perspective*, edited by Doug McAdam, John McCarthy, and Mayer Zald. New York: Cambridge University Press.

———. 2004. "Political Context and Opportunity." In *The Blackwell Companion to Social Movements*, edited by David A. Snow, Sarah A. Soule, and Hanspeter Kriesi. Oxford: Blackwell.

Krut, Riva. 1997. "Globalization and Civil Society: NGO Influence on International Decision Making." Discussion paper. Geneva: United Nations Research Institute for Social Development. Available at: http://cat.inist.fr/?aModele=afficheN&cpsidt=10319354 (accessed August 17, 2011).

Kwon, Roy, Ellen Reese, and Kadambari Anantram. 2008. "Core-Periphery Divisions Among Labor Activists at the World Social Forum." *Mobilization* 13(4): 411–30.

Lewis, Tammy L. 2002. "Transnational Conservation Movement Organizations: Shaping the Protected Area Systems of Less Developed Countries." In *Globalizing Resistance: Transnational Dimensions of Social Movements*, edited by Jackie Smith and Hank Johnston. Lanham, Md.: Rowman & Littlefield.

Lipschutz, Ronnie. 1996. *Global Civil Society and Global Environmental Governance*. Albany: SUNY.

Lynch, Cecelia. 1998. "Social Movements and the Problem of Globalization." *Alternatives: Global, Local, Political* 23(2): 149–74.

Macdonald, Laura. 1997. *Supporting Civil Society: The Political Role of Non-Governmental Organizations in Central America*. New York: St. Martin's Press.

———. 2005. "Gendering Transnational Social Movement Analysis: Women's Groups Contest Free Trade in the Americas." In *Coalitions Across Borders: Negotiating Difference and Unity in Transnational Coalitions Against Neoliberalism*, edited by Joe Bandy and Jackie Smith. Lanham, Md.: Rowman & Littlefield.

Maney, Gregory M. 2001. "Rival Transnational Networks and Indigenous Rights: The San Blas Kuna in Panama and the Yanomami in Brazil." *Research in Social Movements, Conflicts and Change* 23: 103–44.

Manji, Firoze, and Carl O'Coill. 2002. "The Missionary Position: NGOs and Development in Africa." *International Affairs* 78(3): 567–80.

Markoff, John. 1994. *The Great Wave of Democracy in Historical Perspective*. Ithaca, N.Y.: Institute for European Studies.

———. 1996. *Waves of Democracy: Social Movements and Political Change*. Thousand Oaks, Calif.: Pine Forge Press.

———. 2003. "Margins, Centers, and Democracy: The Paradigmatic History of Women's Suffrage." *Signs: Journal of Women in Culture and Society* 29(1): 85–116.

———. 2004. "Democracy." In *Encyclopedia of Social Theory*, vol. 2, edited by G. Ritzer. Thousand Oaks, Calif.: Sage.

———. 2011. "A Moving Target: Democracy." *Archives Européennes de Sociologie* 52(2): 239–75.

Martens, Jens. 2003. "Precarious 'Partnerships': Six Problems of the Global Compact Between Business and the UN." *Global Policy Forum*. Available at: http://www.globalpolicy.org/component/content/article/225/32252.html (accessed October 26, 2011).

Martens, Kersten. 2005. *NGOs and the United Nations*. New York: Palgrave MacMillan.

———. 2007. "Multistakeholder Partnerships: Future Models of Multilateralism?" *Dialogue on Globalization* Occasional Paper. Berlin: Friedrich-Ebert-Stiftung. Available at: http://library.fes.de/pdf-files/iez/04244.pdf (accessed October 26, 2011).

Martinez, Elizabeth (Betita). 2000. "Where Was the Color in Seattle? Looking for Reasons Why the Great Battle Was So White." *Color Lines*, Spring.

Martínez-Torres, María Elena, and Peter M. Rosset. 2008. "La Vía Campesina: Transnationalizing Peasant Struggle and Hope." In *Latin American Social Movements in the Twenty-First Century: Resistance, Power and Democracy*, edited by Richard Stahler-Sholk, Harry E. Vanden, and Glen D. Kuecker. Lanham, Md.: Rowman & Littlefield.

———. 2010. "La Vía Campesina: The Birth and Evolution of a Transnational Social Movement." *Journal of Peasant Studies* 37(1): 149–75.

Marullo, Sam, and John Lofland. 1990. *Peace Action in the Eighties: Social Science Perspectives*. New Brunswick, N.J.: Rutgers University Press.

Marullo, Sam, Ron Pagnucco, and Jackie Smith. 1996. "Frame Changes and Social Movement Contraction: U.S. Peace Movement Framing After the Cold War." *Sociological Inquiry* 66(1): 1–28.

McAdam, Doug. 1982. *Political Process and the Development of Black Insurgency*. Chicago: University of Chicago Press.

———. 1988. *Freedom Summer*. New York: Oxford University Press.

———. 1999. "Introduction to the Second Edition." In *Political Process and the Development of Black Insurgency 1930–1970*, 2d ed. Chicago: University of Chicago Press.

McAdam, Doug, John D. McCarthy, and Mayer Zald. 1996. *Comparative Perspectives on Social Movements: Political Opportunities, Mobilizing Structures and Cultural Framings*. New York: Cambridge University Press.

McAdam, Doug, and W. Richard Scott. 2005. "Organizations and Movements." in *Social Movements and Organization Theory*, edited by Gerald F. Davis, Doug McAdam, W. Richard Scott, and Mayer N. Zald. New York: Cambridge University Press.

McAdam, Doug, Sidney Tarrow, and Charles Tilly. 2001. *Dynamics of Contention*. New York: Cambridge University Press.

McCarthy, John D. 1996. "Mobilizing Structures: Constraints and Opportunities in Adopting, Adapting and Inventing." In *Comparative Perspectives on Social Movements: Political Opportunities, Mobilizing Structures and Cultural Framings*, edited by Doug McAdam, John McCarthy, and Mayer Zald. New York: Cambridge University Press.

McCarthy, John D., David Britt, and Mark Wolfson. 1991. "The Institutional Channelling of Social Movements in the Modern State." In *Research in Social Movements, Conflict and Change*, vol. 13, edited by Louis Kriesberg. Greenwich, Conn.: JAI Press.

McCarthy, John D., and Clark McPhail. 2006. "Places of Protest: The Public Forum in Principle and Practice." *Mobilization* 11(1): 229–48.

McCarthy, John D., and Mayer Zald. 1977. "Resource Mobilization in Social Movements: A Partial Theory." *American Journal of Sociology* 82(6): 1212–41.

———. 1987. "The Trend of Social Movements in America: Professionalization and Resource Mobilization." In *Social Movements in an Organizational Society*, edited by Mayer Zald and John D. McCarthy. New Brunswick, N.J.: Transaction.

———, eds. 1990. *Social Movements in an Organizational Society*. New Brunswick, N.J.: Transaction.

McCright, Aaron, and Riley Dunlap. 2003. "Defeating Kyoto: The Conservative Movement's Impact on U.S. Climate Change Policy." *Social Problems* 50(3): 348–73.

McKeon, Nora. 2009. *The United Nations and Civil Society: Legitimating Global Governance–Whose Voice?* London: Zed Books.

McMichael, Philip. 2006. *Development and Social Change: A Global Perspective*, 4th ed. Thousand Oaks, Calif.: Pine Forge.

———. 2008. "Peasants Make Their Own History, But Not Just as They Please." In *Transnational Agrarian Movements: Confronting Globalization*, edited by Saturino M. Borras Jr., Marc Edelman, and Christóbal Kay. Malden, Mass.: Wiley-Blackwell.

Mendoza, Breny. 2002. "Transnational Feminisms in Question." *Feminist Theory* 3(3): 295–314.

Merry, Sally Engle. 2005. *Human Rights and Gender Violence: Translating International Law into Local Justice*. Chicago: University of Chicago Press.

Meyer, David S., and Sidney Tarrow. 1998. "A Movement Society: Contentious Politics for a New Century." In *The Social Movement Society: Contentious Politics for a New Century*, edited by David S. Meyer and Sidney Tarrow. Lanham, Md.: Rowman & Littlefield.

Meyer, John W. 2000. "Globalization: Sources and Effects on National States and Societies." *International Sociology* 15(2): 233–48.

———. 2007. "Globalization: Theory and Trends." *International Journal of Comparative Sociology* 48(4): 261–73.

Meyer, John W., John Boli, George M. Thomas, and Francisco O. Ramirez. 1997. "World Society and the Nation-State." *American Journal of Sociology* 103(1): 144–81.

Meyer, John W., David John Frank, Ann Hironaka, Evan Schofer, and Nancy Brandon Tuma. 1997. "The Structuring of a World Environmental Regime, 1870–1990." *International Organization* 51(4): 623–51.

Meyer, Mary K. 1999. "Negotiating International Norms: The Inter-American Commission of Women and the Convention on Violence Against Women." In *Gender Politics in Global Governance*, edited by Mary K. Meyer and Elisabeth Prügl. Lanham, Md.: Rowman & Littlefield.

Miller, Alice M. 1999. "Realizing Women's Human Rights: Nongovernmental Organizations and United Nations Treaty Bodies." In *Gender Politics in Global Governance*, edited by Mary K. Meyer and Elizabeth Prügl. Lanham, Md.: Rowman & Littlefield.

Milton-Edwards, Beverley, and Peter Hinchcliff. 2004. *Conflicts in the Middle East Since 1945*. London: Psychology Press.

Minkoff, Debra C. 1993. "The Organization of Survival." *Social Forces* 71(4): 887–908.

———. 1995. *Organizing for Equality: The Evolution of Women's and Racial Ethnic Organizations in America, 1955–1985*. New Brunswick, N.J.: Rutgers University Press.

———. 1997. "The Sequencing of Social Movements." *American Sociological Review* 62(5): 779–99.

———. 2002. "The Emergence of Hybrid Organizational Forms: Combining Identity-Based Service Provision and Political Action." *Nonprofit and Voluntary Sector Quarterly* 31(3): 377–401.

Minkoff, Debra C., and John D. McCarthy. 2005. "Reinvigorating the Study of Organizational Processes in Social Movements." *Mobilization* 10(2): 401–21.

Moghadam, Valentine. 2005. *Globalizing Women: Transnational Feminist Networks*. Baltimore, Md.: Johns Hopkins University Press.

———. 2008. *Globalization and Social Movements: Islamism, Feminism and the Global Justice Movement*. Lanham, Md.: Rowman & Littlefield.

Moody, Kim. 1997. *Workers in a Lean World: Unions in the International Economy*. New York: Verso.

Morphet, Sally. 1996. "NGOs and the Environment." In *The Conscience of the World: The Influence of NGOs in the United Nations System*, edited by Peter Willetts. Washington, D.C.: Brookings Institution Press.

Munck, Ronaldo. 2002. *Globalization and Labour: The New Great Transformation*. London: Zed Books.

Murphy, Gillian. 2005. "Coalitions and The Development of The Global Environmental Movement: A Double-Edged Sword." *Mobilization: An International Quarterly* 10(2): 235–50.

Naples, Nancy A., and Manisha Desai, eds. 2002. *Women's Activism and Globalization: Linking Local Struggles and Transnational Politics*. New York: Routledge.

Nelson, Paul. 1995. *The World Bank and Nongovernmental Organizations: The Limits of Apolitical Development*. New York: St. Martin's Press.

———. 2002. "New Agendas and New Patterns of International NGO Political Action." *Voluntas: International Journal of Voluntary and Nonprofit Organizations* 13(4): 377–92.

Nepstad, Sharon Erickson. 2002. "Creating Transnational Solidarity: The Use of Narrative in the U.S.-Central America Peace Movement." In *Globalization and Resistance: Transnational Dimensions of Social Movements*, edited by Jackie Smith and Hank Johnston. Lanham, Md.: Rowman & Littlefield.

Newell, Peter. 2006. "Climate for Change? Civil Society and the Politics of Global Warming." In *Global Civil Society Yearbook 2005/6*, edited by Marlies Glasius, Mary Kaldor, and Helmut Anheier. Thousand Oaks, Calif.: Sage.

Nordstrom, Carolyn. 2007. *Global Outlaws: Crime, Money and Power in the Contemporary World*. Berkeley: University of California Press.

O'Brien, Robert. 2000. "Workers and World Order: The Tentative Transformation of the International Union Movement." *Review of International Studies* 26(4): 533–55.

O'Brien, Robert, Anne Marie Goetz, Jan Aard Scholte, and Marc Williams. 2000. *Contesting Global Governance: Multilateral Economic Institutions and Global Social Movements*. New York: Cambridge University Press.

O'Neill, Kate. 2004. "Transnational Protest: States, Circuses, and Conflict at the Frontline of Global Politics." *International Studies Review* 6(2): 233–251.

Oliver, Pamela E. 2008. "Repression and Crime Control: Why Social Movement Scholars Should Pay Attention to Mass Incarceration as a Form of Repression." *Mobilization* 13(1): 1–24.

Oliver, Pamela, and Mark Furman. 1989. "Contradictions Between National and Local Organizational Strength: The Case of the John Birch Society." In *International Social Movement Research*, edited by Bart Klandermans. Greenwich, Conn.: JAI Press.

Olzak, Susan, and Kiyoteru Tsutsui. 1998. "Status in the World System and Ethnic Mobilization." *Journal of Conflict Resolution* 42(6): 691–720.

Owusu, Francis. 2003. "Pragmatism and the Gradual Shift from Dependency to Neoliberalism: The World Bank, African Leaders and Development Policy in Africa." *World Development* 31(10): 1655–672.

Pagnucco, Ron, and Jackie Smith. 1993. "The Peace Movement and the Formulation of U.S. Foreign Policy." *Peace and Change* 18(2): 157–81.

Paine, Ellen. 2000. "The Road to the Global Compact: Corporate Power and the

Battle over Global Public Policy at the United Nations." vol. 2005. New York: Global Policy Forum.

Paris, Roland. 2003. "Peacekeeping and the Constraints of Global Culture." *European Journal of International Relations* 9(3): 441–73.

Passy, Florence. 1999. "Supernational Political Opportunities as a Channel of Globalization of Political Conflicts: The Case of the Conflict Around the Rights of Indigenous Peoples." In *Social Movements in a Globalizing World*, edited by Donatella della Porta, Hanspeter Kriesi, and Dieter Rucht. New York: St. Martin's Press.

Peet, Richard. 2003. *Unholy Trinity: The IMF, World Bank and WTO.* New York: Zed Books.

Pellow, David N. 2000. "Environmental Inequality Formation Toward a Theory of Environmental Injustice." *American Behavioral Scientist* 43(4): 581–601.

Phillips, Nicola. 2004. *The Southern Cone Model: The Political Economy of Regional Capitalist Development in Latin America.* New York: Routledge.

———. 2005. "U.S. Power and the Politics of Economic Governance in the Americas." *Latin American Politics and Society* 47(4): 1–25.

Pianta, Mario. 2005. "UN World Summits and Civil Society: The State of the Art." United Nations Research Institute for Social Development, Geneva. Available at: http://www.unrisd.org/80256B3C005BCCF9/%28httpAux Pages%29/5709F9C06F40FDBAC12570A1002DC4D2/$file/pianta.pdf (accessed August 22, 2011).

Pianta, Mario, and Raffaele Marchetti. 2007. "The Global Justice Movements: The Transnational Dimension." In *The Global Justice Movement: Cross-National and Transnational Perspectives*, edited by Donatella della Porta. Boulder, Colo.: Paradigm Publishers.

Pianta, Mario, and Federico Silva. 2003. "Parallel Summits of Global Civil Society: An Update." In *Global Civil Society Yearbook, 2003*, edited by Helmut Anheier, Mary Kaldor, and Marlies Glasius. Oxford: Oxford University Press.

Podobnik, Bruce. 2005. "Resistance to Globalization: Cycles and Evolutions in the Globalization Protest Movement." In *Transforming Globalization: Challenges and Opportunities in the Post 9/11 Era*, edited by Bruce Podobnik and Thomas Reifer. Boston, Mass.: Brill.

Podolny, Joel N., and Karen L. Page. 1998. "Network Forms of Organization." *Annual Review of Sociology* 24: 57–76.

Polletta, Francesca. 2002. *Freedom Is an Endless Meeting.* Chicago: University of Chicago Press.

Porter, Gareth, Janet Welsh Brown, and Pamela Chasek. 2000. *Global Environmental Politics*, 3d ed. Boulder, Colo.: Westview Press.

Porter, Tony. 2005. *Globalization and Finance.* Malden, Mass.: Polity.

Powell, Walter W., and Paul J. DiMaggio, eds. 1991. *The New Institutionalism in Organizational Analysis.* Chicago: University of Chicago Press.

Prashad, Vijay. 2007. *The Darker Nations.* New York: The New Press.

Prügl, Elisabeth, and Mary K. Meyer. 1999. "Gender Politics in Global Governance." In *Gender Politics in Global Governance*, edited by Mary K. Meyer and Elisabeth Prügl. Lanham, Md.: Rowman & Littlefield.

Pugh, Michael, Neil Cooper, and Mandy Turner, eds. 2008. *Whose Peace? Critical*

Perspectives on the Political Economy of Peacebuilding. New York: Palgrave Macmillan.

Quarmby, Katharine. 2005. "Why Oxfam Is Failing Africa." *The New Statesman*, May 30, 2005.

Rajagopal, Balakrishnan. 2003. *International Law from Below: Development, Social Movements, and Third World Resistance*. New York: Cambridge University Press.

———. 2006. "Counter-Hegemonic International Law: Rethinking Human Rights and Development as a Third World Strategy." *Third World Quarterly* 27(5): 767–83.

Reese, Ellen, Christopher Chase-Dunn, Kadambari Anatram, Gary Coyne, Matheu Kaneshiro, Ashley N. Koda, Roy Kwan, and Preeta Saxena. 2008. "Research Note: Surveys of World Social Forum Participants Show Influence of Place and Base in the Global Public Sphere." *Mobilization* 13(4): 431–46.

Reifer, Thomas Ehrlich. 2005. "Globalization, Democratization, and Global Elite Formation in Hegemonic Cycles: A Geopolitical Economy." In *Hegemonic Declines Present and Past*, edited by Jonathan Friedman and Christopher Chase-Dunn. Boulder, Colo.: Paradigm Publishers.

Reimann, Kim. 2002. "Building Networks from the Outside In: International Movements, Japanese NGOs, and the Kyoto Climate Change Conference." In *Globalization and Resistance: Transnational Dimensions of Social Movements*, vol. 6, edited by J. Smith and H. Johnston. Lanham, Md.: Rowman & Littlefield.

———. 2006. "A View from the Top: International Politics, Norms, and the Worldwide Growth of NGOs." *International Studies Quarterly* 50(1): 45–67.

Rich, Bruce. 1994. *Mortgaging the Earth: The World Bank, Environmental Impoverishment and the Crisis of Development*. Boston, Mass.: Beacon Press.

Riles, Annelise. 2001. *The Network Inside Out*. Ann Arbor: University of Michigan Press.

Risse, Thomas. 2000. "Transnational Actors, Networks and Global Governance." In *Handbook of International Relations*, edited by Walter Carlsnaes, Thomas Risse, and Beth A. Simmons. London: Sage.

Risse, Thomas, Stephen C. Ropp, and Kathryn Sikkink, eds. 1999. *The Power of Human Rights: International Norms and Domestic Change*. New York: Cambridge University Press.

Risse-Kappen, Thomas. 1994. "Ideas Do Not Float Freely: Transnational Coalitions, Domestic Structures and the End of the Cold War." *International Organization* 48(2): 185–214.

Robbins, Dorothy B. 1971. *Experiment in Democracy: The Story of U.S. Citizen Organizations in Forging the Charter of the United Nations*. New York: The Parkside Press.

Roberts, J. Timmons. 1996. "Predicting Participation in Environmental Treaties: A World-System Analysis." *Sociological Inquiry* 66(1): 58–83.

Roberts, J. Timmons, Peter E. Grimes, and Jodie L. Manale. 2003. "Social Roots of Global Environmental Change: A World-Systems Analysis of Carbon Dioxide Emissions." *Journal of World Systems Research* 9(2): 276–315.

Roberts, J. Timmons, and Bradley C. Parks. 2006. *A Climate of Injustice*. Cambridge, Mass.: MIT Press.

———. 2007. "Fueling Injustice: Globalization, Ecologically Unequal Exchange and Climate Change." *Globalizations* 4(2): 193–210.

Robinson, William. 2004. *A Theory of Global Capitalism.* Baltimore, Md.: Johns Hopkins University Press.

Robnett, Belinda. 1997. *How Long? How Long? African-American Women in the Struggle for Civil Rights.* New York: Oxford University Press.

Rochon, Thomas. 1998. *Culture Moves: Ideas, Activism, and Changing Values.* Princeton, N.J.: Princeton University Press.

Rohrschneider, Robert, and Russell J. Dalton. 2002. "A Global Network? Transnational Cooperation Among Environmental Groups." *Journal of Politics* 64(2): 510–33.

Rosenau, James N. 2002. "Governance in a New Global Order." In *Governing Globalization: Power, Authority, and Global Governance*, edited by D. Held and A. G. McGrew. New York: Wiley-Blackwell.

Rosenthal, Naomi, Meryl Fingrutd, Michele Ethier, Roberta Karant, and David McDonald. 1985. "Social Movements and Network Analysis: A Case Study of Nineteenth-Century Women's Reform in New York State." *American Journal of Sociology* 90(5): 1022–55.

Rothman, Franklin Daniel, and Pamela E. Oliver. 1999. "From Local to Global: The Anti-Dam Movement in Southern Brazil 1979–1992." *Mobilization: An International Journal* 4(1): 41–57.

Rothman, Franklin Daniel, and Pamela E. Oliver. 2002. "From Local to Global: The Anti-Dam Movement in Southern Brazil 1979–1992." In *Globalization and Resistance: Transnational Dimensions of Social Movements*, edited by Jackie Smith and Hank Johnston. Lanham, Md.: Rowman & Littlefield.

Rupp, Leila J. 1997. *Worlds of Women: The Making of an International Women's Movement.* Princeton, N.J.: Princeton University Press.

Santos, Boaventura de Sousa. 2006a. *The Rise of The Global Left: The World Social Forums and Beyond.* London: Zed Books.

———. 2006b. "Globalizations." *Theory, Culture & Society* 23(2–3): 393–99.

———. 2007a. "Beyond Abyssal Thinking: From Global Lines to Ecologies of Knowledges." *Eurozine* 2007: 35.

———. 2007b. "Human Rights as an Emancipatory Script? Cultural and Political Conditions." In *Another Knowledge Is Possible.* New York: Verso.

SAPRIN. 2002. "The Policy Roots of Economic Crisis and Poverty." Washington, D.C.: Structural Adjustment Participatory Review International Network.

Sassen, Saskia. 1991. *The Global City: New York, London, Tokyo.* Princeton, N.J.: Princeton University Press.

———. 1998. *Globalization and Its Discontents.* New York: The New Press.

———. 2007. *Territory, Authority, Rights: From Medieval to Global Assemblages.* Princeton, N.J.: Princeton University Press.

Schnaiberg, Allan, and Kenneth A. Gould. 1994. *Environment and Society: The Enduring Conflict.* New York: St. Martin's Press.

Scipes, Kim. 2005. "Labor Imperialism Redux?: The AFL-CIO's Foreign Policy Since 1995." *Monthly Review* 57(1). Available at: http://www.zcommunica

tions.org/labor-imperialism-redux-the-afl-cios-foreign-policy-since-1995 -by-kim-scipes (accessed August 17, 2011).

Scott, James C. 1998. *Seeing Like a State: How Certain Schemes to Improve the Human Condition Have Failed.* New Haven, Conn.: Yale University Press.

Seidman, Gay W. 2009. *Beyond the Boycott: Labor Rights, Human Rights, and Transnational Activism.* New York: Russell Sage Foundation.

Sen, Jai. 2007. "The World Social Forum as an Emergent Learning Process." *Futures* 39(5): 507–22.

Sen, Jai, Anita Anand, Arturo Escobar, and Peter Waterman, eds. 2003. *Challenging Empires: The World Social Forum.* Montevideo, Uruguay: Third World Institute. Available at: http://www.choike.org (accessed October 26, 2011).

Seyfang, Gillo. 2003. "Environmental Mega-Conferences: From Stockholm to Johannesburg and Beyond." *Global Environmental Change* 13(3): 223–29.

Shandra, John, Eran Shor, and Bruce London. 2008. "Debt, Structural Adjustment, and Organic Water Pollution: A Cross-National Analysis." *Organization & Environment* 21(1): 38–55.

Shaw, Timothy. 2002. "New Regionalisms in Africa in the New Millennium: Comparative Perspectives on Renaissance, Realisms and/or Regressions." In *New Regionalisms in the Global Political Economy*, edited by Shaun Breslin, Christopher W. Hughes, Nicola Phillips, and Ben Rosamond. New York: Routledge.

Shor, Francis. 2010. *Dying Empire: US Imperialism and Global Resistance.* New York: Routledge.

Sikkink, Kathryn. 1993. "Human Rights, Principled Issue-Networks, and Sovereignty in Latin America." *International Organization* 47(3): 411–41.

———. 2005. "Patterns of Dynamic Multilevel Governance and the Insider-Outsider Coalition." In *Transnational Protest and Global Activism*, edited by Donatella della Porta and Sidney Tarrow. Lanham, Md.: Rowman & Littlefield.

Silver, Beverly J. 2003. *Forces of Labor: Workers' Movements and Globalization Since 1870.* New York: Cambridge University Press.

Silver, Beverly J., and Giovanni Arrighi. 2001. "Workers North and South." *La Rivista del Manifesto* 19(July–August). Available at: http://www.larivistadelmanifesto.it/en/originale/19A20010706e.html (accessed October 26, 2011).

———. 2005. "Polanyi's 'Double Movement': The *Belles Époques* of British and U.S. Hegemony Compared." In *Hegemonic Declines Present and Past*, edited by Jonathan Friedman and Christopher Chase-Dunn. Boulder, Colo.: Paradigm Publishers.

Siméant, Johanna. 2005. "What is Going Global? The Internationalization of French NGOs 'Without Borders.'" *Review of International Political Economy* 12(5): 851–83.

Singh, Jitendra V., David J. Tucker, and Agnes G. Meinhard. 1991. "Institutional Change and Ecological Dynamics." In *The New Institutionalism in Organizational Analysis*, edited by Walter W. Powell and Paul J. DiMaggio. Chicago: University of Chicago Press.

Sklair, Leslie. 2001. *The Transnational Capitalist Class.* Cambridge: Blackwell.

Skogly, Sigrun. 1993. "Structural Adjustment and Development: Human Rights–An Agenda for Change?" *Human Rights Quarterly* 15(4): 751–78.

Smith, Christian. 1996. *Resisting Reagan: The U.S. Central America Peace Movement*. Chicago: University of Chicago Press.

Smith, Jackie. 1995. "Transnational Political Processes and the Human Rights Movement." In *Research in Social Movements, Conflict and Change*, vol. 18, edited by Louis Kriesberg, Michael Dobkowski, and Isidor Walliman. Greenwood, Conn.: JAI.

———. 1997. "Characteristics of the Modern Transnational Social Movement Sector." In *Transnational Social Movements and World Politics: Solidarity Beyond the State*, edited by Jackie Smith, Charles Chatfield, and Ron Pagnucco. Syracuse, N.Y.: Syracuse University Press.

———. 1999. "Global Politics and Transnational Social Movements Strategies: The Transnational Campaign against International Trade in Toxic Wastes." In *Social Movements in a Globalizing World*, edited by Donatella della Porta, Hanspeter Kriesi, and Dieter Rucht. New York: St. Martin's Press.

———. 2000. "Framing the Nonproliferation Debate: Transnational Activism and International Nuclear Weapons Negotiations." In *Research in Social Movements, Conflict and Change*, vol. 22, edited by P. Coy. Greenwood, Conn.: JAI.

———. 2001. "Globalizing Resistance: The Battle of Seattle and the Future of Social Movements." *Mobilization* 6(1): 1–20.

———. 2004. "The World Social Forum and the Challenges of Global Democracy." *Global Networks* 4(4): 413–21.

———. 2008. *Social Movements for Global Democracy*. Baltimore, Md.: Johns Hopkins University Press.

Smith, Jackie, Scott Byrd, Ellen Reese, and Elizabeth Smythe, eds. 2011. *Handbook of World Social Forum Activism*. Boulder, Colo.: Paradigm Publishers.

Smith, Jackie, Charles Chatfield, and Ron Pagnucco, eds. 1997a. *Transnational Social Movements and Global Politics: Solidarity Beyond the State*. Syracuse, N.Y.: Syracuse University Press.

———. 1997b. "Transnational Social Movements and Global Politics: A Theoretical Framework." In *Transnational Social Movements and Global Politics: Solidarity Beyond the State*. Syracuse, N.Y.: Syracuse University Press.

Smith, Jackie, and Nicole Doerr. 2011. "Democratic Innovation in the U.S. and European Social Forums." In *Handbook of the World Social Forums*, edited by Jackie Smith, Scott Byrd, Ellen Reese, and Elisabeth Smythe. Boulder, Colo.: Paradigm Publishers.

Smith, Jackie, and Tina Fetner. 2007. "Structural Approaches in the Study of Social Movements." In *Handbook of Social Movements: Social Movements Across Disciplines*, edited by Bert Klandermans and Conny Roggeband. New York: Springer.

Smith, Jackie, Marina Karides, Marc Becker, Dorval Brunelle, Christopher Chase-Dunn, Donatella della Porta, Rosalba Icaza, Jeffrey Juris, Lorenzo Mosca, Ellen Reese, Peter Jay Smith, and Rolando Vászuez. 2007. *Global Democracy and the World Social Forums*. Boulder, Colo.: Paradigm Publishers.

Smith, Jackie, Rachel Kutz-Flamenbaum, and Christopher Hausmann. 2008. "New Politics Emerging at the U.S. Social Forum." In *The World and US Social Forums: A Better World Is Possible and Necessary*, edited by Judith Blau and Marina Karides. Amsterdam: Brill.

Smith, Jackie, Ron Pagnucco, and George Lopez. 1998. "Globalizing Human Rights: Report on a Survey of Transnational Human Rights NGOs." *Human Rights Quarterly* 20(2): 379–412.

Smith, Jackie, Ron Pagnucco, and Winnie Romeril. 1994. "Transnational Social Movement Organizations in the Global Political Arena." *Voluntas* 5(2): 121–54.

Smith, Jackie, and Dawn Wiest. 2005. "The Uneven Geography of Global Civil Society: Explaining Participation in Transnational Social Movement Organizations." *Social Forces* 84(2): 621–52.

Snow, David, and Robert Benford. 1988. "Ideology, Frame Resonance and Participant Mobilization." *International Social Movements Research* 1(1): 197–217.

Snow, David A., Sarah A. Soule, and Hanspeter Kriesi. 2004. *The Blackwell Companion to Social Movements*. Oxford: Blackwell.

Snow, David, E.B. Rochford, S. Warden and Robert Benford. 1986. "Frame Alignment Processes, Micromobilization and Movement Participation." *American Sociological Review* 51(4): 273–86.

Snyder, Anna. 2003. *Setting the Agenda for Global Peace: Conflict and Consensus Building*. Burlington, Vt.: Ashgate Press.

———. 2006. "Fostering Transnational Dialogue: Lessons Learned from Women Peace Activists." *Globalizations* 3(1): 31–47.

So, Alvin. 1990. *Social Change and Development: Modernization, Dependency and World-System Theories*. Newbury Park, Calif.: Sage Publications.

Soros, George. 2002. *On Globalization*. New York: Public Affairs.

Sperling, Valerie, Myra Marx Ferree, and Barbara Risman. 2001. "Constructing Global Feminism: Transnational Advocacy Networks and Russian Women's Activism." *Signs: Journal of Women in Culture and Society* 26(4): 1155–186.

Staggenborg, Suzanne. 1988. "The Consequences of Professionalization and Formalization in the Pro-Choice Movement." *American Sociological Review* 53(4): 585–605.

Staggenborg, Suzanne, and Verta Taylor. 2005. "Whatever Happened to the Women's Movement?" *Mobilization* 10(1): 37–52.

Starr, Amory. 2000. *Naming the Enemy: Anti-Corporate Movements Confront Globalization*. New York: Zed Books.

Steiner, Henry J. 1991. "Diverse Partners: Non-Governmental Organizations in the Human Rights Movement." In *Retreat of Human Rights Activists*. Boston, Mass.: Harvard Law School Human Rights Program, Human Rights Internet.

Sternbach, Nancy Saporta, Marysa Navarro-Aranguren, Patricia Chuchryk, and Sonia E. Alvarez. 1992. "Feminisims in Latin America: From Bogota to San Bernardo." In *The Making of Social Movements in Latin America: Identity, Strategy, and Democracy*, edited by A. Escobar and S. E. Alvarez. Boulder, Colo.: Westview.

Stewart, Julie. 2004. "When Local Troubles Become Transnational: The Trans-formation of a Guatemalan Indigenous Rights Movement." *Mobilization* 9(3): 259–78.

Stiglitz, Joseph. 2000. "What I Learned at the World Economic Crisis." *The New Republic*, April 17. Available at: http://www.globalpolicy.org/component/content/article/209/42760.html (accessed October 27, 2011).

———. 2003. *Globalization and its Discontents*. New York: W. W. Norton.

Swidler, Ann. 2009. "Dialectics of Patronage: Logics of Accountability at the African AIDS-NGO Interface." In *Globalization, Philanthropy, and Civil Society*, edited by David C. Hammack and Steven Heydemann. Bloomington: Indiana University Press.

Tarrow, Sidney. 1995. "The Europeanization of Conflict: Reflections from Social Movement Research." *West European Politics* 18(2): 223–51.

———. 1996. "States and Opportunities: The Political Structuring of Social Movements in Democratic States." In *Political Opportunities, Mobilizing Structures and Framing: Social Movement Dynamics in Cross-National Perspective.*, edited by Doug McAdam, John McCarthy, and Mayer Zald. New York: Cambridge University Press.

———. 2001. "Contentious Politics in a Composite Polity." In *Contentious Europeans: Protest and Politics in an Emerging Polity*, edited by Doug Imig and Sidney Tarrow. Lanham, Md.: Rowman & Littlefield.

———. 2005. *The New Transnational Activism*. New York: Cambridge University Press.

———. 2011. *Power in Movement: Social Movements, Collective Action and Politics*, 3rd ed. New York: Cambridge University Press.

Taylor, Verta. 1989. "Social Movement Continuity: The Womens' Movement in Abeyance." *American Sociological Review* 54(5): 761–75.

Taylor, Verta, and Leila J. Rupp. 2002. "Loving Internationalism: The Emotion Culture of Transnational Women's Organizations 1888–1945." *Mobilization* 7(2): 141–58.

Thacher, Peter S. 1991. "Multilateral Cooperation and Global Change." *Journal of International Affairs* 44(2): 433–55.

Thom, Mary. 2000. Promises to Keep: Beijing and Beyond." *Ford Foundation Report* 31(1): 30–33.

Thomas, Daniel. 2001. *The Helsinki Effect: International Norms, Human Rights, and the Demise of Communism*. Princeton, N.J.: Princeton University Press.

Tilly, Charles. 1978. *From Mobilization to Revolution*. Reading, Mass.: Addison Wesley.

———. 1984. "Social Movements and National Politics." In *Statemaking and Social Movements: Essays in History and Theory*, edited by Charles Bright and Susan Harding. Ann Arbor: University of Michigan Press.

———. 1995. "Contentious Repertoires in Great Britain, 1758–1834." In *Repertoires and Cycles of Collective Action*, edited by Mark Traugott. Durham, N.C.: Duke University Press.

———. 2004. *Social Movements, 1768–2004*. Boulder, Colo.: Paradigm Publishers.

Trip, Robert, ed. 2009. *Biotechnology and Agricultural Development: Transgenic Cotton, Rural Institutions and Resource-Poor Farmers*. New York: Routledge.

Tsutsui, Kiyoteru, Dawn Wiest, and Jackie Smith. Forthcoming. "Patterns of Transnational Human Rights Organization." Unpublished paper.

Tsutsui, Kiyoteru, and Christine Min Wotipka. 2004. "Global Civil Society and the International Human Rights Movement: Citizen Participation in Human Rights International Nongovernmental Organizations." *Social Forces* 83(2): 587–620.

ul Haq, Mahbub. 1989. "People in Development." In *Redefining Wealth and Progress: The Caracas Report on Alternative Development Indicators*, edited by South Commission. New York: Bootstrap Press.

Union of International Associations. 2004. *Yearbook of International Organizations*. Brussels: Union of International Associations.

United Nations. 2004. *Cardoso Report: We the Peoples: Civil Society, the United Nations and Global Governance*. New York: United Nations Secretary-General.

———. n.d. United Nations Treaty Collection Database. Available at: http://treaties.un.org (accessed August 22, 2011).

United Nations Development Programme (UNDP). 2005. *Human Development Report 2005: International Cooperation at a Crossroads*. New York: Oxford University Press.

Uvin, Peter. 2003. "Global Dreams and Local Anger: From Structural to Acute Violence in a Globalizing World." In *Rethinking Global Political Economy: Emerging Issues, Unfolding Odesseys*, edited by Mary Anne Tétreault, Robert A. Denemark, Kenneth P. Thomas, and Kurt Burch. New York: Routledge.

Vargas, Virginia. 1992. "The Feminist Movement in Latin America: Between Hope and Disenchantment." *Development and Change* 23(3): 195–214.

Vasi, Ion Bogdan. 2007. "Thinking Globally, Planning Nationally and Acting Locally: Nested Organizational Fields and the Adoption of Environmental Practices." *Social Forces* 86(1): 113–36.

von Bülow, Marisa. 2010. *Building Transnational Networks: Civil Society and the Politics of Trade in the Americas*. New York: Cambridge University Press.

Van Rooy, Allison. 1997. "The Frontiers of Influence: NGO Lobbying at the 1974 World Food Conference, the 1992 Earth Summit and Beyond." *World Development* 25(1): 93–114.

Wallerstein, Immanuel. 1976. *The Modern World-System*. New York: Academic Press.

———. 1980. *The Modern World-System II: Mercantilism and the Consolidation of the European World Economy*. New York: Academic Press.

———. 1984. *The Politics of the World-Economy: The States, the Movements, and the Civilizations*. New York: Cambridge University Press.

———. 1990. "Antisystemic Movements: History and Dilemmas." In *Transforming the Revolution: Social Movements and the World-System*, edited by Samir Amin, Giovanni Arrighi, Andre G. Frank, and Immanuel Wallerstein. New York: Monthly Review Press.

———. 1991. *Geopolitics and Geoculture: Essays on the Changing World-System*. New York: Cambridge University Press.

———. 1993. "The World-System After the Cold War." *Journal of Peace Research* 30(1): 1–6.

———. 2004a. *World-Systems Analysis: An Introduction*. Durham, N.C.: Duke University Press.

———, ed. 2004b. *The Modern World-System in the Longue Duree.* Boulder, Colo.: Paradigm Publishers.

Walton, John, and Charles Ragin. 1990. "Global and National Sources of Political Protest: Third World Responses to the Debt Crisis." *American Sociological Review* 55(6): 876–90.

Walton, John, and David Seddon. 1994. *Free Markets and Food Riots: The Politics of Global Adjustment.* Cambridge, Mass.: Blackwell.

Wapner, Paul. 2002. "Introductory Essay: Paradise Lost? NGOs and Global Accountability." *Chicago Journal of International Law* 3(1): 155–60.

Weber, Max. 1994. *Weber: Political Writings,* edited by Peter Lassman. Trans. by Ronald Speirs. New York: Cambridge University Press.

Weber, Tim. 2011. "Davos 2011: World Leaders Struggle to Rebuild Trust," *BBC News,* January 25, 2011. Available at: http://www.bbc.co.uk/news/business-12279769 (accessed April 21, 2011).

Weisbrot, Mark, Dean Baker, Egor Kraev, and Judy Chen. 2002. "The Scorecard on Globalization 1980–2000: Twenty Years of Diminished Progress." *International Journal of Health Sciences* 32(2): 229–53.

Weiss, Thomas G. 1998. *Beyond UN Subcontracting: Task-Sharing with Regional Security Arrangements and Service-Providing NGOs.* New York: Palgrave Macmillan.

Weiss, Thomas G., and Leon Gordenker, eds. 1996. *NGOs, the UN and Global Governance.* Boulder, Colo.: Lynne Reinner.

West, Lois A. 1999. "The United Nations Women's Conferences and Feminist Politics." In *Gender Politics in Global Governance,* edited by Mary K. Meyer and Elisabeth Prügl. Boulder, Colo.: Rowman & Littlefield.

Whitaker, Chico. 2009. "Social Forums — Challenges and New Perspectives." In *The World and the US Social Forums: A Better World is Possible and Necessary,* edited by Judith Blau and Marina Karides. Leiden: Brill.

Widener, Patricia. 2011. *Oil Injustice and Transnational Activism: Resisting and Conceding a Pipeline in Ecuador.* Lanham, Md.: Rowman & Littlefield.

Willetts, Peter. 1989. "The Pattern of Conferences." In *Global Issues in the United Nations Framework,* edited by Paul Taylor and A. J. R. Groom. New York: St. Martin's Press.

———, ed. 1996a. *The Conscience of the World: The Influence of NGOs in the United Nations System.* London: C. Hurst.

———. 1996b. "From Stockholm to Rio and Beyond: The Impact of the Environmental Movement on the United Nations Consultative Arrangements for NGOs." *Review of International Studies* 22(1): 57–80.

———. 2006. "The Cardoso Report on the UN and Civil Society: Functionalism, Global Corporatism, or Global Democracy?" *Global Governance* 12(3): 305–24.

Williams, Marc. 1993. "Re-Articulating the Third World Coalition: The Role of the Environmental Agenda." *Third World Quarterly* 14(1): 7–29.

Wiseberg, Laurie. 1992. "Human Rights Nongovernmental Organizations." In *Human Rights in the World Community: Issues and Action,* edited by Richard P. Claude and Bruce Weston. Philadelphia: University of Pennsylvania Press.

Wittel, Andreas. 2001. "Toward a Network Sociality." *Theory, Culture, and Society* 18(6): 51–76.

Wittner, Lawrence. 1993. *One World or None: A History of the Nuclear Disarmament Movement Through 1953*, vol. 1. Palo Alto, Calif.: Stanford University Press.

Woehrle, Lynne M., Patrick G. Coy, and Gregory M. Maney. 2008. *Contesting Patriotism: Culture, Power, and Strategy in the Peace Movement*. Lanham, Md.: Rowman & Littlefield.

Woodward, David, and Andrew Simms. 2006. "Growth Isn't Working." New Economics Foundation, London. Available at: http://www.neweconomics.org/publications/growth-isn%E2%80%99t-working (accessed October 27, 2011).

World Commission on the Social Dimensions of Globalization. 2004. "A Fair Globalization: Creating Opportunities for All." Available at: http://www.ilo.org/public/english/wcsdg/docs/report.pdf (accessed July 13, 2011).

WorldPublicOpinion.org. 2008. "World Publics Say Governments Should Be More Responsive to the Will of the People." Available at: http://www.worldpublicopinion.org/pipa/articles/governance_bt/482.php (accessed July 13, 2011).

Wuthnow, Robert. 1989. *Communities of Discourse: Ideology and Social Structure in the Reformation, the Enlightenment, and European Socialism*. Cambridge, Mass.: Harvard University Press.

Yanacopulos, Helen. 2005. "Strategies that Bind: NGO Coalitions and their Influence." *Global Networks* 5(1): 93–110.

Zald, Mayer N. 1987. "The Future of Social Movements." In *Social Movements in an Organizational Society*, edited by Mayer N. Zald and John D. McCarthy. New Brunswick, N.J.: Transaction.

Zald, Mayer N., and Roberta Ash Garner. 1987. "Social Movement Organizations: Growth, Decay and Change." In *Social Movements in an Organizational Society*, edited by Mayer N. Zald and John D. McCarthy. New Brunswick, N.J.: Transaction.

Zald, Mayer N., and John D. McCarthy. 1980. "Social Movement Industries: Competition and Cooperation Among Movement Organizations." In *Research in Social Movements, Conflict and Change*, vol. 3, edited by Louis Kriesberg. Greenwich, Conn.: JAI Press.

═ Index ═

Boldface numbers refer to figures and tables.